UFOS
AND THE
DEEP
STATE

50 Years of Disinformation, Saboteurs, Intimidation, and Cover-ups

UFOS
AND THE

A History of the Military and Shadow Government's

DEEP

WAR AGAINST THE TRUTH

STATE

KEVIN D. RANDLE, LT COL, USAR (RET)

NEW
PAGE

This edition first published in 2021 by New Page Books, an imprint of

Red Wheel/Weiser, LLC
With offices at:
65 Parker Street, Suite 7
Newburyport, MA 01950
www.redwheelweiser.com

ISBN: 978-1-63265-190-7

Library of Congress Cataloging-in-Publication Data available upon request.

Cover design by Kathryn Sky-Peck
Interior by Happenstance Type-O-Rama
Typeset in Itc New Baskerville and Franklin Gothic

Printed in the United States of America
IBI

10 9 8 7 6 5 4 3 2 1

CONTENTS

UFOS
AND THE
DEEP
STATE

INTRODUCTION

Almost everyone reading this will know that UFO stands for Unidentified Flying Object. And nearly all of them will think that the term refers to an alien spacecraft rather than to something seen in the sky that can't easily be identified—perhaps nothing more than a streak or pinpoint of light crossing the sky. All of these, however, can correctly be labeled UFOs as well, even though they certainly have nothing to do with alien spacecraft. There are those who have complained about the term UFO, claiming that "flying" implies something manufactured, while "object" suggests something that has mass. Thus "UFO" seems to describe something more real than just a light in the sky—a spacecraft of some sort that, in reality, may actually have been nothing more than a meteor or a weather-related phenomenon.

In the 1970s, the Aerial Phenomena Research Organization (APRO) decided to change the term UFO to Unidentified Aerial Object (UAO) to correct this preconceived notion.[1] This more neutral term still suggested an object, but left open the possibility that what was seen could have been of natural origin rather than something manufactured, thus shedding some of the baggage of the term "UFO." The term "UAO" has, in turn, now evolved into Unidentified Aerial Phenomenon (UAP), which suggests that something was seen in the sky to which no physical attributes could be assigned—something that was not recognized by those who saw it; something that might have had mass or might have been manufactured. It could have been a natural phenomenon with no more mass than a ball of lightning, or a glowing ball of plasma, or a searchlight playing across a cloud seen through a haze of fog.

Those who *do* want to describe what they have seen as an alien spacecraft—something solid, something in flight, and something manufactured on another planet—use the term "flying saucer," an outgrowth of Kenneth Arnold's description of the motion of the objects as being like that of a saucer skipping across a pond.[2] This term is more than simply descriptive, however. It denotes something about what the witness believed, while UAP remains neutral and gives little or no context. Because of this difference, Stanton Friedman, Donald Schmitt, and I began to use the term "flying saucer" to make it clear when we were referring to a craft from another world rather than a more anomolous sighting that might be anything.

That meant, of course, that we had come full circle. When Captain Edward Ruppelt made UFO the preferred term for those investigating the sightings of strange things in the sky, feeling it was more scientific than "flying saucer," the term became a pejorative—as in "You saw a *flying saucer*?"—implying some sort of inability to recognize reality.[3]

THE DEEP STATE—THEN AND NOW

The Deep State is usually defined as a conspiracy through which bureaucrats—appointed by elected officials or hired into various branches of government—are able to manipulate the system, act as a shadow government, influence public policy, decide elections, and provide comfort to those at the very top. These hidden power-players can apply pressure on elected officials whose main concern is to be reelected rather than to govern for the benefit of the electorate.[4] The Deep State rules behind the scenes from administration to administration precisely because they *don't* need to worry about reelection. The system is rigged so that they stay on long after those who appointed them have left government service.

The term is said to have originated in the 1990s as Turkish government officials conspired with drug traffickers against Kurdish insurgents.[5] But the truth is that a Deep State has existed in the United States since the 1930s. It may not have been referred to as such, but the goal of those involved was the same as we see today— to retain power, to increase the personal wealth of those on the inside, and to manipulate the media to bring about a desired result that might not be in the best interests of the United States.[6]

Shortly after the election of President Franklin Delano Roosevelt, a group comprised of very rich industrialists, the KKK, and the American Liberty League worked to overthrow the elected government and replace it with a new regime in what could only be called a bloodless coup.[7] Their plan was to march an "army" of 500,000 veterans on Washington, D. C. under the leadership of retired Marine Major General Smedley Butler. Butler was to be appointed Secretary of General Affairs and the president reduced to a figurehead. Butler would be the real power in the White House, keeping the electorate happy while appearing to be just another bureaucrat working for the president. He and his group would control the direction of the government, while FDR just mouthed the words they wanted him to say and signed the legislation they wanted enacted.

Although Butler had supported Roosevelt during the 1932 election, his fellow plotters believed that his popularity was vital to their plan.[8] He had been awarded two Medals of Honor and would have received a third if not for the fact that Marine officers had not been eligible for the medal during his first action. Butler, they felt, would inspire veterans to join him. They hoped that the sheer size of their force, which was to enter the city disguised as a parade, would compel Roosevelt to accede to their demands.

Butler, however, was horrified by the idea and told reporters, congressmen, and anyone else who would listen about the plot.[9] Although some were reluctant to believe such a wild story, a Congressional committee was convened to investigate. This committee—the

McCormack-Dickstein Committee—held hearings in November 1934 and released its final report to the House of Representatives on February 15 the following year. Their report stated that they had found no evidence to support Butler's claims, perhaps because of their refusal to call key witnesses.[10]

In the context of today's politics, it is interesting that the Committee also stated: "This committee is not concerned with premature newspaper accounts especially when given and published prior to the taking of testimony." In other words, they weren't going to be persuaded by media reports and political rumors. The report continued:

> In the last few weeks of the committee's official life, it received evidence showing that certain persons had made an attempt to establish a fascist organization in this country. No evidence was presented and this committee had none to show a connection between this effort and any fascist activity of any European country. There is no question that these attempts were discussed, were planned, and might have been placed in execution when and if the financial backers deemed it expedient.[11]

The press, including a *New York Times* editorial, called the story a "gigantic hoax."[12] Thomas Lamont of J. P. Morgan called it "pure moonshine."

The point here is that the Deep State, operating in conjunction with elements of private industry, attempted to reduce the elected president of the United States to little more than a figurehead. When the plot was exposed, Congress investigated, but avoided calling witnesses who might have provided corroborating testimony. And finally, the Committee released a report that was designed to keep everyone happy. Names and some testimony were redacted. The attempted bloodless coup had failed and been exposed, but nothing came of it. The embedded structures of the Deep State itself remained in place and they retained some of their power, saved by a compliant media and a Congressional committee that portrayed the coup as little more than rumor.

The next time that the Deep State appeared was in July 1947, when it inserted itself into the events in Roswell, New Mexico and into UFO investigation in general.[13] Retired Brigadier General Arthur Exon tells of a group he called "The Unholy Thirteen"—a team of Washington power-players who controlled the information about UFOs. What is interesting here is that the men he mentioned in connection with this group were all high-ranking members of the military and various civilian branches of government, none of whom held elective office at the time, although some, like Stuart Symington, would later be elected to office. Exon's testimony, which will be explored in depth later, provides fascinating insight into the operation of the Deep State.

The influence of the Deep State becomes clear as we look more deeply into the way investigations of UFOs have been carried out in the last half century. The CIA, the FBI, and even the Air Force Office of Special Investigations (AFOSI) are all arms of the Deep State and have done a great deal to conceal its influence on UFO investigation. During an investigation of two photographs taken in Phoenix, Arizona in July 1947, both the Army Counterintelligence Corps (CIC) and the FBI interviewed witness William Rhodes. But while the Army officer showed Rhodes his credentials, the FBI agent was identified only as another investigator to conceal his affiliation with the agency. This was only discovered by private UFO researchers after the Project Blue Book files were declassified in 1976.[14]

The same thing happened during the Socorro landing in New Mexico in 1964, when the FBI agent involved asked not to be identified, although his ability to remain in the background faded in a matter of hours as the story leaked into the press.[15] Yet no one asked if his desire to remain anonymous was motivated by a desire to protect the Deep State or if it was just a matter of the FBI wanting to keep a low profile in UFO investigations.

There have been many sightings in which witnesses were interrogated by men in civilian clothes who failed to identify themselves or the organizations they worked for. They just arrived at the military facility or law enforcement office with credentials that impressed those in charge and were often granted access that others were denied. Civilian UFO researchers were turned away, but these "mystery men" seemed to take over, listening to witnesses or asking them questions, making suggestions, and sometimes engaging in chemical regression, hypnotic regression, or other forms of memory enhancement. Their attempts stopped just short of physical torture. They have used intimidation, the cloak of national security, and outright lies to get what they want, leaving witnesses confused, frightened, and exhausted.[16]

These shadowy characters are representatives of the Deep State. Their authority supersedes that of any other officials on the scene, including high-ranking military officers. During the Rendlesham Forest investigation (see chapter 12), I was told that an aircraft from Langley Air Force Base had landed at Bentwaters carrying some sort of interrogation team. What was not made clear was who was on the aircraft. Langley's involvement clearly suggests AFOSI; but Langley is also the home of the CIA. Those I asked weren't sure who the men were, other than that they were not part of the personnel assigned to Bentwaters and that they were using the AFOSI facilities on the base as their headquarters.

There is a great deal of evidence that the Deep State has been behind the censorship of UFO information from the very beginning. It is clear that they have attempted to turn attention away from evidence suggesting an interstellar explanation for these phenomena, that they have manipulated the system to provide an unreal assessment of what UFOs are and what they represent, and that they exhibit an authority that intimidates but is never questioned. The

Deep State, often in conjunction with AFOSI as well as many other intelligence agencies, has tried to keep the general public from learning what is going on, despite solid evidence of alien visitation. The reason for this is simple: They want to retain their power. They cannot risk revealing their inability to stop these alien craft from visiting, because that would reveal just how powerless they really are. They need the cloak of invincibility to operate safely in the background.

The goal of this book is to show that the Deep State knows the truth about UFOs but doesn't want the rest of us to know that truth. The following chapters detail evidence that AFOSI and other organizations have colluded with the Deep State to keep key evidence hidden behind a wall of ridicule and a claim of national security. The problem for them is that we now know what is going on, and there are many forces working for a release of this truth.

PART I

UFOS AND THE DEEP STATE

CHAPTER 1

The Cover-Up Begins

I n July 1947, there was no Air Force and therefore no Air Force Office of Special Investigations (AFOSI). But there was a Deep State.[1] At the time, the Army Air Forces (AAF) and the Counterintelligence Corps (CIC) held many of the responsibilities that AFOSI would later acquire. When the Roswell UFO crash recovery was made in July of that year, the initial investigation fell to the senior intelligence officers in Roswell at the time—the 509th Bomb Group intelligence officer, Major Jesse Marcel, Sr., and Captain Sheridan Cavitt, the CIC officer recently assigned to the base.[2]

On July 6, Chaves County Sheriff, George Wilcox, called the Roswell Army Air Field (RAAF). The call was answered, indirectly, by Major Marcel, which is to say that the message from the sheriff was eventually passed to him. Marcel then drove to the sheriff's office to speak with William "Mack" Brazel, a rancher who had found some strange material scattered on the ranch he managed.[3]

According to Phyllis McGuire, Sheriff Wilcox's daughter who was present at the time, Marcel met with the sheriff, his deputies, and Mack Brazel in a small room off the main office.[4] Unable to identify the material brought in by Brazel, Wilcox dispatched two deputies to look for what would become known as the "debris field."[5] When they returned, they reported finding a large, burned area that looked as if something big and circular had landed, but not much in the way of metallic debris. This location was much closer to

Roswell than to the Brazel ranch, suggesting that they had found an entirely different location.

Before the deputies returned, Marcel left the sheriff's office for the base to confer with the base commanding officer, Colonel William Blanchard. He described what he had seen at the sheriff's office in great detail and Blanchard suggested that he examine the field where the debris had been found. He also suggested that Marcel take Cavitt, the newly assigned CIC officer, with him.

Led by Brazel, Marcel and Cavitt approached the field but arrived too late in the day to do anything other than eat a makeshift meal and wait for daylight. The next morning, the three continued to the field, with Brazel and Cavitt on horsback and Marcel, who didn't ride, following in a Jeep Carryall.[6] Although there was no access road, the pastures were fairly flat and posed no threat to the Carryall.

Marcel later reported that the debris field was a couple of hundred yards wide and about three quarters of a mile long. It was filled with strange metallic debris, some of which stirred in the wind, suggesting that it was extremely lightweight. A deep gouge was evident down the center of the field that tapered at both ends and widened out in the middle to about ten feet, giving the impression that something had hit the pasture, slid along for about a half mile, and then bounced back into the air.[7] Curiously, this gouge, later described by Mack's son, Bill, was never mentioned by Marcel in his descriptions of the field.

The three men spent a great deal of time on the field examining the debris, considering the orientation of the gouge, measuring the size of the field, and trying to understand exactly what had happened there. Sometime in the afternoon, Marcel sent Cavitt back to Roswell to brief Blanchard on what they had found, remaining behind to collect debris to take back to the base. There was so much of it that they couldn't possibly carry it all. Finally, as darkness fell, Marcel returned to Roswell.

The next day, July 8, Blanchard ordered Lieutenant Walter Haut, the base public-information officer, to issue a press release saying that the Roswell Army Air Field had recovered a flying saucer on a ranch in the area. Few details were provided other than the names of Sheriff Wilcox and Major Marcel. Later in the day, however, Brigadier General Roger Ramey, commanding officer of the 8th Air Force in Fort Worth, Texas, announced that the debris was from nothing more than a standard weather balloon that had crashed. Pictures of the "balloon," with Marce and Ramey with his chief of staff, Colonel Thomas Dubose, appeared in newspapers around the country. Warrant Officer Irving Newton, who had been called in to identify the debris, was also photographed in Ramey's office.[8] With the debris identified to the satisfaction of the news media, and with none of the officers at the base disputing that identification, the story died.

Marcel, who had been the first on the scene with Cavitt and had been responsible for the initial investigation, was now out of the loop. Although he had the necessary top-secret clearance, once the nature of the find was clarified, his job was done. Ironically, the top intelligence officer on the base was cut out, told he was no longer needed.[9] Others were brought in as Blanchard attempted to contain the information and restrict the number of personnel involved.

Cavitt, though only a captain at the time, was the senior CIC agent in Roswell. His chain of command did not run through the 509th Bomb Group, the parent organization at Roswell, but rather through the CIC. His immediate headquarters and superior officer were located at Kirtland Air Force Base in Albuquerque, New Mexico. Given the nature of the find, however, Cavitt's responsibility didn't end when Marcel's did. His job was to attempt to identify the source of the debris, if possible. In the end, he prepared a report that was sent up his chain of command, first to Colonel Doyle Rees in Albuquerque and then on to CIC headquarters in Washington.

Marcel later told investigators that he confronted Cavitt about being excluded and demanded to see any reports that he might write, reminding Cavitt that he outranked him. But in this particular instance, rank was not the determining factor. This was a need-to-know situation, and Marcel no longer had a need to know. His role had ended when he reported to Blanchard and Blanchard took charge of the investigation. Once the material, whatever it was, had been removed from the site, and once he had finished his report, Cavitt's role ended as well.

The whole tale of the Roswell retrieval remained hidden until 1978, when Marcel began to talk about it to his ham-radio friends, telling them that he had recovered parts of a flying saucer years ago.[10] That information eventually ended up with Stan Friedman and Leonard Stringfield, both of whom began a long investigation into Marcel's claims. During interviews conducted by UFO researchers and the news media, Marcel suggested that the name of the CIC agent involved was Cabot (Cavitt), providing an important clue as to who else had seen the debris and prompting a search for the man. Records eventually identified Cavitt as the man in charge of the CIC office in 1947, contrary to what he had told several different investigators—including me.

When Cavitt was finally identified and interviewed, he said that he had not been in Roswell in July 1947, that he arrived sometime later. During an interview with Don Schmitt and me, he asked: "Are you convinced yet that I wasn't there?" Mary Cavitt added: "If he had been away overnight, at that time, I had just gotten there and I would have remembered it."[11] She later said that she had arrived in Roswell *before* her husband, suggesting that her memory might not have been quite as clear as she thought. Cavitt himself maintained that he had not been there at the right time and that he had never gone out on any balloon recoveries because he was too busy with his serious work. He acknowledged that the description Marcel had given of the man who was there did sound like him, but said he couldn't understand why people wouldn't believe him when he said he wasn't there.

Bill Rickett, the senior sergeant assigned to the CIC office in Roswell in 1947, made it perfectly clear in multiple interviews, however, that Cavitt *was* the man who went with Marcel. In fact, in an interview conducted at his winter home in Arizona, when the tale of aliens was brought up, Cavitt demanded to know: "Did Bill Rickett tell you that?"[12] This suggests that Cavitt was there and had been involved, at least partially, in the recovery operation. But Rickett took it a step further, suggesting that the CIC had an even bigger role in the recovery than Cavitt wanted us to know. According to Rickett, Cavitt took him out to the site on July 8, the day that Ramey released his "balloon" statement. The drive didn't take hours, however, as it had for Marcel and Cavitt two days earlier; it took only about an hour, suggesting they were actually at a different site—one closer to Roswell. Arriving at a military cordon, they showed their military IDs and proceeded to explore the site. Rickett asked Cavitt if it was "hot," meaning radioactive. Cavitt said that it was not.

As he walked the field with Cavitt, Rickett found one piece of debris that was about two feet square and slightly curved. Although it was thin and fairly light, Rickett thought of it as "cold-rolled steel," which meant that it was very strong but not particularly light. Rickett crouched down, braced the metal against his knee and forearm, and attempted to bend it. According to Rickett, Cavitt said to Major Edwin Easley, the provost marshal who was responsible for security at the site: "Smart guy. He's trying to do what we couldn't." Rickett said that the metal was thin and added that it wasn't plastic and didn't feel like plastic. He said that he had never seen anything like it and described it as an exotic metal that he couldn't identify.

Rickett later told both Don Schmitt and Mark Rodeghier, scientific director of the Center for UFO Studies (CUFOS), that he ran into a man a number of years later who had also been at the CIC at the time, but had transferred to the Air Force and AFOSI when the services separated in 1947. When asked about the strange metal found at Roswell, the man answered: "We still don't know what the hell it was."

During investigations that Don Schmitt and I conducted in the 1990s, those who had been involved in the recovery at various levels provided information about what they had seen. Many of them reported that they felt they were dealing with something extraordinary. They didn't know exactly what they had found, but they did know they had never seen anything like it. Most thought at the time that they were dealing with a new type of aircraft made from new types of materials. Some believed, based on flying-saucer reports from around the country, that they were dealing with something interplanetary. No one was thinking in terms of interstellar.

CONTAINMENT

Although Brigadier General Ramey was the one who told the press that the material recovered outside of Roswell was from a weather balloon, the coordination for that explanation originated at a higher command level. Although no one has found any documentation containing actual orders for containment, it is clear that those at the higher echelons of the military and the civilian government became involved quickly. The Deep State was concerned about the impact any revelation about the recovery of an alien craft would have on the general population.

The best documented evidence suggests that Marcel left Roswell sometime after 10:00 AM on July 8, though there are some indications that the flight out of Roswell may have been closer to noon. No matter. He clearly went to the headquarters of the 8th Air Force at Fort Worth on that day and reported to General Ramey, showing him the material that he had brought from the debris field. The story of the find, based on the press release that Blanchard ordered, hit the news wires at about 2:26 PM MST. It quickly became national news, with telephone lines to the Roswell Sheriff's Office, the Roswell Army Air Field, and even the local press jammed by curious reporters.[13]

But by 5:00 PM CST, Ramey had met with J. Bond Johnson, a reporter/photographer with the *Fort Worth Star-Telegram*, and identified the debris as belonging to a weather balloon and the radar reflector used to gauge winds aloft. In Roswell, Sheriff Wilcox refused to answer press inquiries, telling reporters that he was working with the "boys out at the base" and directing them to call out there.

By the next day, the story was officially dead. The press was satisfied with the answer General Ramey had given—just a weather balloon, nothing more unusual than that. The telephones fell silent and the story disappeared from the newspapers and from public consciousness for more than thirty years. Someone, somewhere, had managed to shut the whole thing down in a matter of hours. Given that Marcel—who was no longer in Roswell but in Fort Worth, and so not available for comment—had explicitly said later that the pictures taken in Ramey's office were *not* of the debris he had brought from Roswell, that person had to be fairly highly placed. It had to be someone inside the Deep State.

Evidence of that high placement and Deep State involvement came from George "Jud" Roberts. In 1947, Roberts was the minority owner as well as the station manager of radio station KGFL in downtown Roswell. He and his partner, Walt Whitmore, Sr., managed to record an hour-long interview with Mack Brazel on July 9, but that interview was never aired. Roberts later explained why:

> When there were some questions about releasing it and so forth. Why we got a notice that if we released it, our license would be gone the second day so we didn't do very much on it at that time . . . Walt [Whitmore] took quite a little brunt on that thing. Pretty courageously as a matter of fact . . . Our stuff came from Washington about our license.

Asked who had issued the warning, Roberts said: "I imagine it was [Senator] Clinton Anderson's office. He ran everything from there from the stand point of the state."[14]

This suggests that whoever was involved was very high up in the government. A United States senator would not have been intimidated by a military officer, no matter who it was or how high his rank. The suggestion that Anderson put pressure on the station had to have come from the leadership of the senate, the party headquarters, or the office of the president. For some reason, whoever induced Anderson to call the radio station wanted the information suppressed, and the threat to the station's license was sufficient to stop the broadcast. During interviews conducted in the early 1990s, Easley told me several times that he had been sworn to secrecy, finally declaring: "I can't talk about it. I told you that. I promised the President that I wouldn't."[15] This clearly indicates who had the power to get Anderson to order the Roswell radio station to shut down the broadcast. While the president may not have called Easley directly, he may well have called Anderson, who, in turn, called the station.

This is a clear example of what the Deep State could do, even in the late 1940s. They were able to shut down the Army investigation into the debris that had been recovered. They were able to order the highest-ranking officer in the 8th Air Force to provide a false statement to the press. And they were able to stop a radio broadcast that could have reached no farther than the outskirts of Roswell. All this in a matter of hours. A well thought-out plan shut down interest in the material found outside Roswell, and that was where the story remained for decades. When the Roswell case was mentioned at all, it was normally treated as a hoax. Few, if any, actually remembered the case, although Frank Edwards did mention it briefly in his 1966 book *Flying Saucers—Serious Business*. But cracks began to appear in the wall of secrecy that had been erected around the case, and these would eventually allow the story out—for a time anyway.

CRACKS IN THE WALL

In late 1947, the Air Force separated from the Army and those who had been part of the Army Air Forces were given the option of remaining in the Army or transferring to the new service. Cavitt, along with Rickett, transferred from the CIC into what would become the Air Force Office of Special Investigation (AFOSI).[16] Some of the Army's more highly classified investigations, among them the Roswell recovery, were transferred as well. In other words, the military still had a few fingers in the Roswell pie.

When first approached in the late 1970s and early 1980s, Cavitt claimed that he hadn't arrived in Roswell in time to be part of the investigation. Later, he suggested that he had been assigned to Roswell, but had not arrived there in time to get involved in the investigation or the trips out to the ranch. Eventually, he admitted that he had, in fact, been in Roswell at the time in question. On December 6, 1989, however, Cavitt wrote an interesting letter to Doyle Rees, his commanding officer, first in the CIC and later in AFOSI. The letter is filled with contradictions and half-admissions about the events of July 1947.

In the first paragraph, Cavitt notes that his "new" address is in Sierra Vista, Arizona, which is right outside the gates of Fort Huachuca, home of the Army's intelligence schools. This might be irrelevant except for this comment: "Never fear, I'm not chasing flying saucers again." This suggests that Cavitt *had* been chasing flying saucers at some point in his career, something he lied about when Don and I interviewed him in 1989. Cavitt then added: "I'm sure, however, that you know that you would have known about it [the recovery near Roswell] 'post haste' if I have been in on such a bizarre thing."

Cavitt, in the letter, continues: "Marcel was a smart man; a good friend . . . who was prone to be excitable, and, in this case, was wrong [that Cavitt had been along on the trip to the debris field]." This statement is a bald-faced lie. Later, when interviewed by Colonel Richard Weaver for the GAO investigation of the Roswell case and the search for documents, Cavitt admitted that he had been out there with Marcel, even though he told Don Schmitt and me in January 1990 that he hadn't and didn't know why Marcel had suggested otherwise. Those who put him at the recovery site were wrong, he claimed, and he couldn't understand why so many of us believed he had been there when he had denied it to nearly everyone who asked. Although Rickett told Don Schmitt that he had been with Cavitt at the crash site, Cavitt told us: "It didn't happen. It never happened."[17] Cavitt did say, however, that the *Unsolved Mysteries* episode that covered the Roswell crash was a "bunch of garbage." The question, of course, is: How would he know that if he wasn't there?

One thing did come out of our 1990 interview with Cavitt that suggested that he knew much more than he was willing to say. When I mentioned something about the alien bodies that had been recovered in the days following the crash, Cavitt fidgeted for a moment and then asked: "Bill Rickett tell you that?" Unfortunately, I made a tactical error at that moment. Thinking that we needed to protect Rickett, I said: "No. Edwin Easley did."[18] As soon as I mentioned Easley, Cavitt visibly relaxed. But his reaction to my initial question provided the real answer. Rickett knew more about the crash than he had let on and Cavitt, by extension, knew a great deal more. Rickett was quite candid in his answers to the questions Don Schmitt and Mark Rodeghier put to him, and these were recorded on both audio and video tape.

On June 25, 1994, we visited Cavitt again, this time in his home in Sequim, Washington. I asked him:

> Why do you think that Marcel would identify you as going out there with him? We've got an interview . . . Bob Pratt interviewed Marcel in 1979 . . . the transcript says that he said that he thought your name was Cabot but you were a good West Texas boy from San Angelo.[19]

Cavitt replied: "Sort of nails me doesn't it? . . . I was a West Texas boy and I did ride a horse. But I didn't ride that damn horse out to that crash site."[20] At another point in the interview, Cavitt said:

> It just boggles my mind to think that Rickett could have gone out unless I was not there at Roswell at the time, that Rickett would have gone out with Marcel and I wouldn't have known anything about it.

Finally, it all came down to one statement from Cavitt: "I'm not taking the Fifth but I'm telling you right here that I didn't go out there and pick up any bodies or even see [a] crash like that."

The point here is that Cavitt was denying any involvement in anything that sounded even remotely like the Roswell recovery. He didn't see the debris field. He didn't recover any bodies. And he even denied that he had been out into the field to recover any weather balloons. In fact, he said that, at the time, he was too busy with the investigations for security clearances to be involved with chasing balloons. Cavitt was attempting to take himself completely out of the picture that both Rickett and Marcel had put him in.

During our 1994 interview, Cavitt mentioned that a colonel from the Secretary of the Air Force office had come out from the Pentagon to talk to him. "I gave him a sworn statement," he said. "I guess, incidentally, this colonel used to be in the [AF]OSI." Cavitt, of course, wouldn't discuss what he had told the colonel, who turned out to be Colonel Richard Weaver, the man responsible for the big Air Force report that suggested that there had been no flying saucer recovered at Roswell. That document is important because it contains a transcript of the interview Weaver conducted with Cavitt. And that interview radically changes the tale told by Cavitt to various researchers over the years.

Cavitt's affidavit, which was made on May 24, 1994, proves that he had lied to us repeatedly. It reads:

> Shortly after arriving in Roswell, New Mexico in that time frame [late June or early July], I had occasion to accompany two of my subordinates, MSGT Bill Rickett, CIC, and Major Jesse Marcel, Intelligence Officer the 509th Bomb Group, to a ranchland area outside Roswell to help recover some material. I think this request may have come directly from Major Marcel . . . To the best of my knowledge, the three of us traveled to the aforementioned ranchland area by ourselves (that

is, no other persons, civilian or military, were with us). I believe we had a military jeep that Marcel checked out to make this trip. When we got to this location, we subsequently located some debris which appeared to me to resemble bamboo-type square sticks one quarter to one half inch square, that were very light, as well as some sort of metallic reflecting material that was also very light. I also vaguely recall some sort of black box (like a weather instrument). The area of this debris was very small, about twenty feet square, and the material spread out on the ground, but there was no gouge or crater or other obvious sign of impact. I remember recognizing the material as being consistent with a weather balloon. We gathered up some of the material, which would easily fit into one vehicle. There certainly wasn't a lot of this material, or enough to make up crates of it for multiple airplane flights. What Marcel did with this material at the time was unknown to me, although I know now from reading about this incident in numerous books that it was taken to 8th Air Force Headquarters in Fort Worth where it was subsequently identified as a weather balloon.

I have reviewed the pictures in the 1991 book by Randle and Schmitt on the UFO crash at Roswell wherein Marcel and [Brigadier General Roger] Ramey are holding up this material and it appears to be the same type of material that we picked up from the ranchland. I did not make a report of this to my headquarters since I felt the recovery of a weather balloon was not a big deal and did not merit a written report. In the same referenced book by Randle and Schmitt, I was reputed to have told Rickett (on page 63) that we were never there and this incident never happened. The book seems to imply this was in some sort of conspiratorial tone; however it is more likely I told him not to mention it to our headquarters because we had wasted our time recovering a balloon. I only went out to this area once and recovered debris once, and to the best of my knowledge there were no other efforts to go back out there. If there were, they did not involve me. There was no secretive effort or heightened security regarding this incident or any unusual expenditure of manpower at the base to deal with it.

He goes on to declare:

Many of the things I have mentioned to these people have either been taken out of context, misrepresented, or just plain made up. I did know both Jesse Marcel and Bill Rickett very well (both are now deceased). I consider them to be good men, however both did tend to exaggerate things on occasion. With regards to claims that we tested this material by hitting it with sledgehammers without damaging it, I do no recall any of us doing so. I also did not test the material for radioactivity with a Geiger counter (or anything else). I do not recall attempting to burn any of this debris, but my wife tells me that Jesse Marcel, his wife, and son did have a small piece that they held over the fire when we had a cookout. In short, I did help recover some debris from a crashed balloon. I am not part of any conspiracy to withhold information from anyone, either the U. S. Government or the American public. I have never been sworn to secrecy by anyone concerning this matter and I have received authorization from the Secretary of the Air Force to discuss with Colonel Weaver any information of a classified nature I may have concerning it . . . My bottom line is that this whole incident was no big deal and it certainly did not involve anything extraterrestrial.[21]

Cavitt signed the document and his wife witnessed it. Colonel Weaver signed it as well. But that wasn't the end of it. Cavitt and Weaver then sat down for a tape-recorded interview whose transcript was also published in the massive Air Force study. That transcript contains some interesting comments.

Asked by Weaver if he recalled the Roswell retrieval incident, Cavitt gave a long answer that is somewhat in conflict with his affidavit:

> SC [Sheridan Cavitt]: Well, again I couldn't swear to the dates, but in that time, which must have been July, we heard that someone had found some debris out not too far from Roswell and it looked suspicious; it was unidentified. So, I went out and I do not recall whether Marcel went with Rickett and me. We went out to this site. There were no, as I understand, check points or anything like that (going through guards and that sort of garbage); we went out there and we found it. It was a small amount of, as I recall, bamboo sticks, reflective sort of material that would, well, at first glance, you would probably think it was aluminum foil, something of that type. And we gathered up some of it. I don't know whether we even tried to get all of it. It wasn't scattered; well, what I call, you know, extensively. Like, it didn't go along the ground and splatter off some here and some there. We gathered up some of it and took it back to the base and I remember I turned it over to Marcel. As I say, I do not remember whether Marcel was there or not on the site. He could have been. We took it back to the intelligence room . . . in the CIC office.
>
> RW [Richard Weaver]: What did you think it was when you recovered it?
>
> SC: I thought a weather balloon.
>
> RW: Okay. Were you familiar with weather balloons at the time?
>
> SC: I had seen them. I had seen them. As I recall, I am really reaching back, I think they were equipped with a radio sonde (sic) or something like that, that transmitted data from, when

it got up to altitude (what altitude, I have no idea) and somebody on the ground received it and that way they got some information on what was happening up there.[22]

This interview seems to contradict Cavitt's affidavit. It also seems that his story to Weaver is slightly different from the one he told to Don and me about a month later. There were missed opportunities in this interview that might have clarified some of the situation, but Cavitt and Weaver appear to have been working from a prepared script. Questions were asked, but the answers given weren't necessarily the truth, the whole truth, and nothing but the truth.

The evidence for this appears in the transcript itself, when Weaver asks about what they found on the field. When Cavitt says that he recognized the debris as the remains of a weather balloon, Weaver's next question should have been: "Did you communicate this rather important observation to Major Marcel or to Colonel Blanchard?" Instead, he asks if Cavitt was familiar with weather balloons, which seems to suggest that weather balloons would be hard to identify. The reality is that, of the three people we know who were there on that day, two of them later denied that what they found were weather balloons. Mack Brazel was quoted in the *Roswell Daily Record* on July 9, 1947, as saying that he had found weather balloons on two other occasions and this was nothing like that.

Another discrepancy in this interview lies in Cavitt's claim that the material in the pictures taken in Fort Worth on July 8 looked like what they had picked up on the ranch. However, Marcel, when shown those same pictures by New Orleans WWL-TV reporter Johnny Mann, said that the material was not what they had found on the ranch.[23] He claimed that the materials in the pictures had been brought into Ramey's office while he was in the map room with the General showing him exactly where the debris had been found.

And there are other points on which Cavitt differs from others who were interviewed. He told Weaver, for instance, that "there were no check points or anything like that (going through guards and that sort of garbage)." Of course, when Cavitt drove out to the ranch the first time, there would have been no guards because the importance of the find had not yet been established. However, later, there are multiple witnesses who report that the roads into the area were blocked by military personnel. This may not be a lie by Cavitt and his observation is probably accurate for that first day. But road blocks *had* been established later and his claim was misdirection at best. Moreover, his description of others as "fantastic storytellers" who "tend to exaggerate on occasion" and should not be taken seriously are unfair. These witnesses didn't lie; they just exaggerated because they were excited by the events.

Cavitt, on the other hand, is actually *caught* lying on several occasions as he talked about the Roswell events. His interview with Weaver and his own affidavit are in conflict with statements by many others. At what point should we begin to question what he said rather than taking it as the absolute truth? And at what point do we stop rejecting the testimony of others who corroborate each others' stories?

What we learn from this interview is that AFOSI, even decades after the fact, can be counted on to create doubt about what has been reported by many credible individuals. The interview was scripted from the beginning to give the impression that nothing important occurred at Roswell, although it does verify that something *did* occur. It was carefully crafted to reflect just enough of the truth to make it sound plausible. But it takes us in the wrong direction.

In the interview, Weaver told Cavitt about all the conventional explanations that their investigation had eliminated. It wasn't a stray rocket from White Sands, for instance, because there were no launches "that were not accounted for." He then described a classified balloon experiment run by New York University that lasted for years known as Project Mogul. After Cavitt said that he had never heard of Project Mogul, Weaver went on in greater detail:

> Mogul was designed to run balloons at very high altitude with extremely sensitive acoustic sensors (what we were looking for were nuclear test (sic) on the part of the Russians, because we thought the Russians had gotten the bomb) . . . some of them were up to 600 feet long, not one gigantic balloon, but a series of balloons . . . They had a lot of tin foil on them and a lot of different things.[24]

Weaver then suggests that the weather balloon ruse was perhaps meant to serve as cover for this top-secret project.

This is, of course, complete and utter nonsense. By the time the New York University team arrived in New Mexico in late May 1947, the length of their balloon arrays had been reduced to about 400 feet and the purpose of their experiments was to create a constant-level balloon that would tap into a theorized acoustical level in the upper atmosphere where they believed sound would travel very long distances. They did not contain "a lot of tinfoil," but did contain radar targets that had surfaces covered with a reflective material. Moreover, what was being launched in New Mexico was not classified. The equipment was off-the-shelf and much of it could be found in weather stations across the country. Pictures of the balloon arrays and the launching activities were published in newspapers and those in Roswell did know about the project because, according to Charles Moore, the 509th Bomb Group had been asked to help in balloon recovery.[25] Albert Carey, the NYU man in charge in New Mexico, as well as other members of the NYU team, often stopped at the Roswell Army Air Field to refuel their vehicles when returning from their recovery operations, often with remnants of the arrays in the rear of their vehicles—once again indicating the lack of secrecy surrounding their tests.

The biggest problem with Weaver's suggestion, however, is that none of the balloon flights in the proper time frame were unaccounted for. Flight No. 9 did not fly on July 3 as scheduled but was postponed and was thus too late to have been responsible for the activity on the Brazel ranch. Flight No. 4 did not fly at all, but was cancelled. The next day, when Flight No. 5 was launched, it was designated as the first successful flight in New Mexico.[26] Moreover, if Project Mogul had been the code name for an operation to spy on the Soviets, that information would have been held in secrecy and not communicated to those in New Mexico. But since the project name is mentioned three times in Crary's field diary, there was clearly nothing secret about the project's name at all. Only its ultimate purpose was classified.

While it may be difficult to prove that AFOSI was behind Cavitt's staged interview and affidavit, it certainly contains all the hallmarks of just such a tactic. Both Cavitt and Weaver were former members of AFOSI; both had training in deception and disinformation; both seemed to know what the other was going to say or ask prior to it being said or asked. The interview doesn't have a natural flow, and questions that were suggested by Cavitt's answers were ignored. This interview was designed to mislead those with a limited knowledge of the Roswell case and lead them to the wrong conclusion. It was intended to suggest an alternative answer not supported by the facts. Project Mogul balloons were not the culprit. The debris left by those balloons was recovered. Debris that was not recovered was detailed in Dr. Crary's field notes and none of that points to anything found on the Brazel ranch. Instead, we're told that Marcel and Rickett were "excitable" and sometimes leaped to the wrong conclusions. This red herring clearly pushed a specific agenda intended to hide the truth.

Subsequent AFOSI operations, however, would take on a more aggressive nature that involved more than a few half-truths and little white lies. These tactics would push one man into the hospital as the system worked to discredit his work. And while it is not clear if the Deep State was maneuvering behind the scenes, it is quite clear that AFOSI was involved.

CHAPTER 2

The Shadows Deepen

According to Captain Edward Ruppelt, one-time chief of Project Blue Book, the Pentagon was in a panic in the summer of 1947.[1] Kenneth Arnold had reported nine objects, later described as crescent-shaped, flying over the Cascade Mountains in Washington State. He estimated their speed at around 1,800 miles an hour and he could see nothing on them that looked like a tail. He was puzzled by what he had seen and didn't think it matched anything in the current aviation inventory, although he did think the objects might be part of some sort of secret project.[2]

Had it not caught the attention of the media and "gone viral" as we say today, Arnold's report probably wouldn't have inspired so many other sightings. But in a matter of days, these objects, first called "flying saucers" and then "flying disks," were being reported around the country in great numbers and then around the world. Many of these reports were made by military pilots, and the maneuvers attributed to the objects suggested that they were faster and more agile than anything of known terrestrial manufacture. Military officials believed that they were seeing a leap forward in aviation technology and feared that the United States would be left helpless before that new technology. Perhaps the Soviet Union had developed a new weapons system for which the U. S. had no countermeasures. Top officers and civilians in the Pentagon needed answers and they needed them quickly. The fate of the United States could hang in the balance if the cold war suddenly turned hot.

Unlike today, when we have access to a great deal of classified information, in 1947, much of this information was hidden by the government and the intelligence agencies. UFO sightings remained mysterious in the late 1940s and anything that suggested an alien presence was quickly suppressed. Today, for instance, we know that U-2 test flights, high-altitude balloon research, and the testing of ejection systems were behind some of the more interesting UFO reports in those early years. And we now have access to so much information that we can even identify the influence that the Deep State had on our understanding of UFO phenomena. In fact, understanding the situation as it developed then can help us to interpret the situation as it exists today.

In 1947, while the military was gathering UFO cases, interviewing witnesses, and filing reports, they were also worried about what was causing these sightings. They were worried about invasion—not necessarily from outer space, but by our global adversaries. They needed answers quickly to address potential national security concerns, and they did what they had been taught to do in similar circumstances. They began to evaluate the information that had been gathered— intelligence, as it is called in military circles—and started looking for patterns that could supply the answers they needed. This was the task undertaken first by Project Sign, then by Project Grudge, which finally evolved into Project Blue Book. These projects officially began in January 1948 and continued until December 1969 (see chapter 7). The goals of the projects were to determine if UFOs were a threat to national security and to evaluate UFO-related data scientifically. By the time Project Blue Book ended, it had collected 12,618 UFO reports, most of which were dismissed as misidentifications of natural phenomena or conventional aircraft, although a small percentage of them were classified as "unexplained," even after careful investigation.

Edward Ruppelt wrote:

> The memos and correspondence that Project Blue Book
> inherited from the old UFO [Sign and Grudge] projects told
> the story of the early flying saucer era. These memos and
> pieces of correspondence showed that the UFO situation was
> considered to be serious; in fact, very serious. The paper work
> of that period also indicated the confusion that surrounded
> the investigation; confusion almost to the point of panic. The
> brass wanted an answer quickly.[3]

Questions about the identity of flying saucers weren't left just to
those at the very top of the military chain of command, however.
In fact, questions about flying saucers were also posed to civilians
working at the highest levels of the government, many of whom had
been appointed rather than elected.

Others at the lower levels of both the civilian and military bureau-
cracies who examined these questions came to believe that the
answers they sought were being held in secret at the Air Materiel
Command (AMC) headquarters at Wright Field, or at the very top
levels of command in the Pentagon. Lieutenant Colonel George
Garrett, working with FBI agent S. W. Reynolds, thought he understood what was happening but couldn't understand why. Garrett
and Reynolds wondered why they were being pressured to answer
questions about what they believed to be a secret project conducted
by military scientists. Dr. Michael Swords, who has spent decades
studying the early history of the UFO phenomenon, wrote:

> The cases they were reviewing indicated an unusual aerial
> technology of at least one type, and through the first weeks
> of July [1947] there had been intense pressure exerted down
> the chain of command ("from Topside") to get an explana-
> tion. But by late July and into August, that pressure had sud-
> denly evaporated. Why? Garrett and Reynolds felt the need

to know. The only thing they could think of was that some exceptionally secret U. S. technology was doing all this, and the news had finally been passed along to the Big Wheels topside. If so, why were Garrett, Reynolds, and the FBI wasting their time? Garrett prepared a condensed estimate stating his findings and requested that his superiors, Colonel Robert Taylor and Brigadier General [George] Schulgen, ask all services if they knew about any project to explain all this.[4]

The implication here is clear: If an answer was being held at the top of the command chain, why were those at the other end of that chain gathering sighting reports or attempting to explain what the flying saucers were? In fact, this exercise could conceivably compromise any classified project by exposing it to those not authorized to know about it, whatever it might be. While the phenomena reported were strange, they were not, technically, "unexplained" if they were known to someone at the top—especially if that explanation reached into the Deep State. The last thing that any military officers wanted to do was to expose the next generation of military aircraft to U. S. adversaries through an unintentional leak to the media about flying saucers.

In the weeks that followed, Schulgen and Garrett put together what was known as an Estimate of the Situation (EOTS). This was not the Estimate that Ruppelt and others have talked about, but rather an intelligence analysis of sixteen UFO sightings, many of them made by pilots and other members of the military. In it, they solicited the assistance of the intelligence officers at Wright Field, home of research facilities that would be able to identify whatever it was flashing unchecked over American territory and determine its source.[5]

Typical of the sightings contained in this document is one that involved a Navy veteran and a number of other witnesses who made a report from Manitou Springs, Colorado. This sighting is important because it was made prior to that of Kenneth Arnold, although it was not reported until after the publicity generated by Arnold's sighting.[6] The first mention of the case appeared on June 28 in the *Denver Post*. The witnesses included Dean Hauser, a Navy veteran, and six railroad workers, including Ted Weigand, Marion Hisshouse, T. J. Smith, and L. D Jamison. The group was eating lunch when Weigand spotted a bright silver-colored object approaching rapidly from the northeast. It stopped almost directly overhead and they watched it perform wild gyrations for a number of minutes. Hauser said that the object, after approaching in a straight line, "began to move erratically in wide circles. All this time it reflected light, like metal, but intermittently, as though the angle of reflection might be changing from time to time."

According to these witnesses, it was difficult to get a clear idea of the object's shape and even viewing it through binoculars did not appear to "bring it any closer." They estimated its height at 1,000 feet. For twenty minutes, they watched it climb, dive, reverse its flight course, and finally move off in a westerly direction. "It disappeared in a straight line in the west northwest in a clear blue sky," Hauser reported. At no time did anyone hear any noise.

The first *Post* article was followed by a second the next day. This time, the *Post* reported that witnesses had been interviewed by members of the 15th Air Force Headquarters and that the results of the investigation would be sent on to Washington, suggesting that they would be seen by Garrett, who presumably would be impressed by the number of eyewitnesses and the fact that they were men with some mechanical expertise. Washington's conclusion, however, was that the sighting was of "possible birds," although witnesses observed the object through binoculars over a period of about twenty minutes and would certainly have recognized it as birds if that were true.

The important point here is that there was an investigation by the *military*. Although never explicitly stated, it is likely that the investigators were members of the Counterintelligence Corps (CIC). The report would have remained with the CIC until the separation of the Air Force from the Army, at which point it would have been passed on to AFOSI. Equally significant is the fact that the sighting didn't make its way into any official UFO investigation or into the files of Project Blue Book.

Garrett next cited a report by Bryon Savage, a businessman pilot living in Oklahoma City. Savage said that, on May 17 or 18 at about 8:30 PM, he saw a round flat object that he described in some accounts as "disc-like," traveling nearly due north at a speed estimated at three times that of a jet.[7] It disappeared from view in about fifteen to twenty seconds. The *Oklahoma City Times* gave the story prominent space on June 26th. At the time of his sighting, Savage was out in his yard near dusk when he saw the object "come across the city from just a little east of south":

> Its altitude was very high somewhere around 10,000 feet, I couldn't be sure. Funny thing about it, it made no noise. I don't think it had [any] kind of internal combustion engine. But I did notice that right after it went out of sight, I heard the sound of rushing wind and air. I told my wife right away, but she thought I must have seen lightning.

Savage said that the object was "a shiny, silvery color," and very large—"bigger than any aircraft we have." He described it as "perfectly round and flat" and "frosty white." Although the sighting details Savage provided are far more complete than those given for many of the official cases listed by Project Blue Book as "explained," this report was placed in the category of "insufficient information."

Garrett's report included a sighting from Greenfield, Massachusetts on June 22:

> Edward L. de Rose said . . . there appeared across his line of vision a "brilliant, small, round-shaped, silvery white object"

moving in a northwesterly direction as fast as or probably faster than a speeding plane at an estimated altitude of 1,000 feet or more. The object stayed in view for eight or ten seconds until obscured by a cloud bank. It reflected the sunlight strongly as though it were of polished aluminum or silver . . . He said it did not resemble any weather balloon he had ever seen and that "I can assure you it was very real."

This case had been secretly investigated by the FBI and, given Special Agent Reynolds' participation with Schulgen and Garrett, this is not surprising. This demonstrates an FBI interest in UFOs that began early on—something the FBI sometimes suggests they wanted to hide. It may also be an indication that the Deep State was taking an interest in UFO sightings from the start, because keeping the FBI out of any public discussion of UFOs would also keep the Deep State's interest secret.

One of the most telling cases in Garrett's report involved multiple witnesses and pilots, including Wilson H. Kayko, John H. Cantrell, Theodore Dewey, and someone identified only as Redman. Project Blue Book files show that two Air Force (at the time, Army Air Forces) pilots and two intelligence officers saw a bright light zigzagging in the night sky over Maxwell Air Force Base on June 28, 1947. The sighting lasted for about five minutes, which gave them an opportunity for a solid observation that ruled out many mundane explanations like meteors. Ed Ruppelt, in his book *The Report on Unidentified Flying Objects*, reported it this way:

> That night [June 28] at nine-twenty, four Air Force officers, two pilots and two intelligence officers from Maxwell AFB in Montgomery, Alabama, saw a bright light traveling across the sky. It was first seen just above the horizon, and as it traversed toward the observers it "zigzagged," with bursts of high speed. When it was directly overhead, it made a sharp 90-degree turn and was lost from view as it traveled south.

The Blue Book files contain just ten pages of information about the case, including the project card and weather data. A letter dated July 7, 1947, to the Assistant Chief of Staff for Intelligence at Air Tactical Command (ATC) gave additional information:

> At approximately 2120 Central time, a light, with a brilliance slightly better than a star, appeared in the West. It was first noted above the horizon of the clear moon-light night, traveling in an easterly direction at a high rate of speed. There was no audible sound and it was impossible to determine the altitude, except that it appeared to be at great height. It traveled in a zig zag course with frequent bursts of speed, much like a water bug as it spurts and stops across the surface of water. It continued until it was directly overhead and changed course 90 [degrees] into the south. After traveling in the above manner for approximately five (5) minutes, it turned southwest and was lost in the brilliance of the moon. [sic] at 2145 Central it was no longer possible to observe.

The letter, which was signed by one of the witnesses, Wilson Kayko, noted: "No plausible explanation is offered for the unusual action of this source of light, which acted contrary to common aerodynamic laws."

And here's another interesting note. On the "checklist" that contains many questions about the sighting, there is one question about photographs. The answer? "None in our file altho letter of transmittal indicates one was sent." That photograph has never surfaced and may well have found its way into the files of the Deep State.

The eventual explanation for this case was that this was a balloon, although it seems that four officers, including two intelligence officers, would have been able to identify a balloon when they saw one. It would also seem that the maneuvers of the object would rule out a balloon, regardless of how strong the winds aloft were or how variable they may have been at different altitudes. Moreover, there is nothing to suggest a lighted balloon in the area, although weather balloons did sometimes carry lights to make them easier to see after dark.

In another case reported by Garrett, a police officer and others in Grand Falls, Newfoundland reported an egg-shaped object with a barrel-like leading edge, as well four objects that had a phosphorescent glow. The sighting occurred about thirty minutes before midnight on July 9, 1947. The next day, a series of sightings were reported across Newfoundland. One of these took place about 4:00 PM and was seen by a "TWA Representatives and a PAA Representative [identified as J. N. Mehrman, A. R. Leidy, and J. E. Woodruff] on the ground." The object was "circular in shape, like a wagon wheel"—bluish-black with a fifteen-foot-long trail. It "seemed to cut clouds open as it passed thru [sic]. Trail was like beam seen after a high-powered landing light is switched off."

This case took on added importance because there were color photographs of the disk as it cut through the clouds. Swords reported the event in the *Journal of UFO Studies*:

> The bluish-black trail seems to indicate ordinary combustion from a turbo-jet engine, athodyd [ramjet] motor, or some combination of these types of power plants. The absence of noise and apparent dissolving of the clouds to form a clear path indicates a relatively large mass flow of a rectangular cross section containing a considerable amount of heat.

The report reached General Schulgen on July 16, with a more detailed version following on July 21. The updated information was sent on to the Pentagon. Schulgen ordered T-2, part of the intelligence function at Wright-Patterson, to take a top team to Harmon AFB in Newfoundland to investigate.[8]

This response provides a hint as to what Garrett and others were thinking in 1947. They believed that the answers lay in terrestrial technology—in other words, this was something of Soviet manufacture. The sightings, first in Canada and then in Alaska, led them to suspect that the Soviets were flying something along what was known as "the great circle route." While the sighting itself is interesting for the photographs, it was important because it seemed to indicate Soviet rather than alien activity. The original investigation had excluded meteors or fireballs as possible explanations. Later, as Blue Book officers became more interested in explanations than facts, however, the case was written off as a meteor.

Garrett sent his report, through Schulgen, to the Air Materiel Command at Wright Field for review. The top intelligence officer there was Colonel Howard McCoy, who, in World War II, had been involved in the investigation of the Foo Fighters, those strange lights and anomalies seen by flight crews during the war.[9] McCoy was aware that no explanation for the mysterious phenomenon had ever been found; when the war ended, the urgency for providing one evaporated. No one cared what the Foo Fighters had been, because they no longer posed a threat. Reports of them tapered off and finally disappeared.[10]

In 1946, McCoy was involved in a similar mystery that involved what were dubbed Ghost Rockets—strange missiles that were reported first in Finland and later in Sweden, and then across most of northern Europe. No explanation was ever found for them either, although some believed them to be a Soviet attempt to intimidate the Scandinavians. When the Soviet Union collapsed in the 1990s and many of their classified files were opened to UFO researchers, however, it became clear that the Ghost Rockets had not been launched by the Soviets.[11] McCoy spent time in Sweden gathering intelligence on them and he took that intelligence with him when he returned to Wright Field.

McCoy had also been gathering information on similar phenomena reported, not only in Europe, but in the United States. His sources were, quite naturally, the military's aviation units. According to the best information available today, McCoy was directed to open an unofficial investigation into the ongoing problem of these unidentified aerial phenomena in December 1946.[12] When these strange things, whatever they might be, hit the media in the United States in June 1947, it was McCoy who inherited the problem of identification. Since he was already, in a sense, a "subject matter expert," those in the Pentagon turned to him for explanations. When Schulgen's and Garrett's Estimate arrived at Wright Field for evaluation, Lieutenant General Nathan F. Twining, commanding officer of the Air Materiel Command at Wright Field, passed the document to McCoy for his analysis.

While it seems that both Schulgen and Garrett expected to be told that there was no reason for concern, that the sightings were part of a classified project, the answer they received from Twining was something completely different. Rather than ordering them to back off their investigation, a letter dated September 23 that was signed by Twining but written by McCoy seemed to confirm their findings:[13]

1. As requested by AC/AS–2 there is presented below the considered opinion of this Command concerning the so-called "Flying Discs." This opinion is based on interrogation report data furnished by AC/AS–2 and preliminary studies by personnel of T–2 and Aircraft Laboratory, Engineering Division T–3. This opinion was arrived at in a conference between personnel from the Air Institute of Technology, Intelligence T–2, Office, Chief of Engineering Division, and the Aircraft, Power Plant and Propeller Laboratories of Engineering Division T–3.

2. It is the opinion that:

   a. The phenomenon reported is something real and not visionary or fictitious.

   b. There are objects probably approximately the shape of a disc, of such appreciable size as to appear to be as large as man-made aircraft.

c. There is a possibility that some of the incidents may be caused by natural phenomena, such as meteors.

d. The reported operating characteristics such as extreme rates of climb, maneuverability (particularly in roll), and action which must be considered evasive when sighted or contacted by friendly aircraft and radar, lend belief to the possibility that some of the objects are controlled either manually, automatically or remotely.

e. The apparent common description of the objects is as follows:

(1) Metallic or light reflecting surface. . .

(2) Absence of trail, except in a few instances when the object apparently was operating under high performance conditions.

(3) Circular or elliptical in shape, flat on bottom and domed on top.

(4) Several reports of well kept formation flights varying from three to nine objects.

(5) Normally no associated sound, except in three instances a substantial rumbling roar was heard.

(6) Level flight speeds normally above 300 knots are estimated.

f. It is possible within the present U. S. knowledge—provided extensive detailed development is undertaken—to construct a piloted aircraft which has the general description of the object in subparagraph (e) above which would be capable of an approximate range of 7000 miles at subsonic speeds.

g. Any developments in this country along the lines indicated would be extremely expensive, time consuming and at the considerable expense of current projects and therefore, if directed, should be set up independently of existing projects.

h. Due consideration must be given the following:

(1) The possibility that these objects are of domestic origin—the product of some high security project not known to AC/AS–2 or this command.

(2) The lack of physical evidence in the shape of crash recovered exhibits which would undeniably prove the existence of these objects.

(3) The possibility that some foreign nation has a form of propulsion possibly nuclear, which is outside of our domestic knowledge.

3. It is recommended that:

a. Headquarters, Army Air Forces issue a directive assigning a priority, security classification and Code Name for a detailed study of the matter to include the preparation of complete sets of all available and pertinent data which will then be made available to the Army, Navy, Atomic Energy Commission, JRDB, the Air Force Scientific Advisory Board Group, NACA, and the RAND and NEPA projects for comments and recommendations, with a preliminary report to be forwarded within 15 days of receipt of the data and a detailed report thereafter every 30 days as the investigation develops. A complete interchange of data should be effected.

4. Awaiting a specific directive AMC will continue the investigation within its current resources in order to more closely define the nature of the phenomenon. Detailed Essential Elements of Information will be formulated immediately for transmittal thru channels.[14]

The second page of the report begins with the following heading: "basic Ltr fr CG, AMC WF to CO, AAF, Wash. D.C. subj "AMC Opinion Concerning 'Flying Discs.'"

This letter marks the beginning of the official investigation into flying saucers. It was, at that time, limited to the military—specifically, what was now the Air Force—to determine what was being seen. Although it suggests that this was a priority project, it was not scheduled to begin its work until January 1948, or three months from the writing of Twining's letter. The involvement of the Deep State, as it applied to flying saucers, was buried under layers of bureaucracy. The first hints of Deep State interference came with the fabled Estimate of the Situation created for Air Force Chief of Staff General Hoyt S. Vandenberg the following year.

PROJECT SIGN

During the first months of 1948, as the Air Force investigated a number of UFO sightings, the mood of investigators was serious. They believed they were doing important work and the fact that they were receiving sightings by qualified people suggested that something quite real was flying around in the atmosphere. They weren't sure about the source of these strange craft, only that reliable people were reporting them and that top brass, not to mention civilians in the chain of command that led up to the president, were worried about what was being reported.

Part of the inspiration for Schulgen's and Garrett's Estimate was a sighting made on July 20, 1948, that was reported the next day to Project Sign, an official Air Force study of UFOs that was active until February 1949, when it became Project Grudge. That sighting, made by several people in The Hague, Netherlands said they had seen a UFO as it maneuvered among high, broken clouds. It was rocket-shaped and had two rows of windows along its side. No further details were given and the sighting itself is not found in the Project Blue Book files. Clearly, however, it was reported in some form to the Air Force.[15]

This report would probably have escaped notice if not for another sighting just days later by airline pilots Clarence Chiles and John B. Whitted. Chiles and Whitted were flying in a commercial DC-3 at 5,000 feet on what they described as a bright, nearly cloudless night. About twenty miles southwest of Montgomery, Alabama, they saw a bright light slightly above and to the right of their aircraft. Their first reaction, given the brightness of the glow, was that they were seeing one of the military's new "jet jobs." Chiles called Whitted's attention to it by saying: "Look, here comes a new Army jet."

As the object approached in what appeared to be a slight dive, it deflected to the left and then passed them on the right. They believed that the object was at their flight level. As it passed, they could see a double row of square windows on a torpedo-shaped craft. Then the craft seemed to pull up slightly and disappear into the clouds.

Whitted spoke to Air Force investigators just hours after landing:

> The fuselage appeared to be about three times the circumference of a B-29 fuselage. The windows were very large and seemed square. They were white with light which seemed to be caused by some type of combustion. I estimate we watched the object for at least five seconds and not more than ten seconds. We heard no noise nor did we feel any turbulence from that object.

Two weeks later, on August 3, Chiles made a written statement: "It was clear there were no wings present, that it was powered by some jet or other type of power showing flame from the rear some fifty feet . . . Underneath the ship there was a blue glow of light."[16]

Ruppelt noted in his book that this case, in which it seemed that a UFO nearly collided with a commercial passenger airliner, caught the attention of those working on Project Sign:

> According to old-timers at ATIC [Air Technical Intelligence Center], this report shook them worse than the Mantell incident [the case of an Air Guard pilot who was killed chasing a UFO]. This was the first time two reliable sources [meaning Chiles and Whitted] had been really close enough to anything resembling a UFO to get a good look and live to tell about it.[17]

This sighting prompted the Estimate that eventually made its way to Vandenberg.

Those assigned to the UFO investigation at Wright-Patterson pulled together data received from dozens of sources for a careful analysis. They decided that these reports indicated that some sort of interplanetary, as opposed to interstellar, craft was visiting Earth. Those making that assumption had access to all the details of secret aircraft currently under development. They knew what was being done at White Sands Proving Ground, and had a good handle on what other nations were doing to create the next generation of military aircraft and missiles. No one they knew of had anything that matched the reported capabilities of the UFOs. The only conclusion they could draw was that they were craft built on another planet.

The Estimate was passed up the chain of command until it reached the desk of the Air Force Chief of Staff, who was not impressed with the evidence. Despite discussions of radar sightings, photographs, and the testimony of some very reliable and credible people—including Air Force pilots—the report was "batted" back down. Vandenberg said that the case had not been made; they "lacked proof." But that wasn't the end of it. Those responsible for the Estimate were ordered to Washington for a meeting with the "relevant" members of the intelligence community. Captain Robert Sneider led those from Project Sign. Others from that project and from the Air Materiel Command (AMC) probably included Loedding, Deyarmond, Lawrence Truettner, and Colonel Howard McCoy.[18] Opposing them were people from the Office of Naval Intelligence and possibly members of the CIA—that is, representatives of the Deep State.

Apparently, those in Washington, including both military officers and civilian agencies, were also unimpressed. Project Sign was required to send copies of all their reports to various individuals and agencies in Washington for analysis. The Deep State was taking away the ability of those left at AMC and the Air Technical Intelligence Center (ATIC) to investigate and to analyze the sightings.

This marked the end of Project Sign. Deyarmond and Truettner returned to Ohio to rewrite the report, excluding any mention of the interplanetary theory. The project's name was changed to Project Grudge and, according to Swords: "Within a month or two, all of the main contributors to the Sign project were reassigned to other duties, leaving only the two lowest ranks (a Lieutenant Smith and a civilian, Towles) to maintain a case filing activity under the term Grudge."[19]

According to Ruppelt, a few months later, sometime in December, the Estimate was declassified and ordered destroyed, perhaps due to machinations of the Deep State. After all, if the report proved nothing and was not classified, it could pose no threat to national security. So why was it necessary to destroy it? The answer is simple. The destruction of classified material requires a document signed by the officers who carry out the order. This destruction order gives the title of the document, its classificiation status, and a control number, all of which prove that the document existed. By declassifying and then destroying the report, they destroyed the paper trail and the evidence disappeared.

Ruppelt, however, doesn't mention any of this. Nor does he mention the carnage that followed Vandenberg's negative reaction, which seemed to be disproportionate. The Estimate was, after all, a report based on the sightings by dozens of people around the United States. Those who had written the report, however, were soon transferred from ATIC. When the purge was over, only one or two of the lowest ranking members of the ATIC team remained. After all, UFO investigations couldn't be very important if only a lieutenant and a civilian were left in charge of them.

The Deep State had taken control of the UFO problem. They now decided who should do what and directed how questions and problems should be handled. Moreover, they actually decided what the answers should be. But the involvement of the Deep State would become even more apparent in the summer of 1952, when flying saucers swarmed over Washington on two consecutive Saturday nights in July.

CHAPTER 3

The Deep State Takes Control

After the rejection of the ATIC Estimate, UFO investigation was left largely in the hands of the Air Force and various Air Force projects, both public and classified. Although there are documents in the Project Blue Book files, not to mention in various government and university archives, that prove the FBI's interest in the inquiry, there is little evidence at this point that the Deep State had any interest in investigating UFOs or in directing how that research should be conducted. There are hints of CIA involvement in the rejection of the Estimate, but no real hard evidence of it. To all appearances, the CIA, as well as other government intelligence agencies, just didn't seem to be concerned about UFO sightings.

Then, on two consecutive Saturday nights in July 1952, UFOs were seen over Washington, D. C. They were tracked on radar and intercepted by jet fighters scrambled from nearby Air Force bases. According to CAA logbooks (forerunner of the Federal Aviation Administration), it all began at 11:40 PM on the evening of July 19, when radar at the Air Routing and Traffic Control Center (ARTC) picked up eight unidentified targets near Andrews Air Force Base.[1]

GAME ON

When air traffic controller Edward Nugent spotted seven unidentified and uncorrelated blips clustered in the corner of his radar screen, indicating they were in an area about fifteen miles south-southwest of Washington, D. C., he knew they were not airplanes because they appeared to accelerate far faster than any conventional aircraft could at the time. After moving along at about 100 miles an hour, they suddenly seemed to accelerate to unbelievable speeds. According to calculations made by the men watching the screens, one of the objects was tracked at around 7,000 miles an hour. Nugent called Harry C. Barnes, the senior air traffic controller on duty, who later wrote:

> We knew immediately that a very strange situation existed . . . They [the unidentified blips on the radar] followed no set course [and] were not in any formation, and we only seemed to be able to track them for about three miles at a time. The individual pip would seem to disappear from the scope at intervals. Later I realized that if these objects had made any sudden burst of extremely high speed, that would account for them disappearing from the scope.[2]

That put the speed of the craft right in the range of the 7,000 mile-an-hour bursts noticed by Nugent earlier.

After two other controllers, both trained in basic radar maintenance, found nothing wrong with their equipment, Barnes called Howard Cocklin, his counterpart in Tower Central. This facility was located about a quarter mile away at the same airport, so, even if the radar at the ARTC were malfunctioning, those at Central should not be affected. Cocklin told Barnes that they had spotted and were tracking the same objects, and that he had looked out the windows of the control tower and seen one of them high overhead. He described the object later as a bright orange light, but said he could see no shape behind the light and could offer no details about it other than that it was bright and overhead. Cocklin's report seemed to confirm that, in fact, something *was* in the sky near the airport.

Barnes next called nearby Andrews Air Force Base and asked if they had seen anything on their radar, but was told that they were seeing nothing out of the ordinary—just a C-47 (the military version of the DC-3) that was scheduled to land at Andrews in about an hour. Moments later, Barnes made another call to Andrews and suggested that they look outside, because there was something strange in the sky near the base. When Airman William Brady did just that, he saw what he later described as "an object which appeared to be like an orange ball of fire, trailing a tail. It appeared to be about two miles south and one-half mile from the Andrews range. It was very bright and definite and unlike anything I had ever seen."[3]

Brady tried to get others at the Andrews facility to verify his sighting, but, even as he shouted to them, the brightly glowing object stopped moving and then just seemed to vanish. According to Brady, it "took off at an unbelievable speed" and disappeared in a split second.[4] No one else in the tower saw anything, although later there were other sightings made from the tower. This may have been because things happened so quickly, or it may have been that Brady saw nothing more than a few stars through a thin layer of haze. In fact, this was the explanation later offered by Air Force investigators to reduce the importance and number of sightings reported that night. Nonetheless, a memo in the Project Blue Book files reports a sighting at about 12:30 AM of "an orange disk about 3,000 feet . . . at 360 degrees [due north]."[5] This report could be independent confirmation of Brady's sighting, made at Andrews at about the same time. But, as so often happens, the report was too short on important details to make the necessary connection.

At about 2:00 AM on July 20, or just a little over two hours later, Captain Harold C. Way, radar officer at Andrews Approach Control, learned that the ARTC had a target just east of the base. He went outside and saw a strange light. At the time, he didn't believe it was a star, but said that he thought it was changing colors, from "red to orange to green to red again," and that it seemed to lose altitude rapidly and then climb again.[6] When he went back out, however, he decided that he was, in fact, looking at a star and that the sky conditions had fooled him—at least this is what he later told Air Force investigators. It now seems, however, that pressure was exerted on witnesses to explain all the sightings reported that night as stars, thus obscuring what was really going on. The Air Force didn't want to admit that they were powerless to stop an invasion of the sky over Washington. And to make things worse, they couldn't even identify what the objects were.

Bolling Air Force Base, another Air Force installation in the D. C. area, became briefly involved at about the same time that Way went outside. The tower operator there reported seeing a roundish object drifting low in the sky to the southeast of the base. Although there is no radar confirmation of his sighting and it is unclear if he had heard the radio exchanges between other facilities, this report does implicate a third government facility in the events of that evening.

Then ATRC radar operators at National Airport began to detect targets near Bolling and informed the tower operators, including SSgt Richard Lacava, the operations dispatcher at Bolling. From a mobile control tower—a truck-mounted tower that can be repositioned as needed—SSgt Don Wilson spotted a round, white-amber light about the intensity of a star that he believed was drifting slowly about seven miles to the southeast of the airfield. Although it remained visible for a few minutes, Wilson could see no details other than the bright light itself. This does sound suspiciously like a star seen through a partially cloudy sky, giving the light the appearance of motion.

In still another sighting from that area, a guard who was going off-duty saw an object to the southwest:

> [It] looked to be the size of a golf ball . . . bright orange in color. The object moved from the west to the northeast in a half circle pattern and was traveling at such speed that I knew

that it could not be a jet aircraft . . . It would be hard to judge the altitude the object was flying because it seemed to lose and gain altitude. The object moved in this pattern several times and then disappeared into the west. From the time I saw the object and then lost it, I would say it was about 15 to 20 minutes.[7]

This meant that the guard had gotten a very good look at the object. This was no fleeting light seen for only a few seconds or a star seen through the clouds. This report suggests something more than a misidentified star.

These multiple radar-facility reports, which tend to rule out many of the more mundane explanations for the sightings, were quite important. At one point during the night, the radars at the ARTC, Washington National Airport, and Andrews were all fixed on an object hovering over the Riverdale radio beacon. It remained for thirty seconds, allowing the radar operators in all three locations to check their readings and their equipment against one another's observations. The target vanished from the screens at all three radar facilities at the same time, suggesting that something real had been detected as opposed to some sort of weather-induced return.

Associated Press stories written hours after the sightings and based on information supplied by the Air Force claimed that no intercepts had been attempted that night, but those stories were inaccurate. Documents in the Project Blue Book files, as well as eyewitnesses interviewed at the time, confirm that intercepts were attempted. Barnes, in fact, believed that the UFOs were monitoring the radio traffic, because, at about 3:00 AM, all the mysterious targets suddenly disappeared from the radar screens. Moments later, two F-94 jet interceptors, scrambled from New Castle Air Force Base in Delaware, streaked across the sky. Although the interceptor pilots searched for the UFOs, they found and saw nothing and low fuel levels finally forced them to return to base. As the jets left the area, however, the UFOs reappeared—which suggested to some that the objects were under intelligent control. It also seemed to confirm Barnes's belief that they were monitoring radio traffic.

Moreover, it wasn't just men on the ground and in the towers at Andrews and Washington National or those at radar screens inside those facilities who reported seeing UFOs that night. Airline pilot Captain Casey Pierman on Capital Airlines Flight 807 also spotted the lights. On a flight between Washington, D. C. and Martinsburg, West Virginia on July 20 at around 1:15 AM, he and the rest of the crew saw seven objects flash across the sky in front of them. Pierman said: "They were like falling stars without trails."[8]

Capital Airline officials confirmed that National Airport radar had picked up the objects and asked Pierman to keep an eye on them. Shortly after take-off, Pierman radioed that he had them in sight. He was flying at 180 to 200 mph and reported that the objects were traveling at tremendous speed. Official Air Force records confirm this, which means that Pierman did make the report to Air Force officers. This also suggests that the UFOs were not weather-related, because Pierman and his crew saw the same thing that the radar had picked up, and those returns were repeatedly confirmed as solid objects. As further confirmation, the number of objects and the maneuvers they performed matched what was seen on radar.

Throughout the night, Barnes repeatedly attempted to alert military authorities at various military facilities about the series of UFO sightings. He wanted the closest Air Force intelligence officer alerted so that a proper military record could be made of them. When he spoke to the duty officers at those facilities, they told him that the information was being forwarded up the chain of command and that they had no authority to do anything other than take his call—which would, of course, be logged. It is clear, however, that military officials were already responding to the sightings, because they were attempting intercepts. Just before daylight, after repeated requests from the ARTC, another F-94 interceptor arrived on the scene, but it was too little too late. All the targets were now gone. Although the flight crew made a short search of the local area, they found nothing unusual or exciting, and returned quickly to base. At about 5:30 AM, seven or eight of the objects reappeared on the ARTC radar, but they faded quickly from sight. At about this same time, radio engineer E. W. Chambers saw five huge disks circling in a loose formation over the Washington, D. C. area. As he watched, the disks climbed steeply and disappeared.

Barnes confirmed these events nearly fifteen years later when he talked to investigators for the Condon Committee. This was part of the University of Colorado UFO Project funded by the Air Force from 1966 to 1968 under the leadership of physicist Edward Condon (see chapter 6).

> A number of objects, some seven or eight, would be in a place as a group, then seem to go over to an aircraft to take a look. If the aircraft attempted evasive action by turning, the objects would turn too. They seemed, furthermore, to have monitored messages between the aircraft and the tower. When a particular pilot was told to look for an object the pilot would see it, but would report that it was zooming off at just about the time at which the target also disappeared from the radar set. Many of the objects were extremely maneuverable.[9]

Barnes also told the committee that he didn't believe that the objects they had detected were "ghost" or weather-related phenomena. He ruled out a malfunction as well, pointing out that Washington National, Andrews, and Andrews approach control had all independently sighted the objects at about the same time and at the same place. All the radars were operating normally and men at all three facilities were in contact and confirming the sightings.

In fact, during one of the attempted intercepts, the onboard radar of one of the jet fighters obtained a lock on one of the objects, which increased the number of radars involved. The pilot, however, did not have a visual sighting and the records don't seem to confirm this radar contact. The three radar facilities apparently only once reported seeing the targets on all three radars at the same time and in the same place. There were, however, a number of times when the ARTC and Washington National radars recorded simultaneous contacts, and it seems that they were displaying the same targets reported by the crew of the Capital Airlines flight. Later, Barnes told investigators for both the military and for the Condon Committee that the experience of finding unidentified radar and visual targets where there was supposed to be nothing but thin air had been frightening. He also mentioned that the UFOs had flown in the vicinity of the White House, which would later become a point of interest to many, as it was a clear violation of various FAA regulations.[10]

The bottom line is that, during that eventful night, multiple radars and multiple eyewitnesses saw and recorded objects in the sky over the Washington, D. C. For those in the Deep State, this in itself was disturbing. But when the White House was "buzzed," it became more than just an interesting series of sightings. And this brought the situation to the attention of President Truman.

ROUND TWO

The night of July 19 finally ended and the sightings on the radars at the various facilities faded. But the respite was a short one. The second round of sightings over Washington began a week later, on July 26. This wave of sightings didn't begin at night, however, nor were they first seen by radar operators at National Airport.[11] At about 2:30 PM, two radar operators at Langley Air Force Base, not far from Washington, watched an object on their radar for about two minutes. They estimated that it was approaching Langley from the south at a speed of 2,600 miles an hour at an altitude just under 5,000 feet. It disappeared from their screens when it was only eight miles away, which means that it either accelerated too fast for the radar to detect it, or it fell below the radar coverage.

About twenty minutes later, those same radar operators watched another target for about four minutes as it headed toward the east. It suddenly stopped, hovered for two minutes, and then continued its flight to the east, finally disappearing from the radar when it was about fifteen miles away. The operators believed that the object had simply dropped below 5,000 feet, which was the lower limit of the radar's capability. They tried to spot the object using binoculars, but were unable to find it. They also noted that the return on their screen was larger than that of an aircraft, and that it had a fuzzy appearance, suggesting to some that the blip was a weather anomaly.

About 10:30 PM (although some sources suggest it was as early as 8:00 PM), the same radar operators who had been on duty the week before again spotted several slow-moving targets on their radar at Washington National. The objects were spread out in a large arc over the city. This time, the controllers carefully marked each of the unidentified objects on their screens, then called the tower to confirm that the targets were appearing on their screens as well. A call to Andrews further confirmed that they were watching the same unknowns. That meant that three separate radar systems were displaying the same objects at the same time, thus ruling out equipment malfunction.

Senior controller Harry Barnes alerted the Pentagon that the unidentified targets were back. Given the experience of the week before, and given the number of sightings reported in the area during the intervening week, a number of military officers and other officials were put on alert. The first to respond was Al Chop, civilian Pentagon spokesman for UFO phenomena. Later in the evening, Major Dewey Fournet, UFO liaison officer at the Pentagon, and Navy Lt. John Holcomb made their way to National Airport. Holcomb, an electronics specialist temporarily assigned to the Air Force Directorate of Intelligence, was the resident radar expert.

After an hour of tracking the targets, the controllers called for jet interceptors. Chop said that he was in communication with the main command post at the Pentagon and had requested the interceptors, but that, as a civilian, he could only make the request and then wait for the flag officer (general or admiral) in command to make the official decision. He did, however, have connections at the Pentagon who took what he said seriously rather than just ignoring his request.[12]

The situation, at that point, was only mildly better than it had been a week earlier. As before, there was a delay in responding. But by midnight, two F-94 jet interceptors were on station over Washington. Reporters who had learned of the sightings and had arrived at the airport were asked by Chop to leave the radar room and told that classified radio and intercept procedures would be in operation during the intercept. Although this fact was well reported, Ed Ruppelt later wrote that this was absurd:

> [A]ny radio ham worth his salt could build equipment and listen in on any intercept. The real reason for the press dismissal, I learned, was that not a few people in the radar room were positive that this night would be the big night in UFO history—the night when a pilot would close in on and get a good look at a UFO—and they didn't want the press to be in on it.[13]

Chop disagreed, however:

> [B]ecause an intercept is run under classified [regulations], it was not privy to the reporters so I made them leave . . . We would allow them to come in there and look at the radar scopes until we ran into an intercept. At that time, they had to leave the room.[14]

Chop claimed he wasn't worried about the reporters overhearing supposedly classified intercept conversations. Rather he was concerned about them watching the intercepts as they played out on the radar screens, which might give away classified tactics and compromise classified information, depending on who said what during the intercepts. Whatever the reason, reporters were not allowed to watch the intercepts that evening.

Chop described the first of these intercepts for me during an interview in 1995. The fighters, according to him, came from New Castle, Delaware.

> The first two that came in, when they came in, we had about, I'd say, fourteen or fifteen UFOs, targets that we could not identify on the radar scopes. We had them marked. Well, we didn't mark the unknowns. They marked the known flights. Everything else on the scope was a UFO, of course . . . Now [Andrews] were tracking the objects or what appeared to be the same objects. We couldn't conclusively say they were exactly the same but the conversations between the flight controllers at Washington National and at [Andrews], they would say, "Do you have these four up at the southeast section of your scopes," and [Andrews] would say, "We have those."[15]

It's not clear whether Holcomb or Fournet telephoned the analysis to New Castle. Either way, the F-94s were scrambled and, on arrival, were vectored toward the various targets, which were now weaker. The pilots didn't see anything except an object in the distance that was identified as an aircraft and a hovering white light that disappeared when approached by the jets.

As had happened the week before, when the fighters arrived, all the UFOs vanished from radar. The jets were vectored to their last known position, but, even though visibility was unrestricted in the area that night, the pilots could see nothing interesting. The fighters made a systematic search, but since they could see nothing out of the ordinary, and because the targets had disappeared from all the radars, they returned to base. Their fuel was running low and their time over the target was limited because of the distance they had to travel to and from base. All this affected their ability to make intercepts.

Chop, describing the situation for me years later, said:

> The minute the first two interceptors appeared on our scope all our unknowns disappeared. It was like they just wiped them all off. All our other flights, all the known flights were still on the scope . . . We watched these two planes leave. When they were out of our range, immediately we got our UFOs back.[16]

Again, the Air Defense Command was alerted and again jet fighters were scrambled. This time, however, the pilots were able to see the objects and were vectored toward them by the air traffic controllers. But the fighters couldn't close on the lights. The pilots saw no external details behind the bright glow, and saw nothing other than lights where the radar suggested that something strange should be seen. Clearly these were not stars seen through haze or in some sort of unusual configuration. Nor did the situation seem to match many of the other standard explanations offered by the military and later by Project Blue Book.[17]

After several minutes of failing to get close to the targets, one of the lights was spotted loping along alone. Fighter pilot Lieutenant William Patterson turned, kicked in his afterburner for additional speed, and tried to catch the lone object. But it disappeared before he could see much of anything other than that it was a solid object. In an interview the next day, Patterson told reporters:

> I tried to make contact with the bogies below one thousand feet, but they [the controllers] vectored us around. I saw several bright lights. I was at my maximum speed, but even then, I had no closing speed. I ceased chasing them because I saw no chance of overtaking them. I was vectored into new

objects. Later I chased a single bright light which I estimated about ten miles away. I lost visual contact with it.[18]

Patterson finally had to break off his attempts, although there were still lights in the sky and objects on the radar screens. According to Chop, he radioed that he was running low on fuel and headed back to base. The last of the objects disappeared from radar at about the time the sun came up. "They stayed [under] observation on our radar scope until dawn," Chop said, "about five or six o'clock [that morning]. When it got light, they just gradually disappeared."[19]

Ruppelt later quizzed Dewey Fournet about the activities that night. He and Holcomb were apparently both convinced that the targets were solid, metallic objects. Fournet told Ruppelt that there were weather-related targets on radar that night as well, but that all the controllers were ignoring them. Holcomb and the radar operators could all tell the difference between weather-related targets caused by light-inversion layers and those they believed to be solid, real objects. Everyone in the radar rooms was convinced that the targets were real.[20]

On July 29, news outlets around the world told the whole story. In a banner headline that could have come from a science-fiction movie, *The Cedar Rapids Gazette* reported: "Saucers Swarm over Capital." The problem, however, is that no one was sure what had happened that night. Both Fournet and Chop, interviewed in 1995, told me that the radar returns were solid not weather-related, and that the objects seemed to react to the appearance of the jet interceptors. The radar operators and the Navy radar expert all thought they were looking at real objects and not echoes or refracted returns.[21]

When the night ended, the story did as well. While UFOs continued to be reported all over the United States for several weeks, the real interest was centered on the Washington sightings and those in power knew it. The consensus seemed to be that UFOs over almost anywhere else in the United States was interesting, but UFOs over Washington were frightening. The Air Force realized that these particular sightings had to be explained as quickly as possible, even if that explanation was less than plausible. The result was the largest military press conference held since the conclusion of World War II.

END GAME

At 4:00 PM on July 29, Major General John A. Samford, Chief of Air Intelligence, accompanied by Major General Roger Ramey, the same man who had been involved in the Roswell events in 1947, held a press conference at the Pentagon on orders from those in the civilian chain of command, which would have included the Secretary of Defense and probably the president.[22] Of that press conference, Ruppelt later wrote:

> General Samford made an honest attempt to straighten out the Washington National Sightings, but the cards were stacked against him. He had to hedge on many answers to questions from the press because he didn't know the answers. This hedging gave the impression that he was trying to cover up something more than just the fact his people fouled up in not fully investigating the sightings. Then he brought in Captain Roy James from ATIC to handle all the queries about radar. James didn't do any better because he had just arrived in Washington that morning and didn't know very much more about the sightings than [what] he'd read in the papers. Major Dewey Fournet and Lieutenant Holcomb, who had been at the airport during the sightings, were extremely conspicuous by their absence.[23]

Samford, backed up by his radar expert, suggested that there were temperature inversions over Washington on the nights in question, and that piece of weather information soon morphed into a full-blown explanation for the sightings that was shouted by newspapers that evening.

While Ruppelt seems to be covering for his superiors by suggesting a lack of insight into the sightings and a failure of staff to provide suitable information, the real reason may be something much more nefarious. It may be that General Samford had been directed to fumble for answers and wait until the radar expert provided some background on how radar works and how temperature inversions can "bend" the radar beams so that they provide false targets. They did, in fact, have one sighting that seemed to bear this out. One of the pilots had been told where to look for one of the UFOs, but the only thing he could find was a riverboat maneuvering on the river far below him. Each time he passed over it, he was told that he had just passed above the target. This explanation had been developed, not by the Air Force officers involved, but by those at a higher level—those hidden within the Deep State—who provided the "script" for the press conference. And while Ruppelt thought that Samford had fumbled the ball, the truth is that the press bought the answer. This, of course, suggests that those in the Deep State understood the news media and human psychology much better than Ruppelt did.

The truth is that the temperature-inversion explanation simply doesn't work, especially since there were both radar and visual observations made many times of the same thing. It doesn't work because, at some points, the interceptor pilots *did* see lights and objects right where the radar operators said they would be. But the weather explanation made those in charge in the Deep State happy and gave the news media an answer. So the sightings could now be ignored, which was the whole point to begin with. Besides, those in the Deep State were already planning to move UFOs from the front pages and supplant them with other events that seemed more important. A word or two in the ears of the senior editors and publishers of the print media would be sufficient.

And if all else failed, they could always fall back on the idea that those seeing UFOs were uneducated, unsophisticated, or simply a little drunk. After all, those who saw UFOs or who believed in them weren't the brightest people. It didn't matter to those in the Deep State how they diverted or deflected interest, just as long as they kept the nation thinking that there was nothing to the whole UFO saga and kept people from asking questions that might be difficult for them to answer.

After the Roswell crash, someone outside the military—someone in the upper reaches of the government—had decided that the public's interest in flying saucers was somehow dangerous. That person or group ordered that stories about flying saucers be kept off the front pages of the newspapers. One United Press story even announced on July 9, 1947: "Reports of flying saucers whizzing through the sky fell off sharply as the Army and the Navy began a concentrated campaign to stop the rumors."[24] Ironically, the newspaper reports on this request revealed to those paying attention that someone didn't want the information circulated. The effect of that strategy, while not immediate, can be seen in the sudden drop-off in the number of sighting reports made afterward. In July 1947, there were some days when reports of sightings covered an entire page of single-spaced entries in the Project Blue Book index. Beginning in August, however, that number fell off dramatically and, by September, the sightings on a single page might cover eight days or more.

While it is true that many of the sightings that were reported in July 1952 have credible explanations, it is also true that there is a great deal of information available in the Blue Book files that has not been made publicly available. An examination of those files— which include documentation, eyewitness statements from airline pilots and military officers, and even the complete transcript of Samford's press conference—provides a different perspective on the case. It is not easy to accept a simple temperature-inversion explanation in the face of radar data or pilot observations. There is too much data that argues against it, all of which is available in the Blue Book files. That information only survives because of the assumption that none of it would ever be seen by the public or by private UFO investigators.

In fact, by 1952 the Deep State was ready to make a major move to end interest in UFOs and remove them once and for all from the public consciousness. The CIA was about to emerge from the background and become publicly involved, at least briefly, in this systematic suppression. Their plan, which began to develop at the beginning of 1953, would be known as the Robertson Panel. And this panel was designed to toll the death knell of UFO investigations.

CHAPTER 4

Presidents and the Deep State

A lthough the Deep State is comprised of unelected bureaucrats who are entrenched in positions of power, it is also true that presidents, because of their executive power, must be carefully managed by the Deep State. If a president asks for specific information, the agency holding it can't withhold it on the grounds of classification. Presidents are cleared for everything. They can simply fire the head of any agency that denies them access to information they want to see. But presidents also need to be careful, because, in our system, there are penalties for getting too far out of line, and this is how the Deep State uses its power to discredit those who oppose it.

In March 1966, a series of sightings occurred in the congressional district that had elected Gerald Ford to the House of Representatives. Ford, who wouldn't be president for another decade, took notice and called for a Congressional investigation. On March 20, Frank Mannor and his son reported seeing a strange glowing object hovering over a swampy area near their farmhouse. Mannor, members of his family, and dozens of others later told reporters and UFO investigators that a domed disk with a "quilted" or "waffled" surface was seen close to the ground. Mannor and his 19-year-old son, Ronald, went into the swamp to try to identify the object.

At about 8:00 PM, their attention was first caught by what they described as a ball of fire that came from the west and fell below a clump of trees. They were only able to approach within 500 yards of the object, but claimed they got a good look at it. According to *The APRO. Bulletin*, Mannor said that neither he nor his son had weapons or lights with them, adding:

> We came over that knoll and there it was, about eye-level with us, no more than 500 yards away. It had a blue light in front, and in the back a light that kept changing from red to white, like it was rotating.
>
> It was almost flat on the bottom and kind of high and peaked at the top. We couldn't see much except the outline and the lights at the ends, because the whole thing was wrapped in a light like a halo and it kept shimmering. It was like watching something across the desert . . . Ronnie said, "Look at that horrible thing there!"—And just like that it was gone. We went down into the swamp but there was nothing. No smell of exhaust. Nothing.[1]

Mannor said the object was about the size of a car, with a raised portion on top and a twin antenna on the bottom. Drawings of the object based on witness descriptions showed that the surface seemed to be cross-hatched, or waffle-like. Mannor described it as pyramid-shaped, but the drawings show a domed disk rather than something resembling a pyramid.

On March 22, the objects were seen again in the area of Ann Arbor, Michigan by students at Hillsdale College. Two girls, one later identified as Jo Wilson in the Blue Book files, reported that a "casual glance out the window" revealed what looked like a house on fire.[2] They saw a fairly bright red light and two that were described as yellowish and close to the ground. They both knew, however, that there was no house in that area and that there should be no lights there. They saw no object, just the lights. Several other students reported seeing a very bright light sweep past a window as well. Air Force consultant Dr. J. Allen Hynek, who talked to many of the students, said that he "could get no consistent story relative to this, in contrast to the fairly consistent description to the lights in the swamp."[3]

Civil Defense Director William Van Horn, who responded to the reports, said that his first impression of the lights was that they were marsh gas, or swamp gas, also known as fox lights. As he watched, the red and white lights started to brighten and then began to rise. They rose and fell four times between about 11:30 PM and 1:45 AM. He thought he could see a mass that had a convex shape, but wasn't sure.[4]

Television reports of these sightings rekindled a national interest in UFOs. Because they occurred in his congressional district, they caught the attention of Congressman Weston Vivian, who, like Ford, asked for an official investigation. Hector Quintanilla, then chief of Project Blue Book (see chapter 7), sent Hynek to Michigan. On March 25, Hynek, in a crowded press conference, said:

> It would seem to me, that the association of the sightings with swamps . . . is more than coincidence . . . [The sightings] could have been due to the release of variable quantities of marsh gas.[5]

Hynek's pronouncement was met with open hostility. Rather than diverting attention from the sightings as intended by the Air Force (and probably the Deep State), it sparked additional interest in UFOs, prompting then House Minority Leader Gerald Ford to ask the House Armed Services Committee to hold hearings, suggesting that the American public deserved a better explanation.

That hearing was held on April 5, just a couple of weeks after the sightings ended. Only three witnesses were called: Secretary of the Air Force Harold Brown, Project Blue Book director Hector Quintanilla, and Scientific Consultant J. Allen Hynek. Brown, as an unelected official and possibly a member of the Deep State, said the same things that those at Blue Book had been saying all along. There were no national security issues involved, and UFOs, whatever they might be, were not from another world. He insisted that the Air Force had made a thorough investigation of thousands of sightings, but said nothing about the great gaps in the case files or the ridiculous answers offered for some of the more spectacular reports. His script played straight into the hands of members of the Deep State, who wanted to divert attention away from the UFO problem for reasons known only to them.

Hector Quintanilla offered no official statement, but Hynek had had enough of the criticism directed at him by nearly everyone. After pointing out that the press had accused him of being a puppet of the Air Force, he read a statement that had not been prepared by either the Air Force or the Deep State:

> I felt I would be derelict in my scientific responsibility to the Air Force if I did not point out that the whole UFO phenomenon might have aspects worthy of scientific attention . . . it is my opinion that the body of data accumulated since 1948 . . . deserves close scrutiny by a civilian panel of physical and social scientists and that this panel should be asked to examine the UFO problem critically.[6]

L. Mendel Rivers, committee chairman, thought the idea was a good one, as did the Air Force, which saw this as a way to get rid of the UFO investigation, as it had been suggesting for more than a decade. The eventual result of the hearing was the establishment of the Condon Committee (see chapter 6).[7]

JIMMY CARTER

Gerald Ford became involved in the investigation of UFOs because of the sightings in his home district. But Jimmy Carter experienced his own UFO sighting while governor of Georgia. Skeptics claim that what Carter actually saw was Venus, but that is irrelevant for the purposes of this discussion. What is important is that, when Carter was elected president, he believed he had seen something that was of extraterrestrial origin. He believed he had seen an alien spacecraft. During his presidential campaign, he said:

> One thing's for sure, I'll never make fun of people who say they've seen unidentified objects in the sky. If I become President, I'll make every piece of information this country has about UFO sightings available to the public and the scientists.[8]

When he won the election, many thought that "full disclosure" of all UFO-related information was just around the corner.

In February 1977, Carter asked his science advisor, Dr. Frank Press, to write to NASA Administrator Dr. Robert Frosch. Press had suggested that NASA would be the perfect organization to become the "focal point for the UFO question."[9] NASA replied that it would continue to take sighting reports from the public, but that it would not conduct any real research. Frosch may have feared becoming mired in the same difficulties that the Air Force had encountered for twenty-two years, and it is probably safe to say that NASA didn't want to waste any of their limited budget chasing UFOs. It is worth asking, however, whether Frosch knew about Project Moon Dust (see chapter 8) and could see no reason to duplicate that effort. There is some evidence to support this. Colonel Charles Senn, Chief of the Air Force Community Relations Division, wrote in a letter to Lieutenant General Duward Crow of NASA: "I sincerely hope that you are successful in preventing a reopening of UFO investigations."[10] This may indicate that the Deep State wanted to prevent Carter from living up to his campaign pledge. They certainly knew what had to be done to suppress the information and they knew just how to do it.

President Carter wasn't just another interested party, however, and he wasn't through with his inquiries. According to Daniel Sheehan, president-elect Carter approached George H. W. Bush, who was then Director of Central Intelligence (DCI), about possible ways to proceed:

> [S]hortly after November, late November, early December . . . Carter . . . asked George H. W. Bush to communicate the content of what the CIA knew about the issue of extraterrestrial intelligence and or the UFO phenomenon.

According to Sheehan, George Bush replied:

> Wait a second. Hold the line . . . [Before I] decide to tell you this or not, I'd like to ask you to leave me on as your Central Intelligence Agency director.

But Carter declined and Bush refused to comply until Carter was actually sworn in as president.[11] Remember, at this time, Bush was not an elected official, but rather a political appointee who probably wouldn't be held over by the incoming administration. Since he saw no personal benefit in providing the information, he advised Carter to follow a different path:

> If you want to get this information now, prior to you being the president, you'll have to go the House Science and Technology Committee . . . They will go to the Congressional Research Service and ask to undertake to gather that information for you and they will have to try to get it declassified if you want to have it.

So, that's what Carter did.

When asked about how he, Sheehan, became involved in UFO research, Sheehan said:

> It started with a conversation with Rosemary Chalk. Rosemary Chalk was the executive secretary of the . . . National Science Foundation or something. One of those groups in Washington, D. C. I was general counsel for the General Counsel to

the United States Jesuit National Headquarters. Rosie and I used to go to the same Catholic Church in Washington and she invited me to lunch one day . . . [When she asked if I] always wanted to be a lawyer . . . [I replied that I] always wanted to be an astronaut [and] to go into outer space and to reach out to the people from other civilizations up there . . . all before the discovery of all the exoplanets.

Chalk then told him that President Carter had asked that a special research project be established to investigate UFOs and extraterrestrial life and that one of her good friends had been tasked with putting together two separate reports—one on the probability of the existence of extraterrestrial intelligence and one on whether UFOs might actually be vehicles from extraterrestrial civilizations. Chalk then asked if Sheehan would be willing to take a call from this friend.

"In a matter of a couple of days," Sheehan remembers, "[I] get a call from Marcia Smith and she asked me to go to lunch with her." At this meeting, Smith asked him to "participate in a highly classified, major evaluation of the UFO phenomena." This end run around Bush could shorten the time it would take for the president to receive the intelligence he wanted. Moreover, this "different path" might provide better data, since Sheehan might be able to use his connections with the Jesuits to gain access to the Vatican's extensive collection of materials related to extraterrestrial intelligence and, by extension, UFOs. Sheehan reported, however, that, to his surprise, his request to the Vatican was denied.

Sheehan originally thought that the Science and Technology Committee might not have understood that the Congressional Research Service had been acting for the President when it made its request for information, so he attempted to make it clear that the request was coming from the President, who wanted to fulfill a campaign promise. But the request was denied again, demonstrating that the Deep

State could operate outside normal diplomatic channels and at the highest levels of government.

Sheehan wasn't finished with his UFO endeavors, however. Months after his failure to gain access to the materials in the Vatican Library, Marcia Smith called with new information. She told him that the budget for the Search for Extraterrestrial Intelligence (SETI) had been cut by the new congress. Smith was putting together a small group of astronauts to lobby on behalf of the program and she thought that Sheehan might be able to provide some additional support. Eventually, the lobbying effort was successful and the SETI budget was restored. Scientists at the Jet Propulsion Laboratory, who were grateful for Sheehan's help, then asked for some additional information on extraterrestrial intelligence and UFOs. Sheehan agreed to provide it, but said he wanted to see the classified sections of the Project Blue Book files before he made any presentation.[12]

I was surprised by this request. I didn't think there were any highly classified Blue Book files that hadn't been released. Other projects that dealt with UFOs, including Project Moon Dust, still remained classified, but the Blue Book files were all supposed to have been cleared. Sheehan made it clear, however, that the Air Force had agreed to his request and insisted that he had seen classified material that was not part of the publicly available Blue Book files—not at Maxwell AFB, but in Washington, D. C.[13]

> All I know is that as of the spring, March, April of 77 that I was informed they were making the classified portions of Blue Book available . . . I was supposed to go over to this Madison Wing of the Congressional Library on Saturday morning, I had to bring two forms of photo ID with me. So, I brought my passport and my driver's license and my ID from the Jesuit Headquarters and went over there. There were these two guys in suits. They're just inside the door, so I knocked on the door,

> showed my ID. They clearly were anticipating my being there.
> They took me in and told me to . . . just go down the hall
> to the elevator . . . and go down to the basement floor . . .
> [A]s I going down in the elevator, I just instinctively opened
> up my briefcase and took out a yellow pad . . . and put it under
> my arm and closed my briefcase.

Sheehan looked down the hall as he came out of the elevator and saw two men standing in front of a door about twenty yards away. They told him to leave his briefcase and that he couldn't take any notes. They didn't say anything about the yellow pad under his arm, however. They let him into a room that was about eighteen to twenty feet wide and ten to twelve feet deep. In it were four or five folding tables stacked with unlabeled boxes the size of shoe boxes, along with a microfiche machine.

> I opened up one of the boxes and I looked in and there were
> these little metal film canisters . . . each one containing micro-
> fiche film footage. I opened them up and brought one over
> to the microfiche machine and put it in and went through it.
> There were documents.

Realizing the kind of job he had ahead of him, he began cranking through the microfiche looking for photographs. After going through several canisters, he finally came across one.

> It was a photograph of a what was absolutely, no doubt about
> it, a UFO . . . It had hit the ground and it had plowed a
> furrow right through this field. The field was, I don't know,
> maybe half an acre . . . and you could see where it had hit
> and it plowed this big furrow in the snow on the ground.
> There must have been two feet of snow on the ground but
> there was this big dirt furrow all the way through the field
> and this UFO was stuck in the side of an embankment . .
> . [at] a 45-degree angle. Like it came across this field and

hit into the side of this embankment and then lifted up a little bit and was sticking out of the side of this hill. There were Air Force people around it. They were in winter jackets with the big furry things around the hood and little name plates . . . sown on their jackets. . . I was thinking here is an actual photograph of a saucer . . . a classic disk shape and had a dome on the top of it.

Sheehan was stunned to find four photographs of the same craft taken from different angles. Then he realized that he could see what looked like some kind of writing or symbols on the bottom of the dome and on the top of the disk. He took out the yellow pad he had been carrying, laid it down on the viewing screen of the microfiche machine, and proceeded to trace the symbols, which were made up of combinations of lines and dots. They looked as if they might be letters or characters, but were not hieroglyphics. In fact, they were like nothing he had ever seen. When he finished tracing them, he put the film back in the canister, convinced that he had found evidence of what was undoubtedly a UFO. Stunned by his find, Sheehan put the yellow pad lengthwise under his arm to partially conceal it and left the room.

As he left the building, he considered what he had seen:

It was winter time and they were US Air Force guys . . . One of the photographs had a picture of a guy was filming it and the camera he had was one of those that had those two big round circles on top of it . . . like reels inside a metal container. So, I don't know. That must have been like the 40s or early 50s or something . . . [but] I couldn't figure out where it was.

That was the end of Sheehan's involvement with the Carter Administration's search for truth about UFOs. He did have other contacts and became involved in other activities, but he learned nothing further to support Carter's interest in the topic. He could never understand why, despite the president's interest, nothing new was ever learned from any U. S. government or foreign agency.

Some interesting things are often overlooked by those in pursuit of this story. Bush refused Carter's request as president-elect because of the high classification of the information and Carter's lack of a need to know at the time the request was made. But after Carter was inaugurated, he requested information from other agencies like the DIA and the NSA. None of these requests were refused; they were simply stalled and delayed. The information would have to be gathered and reviewed, and then put into a form acceptable for a presidential briefing. And, of course, it would take time to coordinate all this with the various agencies involved. The new DCI might suggest that the best information was held by the DIA rather than the CIA. And the DIA would need to pull all the data together from various facilities. Multiple scientists and military officers would have to be consulted to determine possible impacts on national security. And if all else failed, there was the old lawyer trick of burying the inquiry under a flood of paperwork. After all, you don't reach the highest echelons of the Deep State if you aren't smart enough to find ways to fend off potentially dangerous requests—even those from the president.

And the tactic worked. It avoided any outright refusal that might have led to a confrontation that could have been disastrous for the Deep State. And although Carter was interested in finding answers about UFOs, there were other problems of state that took precedence. Indeed, it could be weeks or months before he returned to the less pressing issue of flying saucers. The Deep State was safe.

To the relief of the Deep State bureaucrats, Carter was out after only four years, and Ronald Reagan was in. Although Ronald Reagan was also interested in UFOs, he didn't have the driving need to learn all about them that Carter had. Besides, his vice-president was George H. W. Bush, the same man who had refused to provide the intelligence to Carter in the first place.

REAGAN AND BUSH

Like Jimmy Carter, Ronald Reagan had experienced at least one, and possibly two, UFO encounters. One happened sometime between 1967 and 1975, while he was still governor of California. According to Reagan, he and his wife, Nancy, were driving to a party when they saw a weird light. Reagan stopped to get a better look and both of them watched the object for several minutes. They arrived at the party about an hour late. Some have speculated that this was actually an episode of "missing time," and was possibly related to an alien abduction, but I think that highly unlikely. While they may have seen a strange light that seemed to pace their car, there is no evidence that Reagan and his wife were abducted. They were just fascinated by the light.

The second sighting occurred in 1974 when Reagan was aboard a private plane flown by retired Air Force Colonel Bill Paynter, who would later confirm the sighting. According to the original report in the *National Enquirer,* Paynter said:

> We were flying a Cessna Citation. It was maybe nine or ten o'clock at night. We were near Bakersfield when Governor Reagan and the others called my attention to a big bright light flying a bit behind the plane. It appeared to be several hundred yards away. It was a fairly steady light until it began to accelerate then it appeared to elongate. The light took off. It went up at a 45-degree angle at a high rate of speed. Everyone on the plane was surprised. Governor Reagan expressed amazement. I told the others I didn't know what it was. The UFO went from a normal cruise speed to a fantastic speed instantly. If you give an airplane power it will accelerate but

not like a hot rod and that is what this was like. We didn't file a
report on the object because for a long time they considered
you a nut if you saw a UFO.[14]

This may explain why Reagan had an interest in UFOs and why,
when he was elected president, he made some inquiries about
them. Paynter recalls that he periodically discussed the sighting
with Reagan over the years. It is also true that Reagan and his wife
shared an interest in the paranormal and that meetings, trips, and
political announcements were sometimes coordinated with psychics
and astrologers by Nancy Reagan.

Reagan, knowing that his vice-president had been DCI, may have
consulted with him about UFOs. While Bush hadn't given Carter
access to the CIA files, he couldn't have used the same dodge with
Reagan. Bush may have filled him in or pointed him in the right
direction—or perhaps told him just enough to satisfy his curiosity.

We do know that Reagan worried about contact with alien races
and the possibility of some sort of conflict growing out of that contact. In fact, he mentioned it several times during his presidency.
When Charlie Rose interviewed George Schultz, Reagan's Secretary
of State, he asked him about a private conversation that Reagan had
with Mikhail Gorbachev. Taking a break from diplomatic talks, the
two world leaders walked off together accompanied by no one but
their personal interpreters. Reagan allegedly turned to Gorbachev
and said: "What would you do if the United States were suddenly
attacked by someone from outer space? Would you help us?" Gorbachev responded: "No doubt about it."[15]

Like those who preceded him, Reagan never made statements
about what UFO information might be held in secret by the U. S.
government. He made no promises to open files for public scrutiny. While some suggest that the Strategic Defense Initiative was the
result of Reagan's fear of an alien invasion, Reagan knew that the
real threat was the Soviet Union.

As vice-president, Bush was still a member of the Deep State. Moreover, he was now in an even better position to blunt any attempt by the president to see secret UFO files. Reagan's attention was easily diverted with the same tactics used to deflect Carter's requests. With Bush in position, the Deep State's knowledge of UFOs was secure and they had nothing to fear from Reagan—assuming, of course, that he wasn't a member of the Deep State himself. And in that case, he was no threat at all.

BILL CLINTON

While he was in Belfast, Ireland, a boy asked President Clinton about the Roswell crash. Clinton replied: "No, as far as I know, an alien spacecraft did not crash in Roswell, New Mexico, in 1947. And, Ryan, if the U. S. Air Force did recover alien bodies, they didn't tell me about it either, and I want to know."[16]

In fact, when President Clinton took office, there were two questions he wanted to probe. He wanted to know what the government had been hiding about the Kennedy assassination and he wanted to know what they were hiding about UFOs. He tasked Webster "Webb" Hubbell with finding the truth about UFO investigations. Hubbell wrote in his memoirs that he failed to learn anything new about them and was never satisfied with the answers he received. Before he could push for additional information, the administration found itself mired in a number of scandals, and time, personnel, and resources were focused on dealing with all that turmoil. Some wonder if the goal of these controversies was, in fact, to divert Clinton's attention from his interest in UFOs and keep him focused on preserving his presidency.

Could these scandals have been part of a Deep State plot to divert the president's attention? While Carter had found himself the victim of delays and obfuscation, Clinton found himself dealing with issues that had nothing to do with running the country or engaging in foreign affairs. In both cases, UFOs were pushed to the side. Were these different strategies intended to keep different presidents from learning what might be held by various government agencies? These diversions occupied time and required responses as the news media and constituents demanded answers. A president can't be chasing after UFOs if he is busy trying to maintain his power and defend his integrity. Perhaps the Deep State was just keeping Clinton off balance until his term ran out and his power dissolved.

The Deep State does, in fact, have the power to thwart attempts to disclose secret UFO information. If a president expresses a desire to disclose the data, the Deep State can provide any number of explanations for why that information shouldn't be released. If that doesn't work, they can create situations that demand immediate action and divert attention away from disclosure. And these are most likely just a few of their tactics.

PART II

SUPPRESSION
AND
DISINFORMATION

CHAPTER 5

The Robertson Panel

The Robertson Panel, which can be considered the first public attempt by the Deep State to convince the population that there was nothing to the UFO phenomenon, was the result of the sightings that occurred over Washington, D. C. in July 1952. While the public was told that the Air Force was hard at work investigating the sightings, those behind the scenes were concerned that the events posed a threat to their positions in the Deep State. To address that threat, they convened a panel of experts to conduct a "scientific examination" of the UFO phenomenon. The experts on the panel were men at the top of their fields whose names were recognized around the world—men who could be counted on to end any public interest in UFOs. The panel's official name was the Scientific Advisory Panel on Unidentified Flying Objects, but it became known as the Robertson Panel, named for its chairman, Howard P. Robertson, a well-respected scientist who was also a member of the Deep State.[1]

The CIA, suggesting that a potential intelligence problem was developing because of UFO sightings—or more accurately, sighting reports—began a series of "informal discussions" chaired by H. Marshall Chadwell, the CIA's Assistant Director of Scientific Intelligence at the time. In September 1952, Chadwell wrote to the Director of Central Intelligence (DCI):

> Recently an inquiry was conducted by the Office of Scientific
> Intelligence to determine whether there are national security

implications in the problem of "unidentified flying objects," i.e., flying saucers; whether adequate study and research is currently directed to this problem in its relation to such national security implications; and what further investigation and research should be instituted, by whom, and under what aegis.[2]

Chadwell went to Wright-Patterson Air Force Base with Frederick Durant (who surfaces later on the Robertson Panel) for a series of briefings by UFO investigators. (When all else fails, find fault with those charged with conducting the investigations![3]) These briefings opened the door to interference in the investigation, allowing the CIA to manipulate events at the lower levels of the bureaucracy and giving the Deep State an opportunity to become involved in creating policy.

This tells us that officials at the highest levels of the intelligence community were being briefed about UFOs and makes evident the problems this could pose. Moreover, Chadwell was suggesting that they needed to determine what should be done about these problems. This seems to be a reasonable worry, given the nature of the world situation at the time. But his concern also created a need to review the topic where no such need actually existed.

Chadwell went on to address some of the issues he had posed himself:

[P]ublic concern with the phenomena indicates that a fair portion of our population is mentally conditioned to the acceptance of the incredible. In this fact lies the potential for the touching-off of mass hysteria . . . In order to minimize the risk of panic, a national policy should be established as to what should be told to the public regarding the phenomena.[4]

In other words, the public can't be trusted to think for themselves. They are easily led. The men and women of the CIA—and, by extension, the Deep State—should therefore determine how much of the truth the public should be told.

In fact, these are the same conclusions that would be reached by the Robertson Panel itself some five months later. The theory that average citizens can't be trusted to make intelligent and rational decisions is a perfect example of the Deep State mentality. Those at the highest levels of the government determined that the public was not smart enough to be told the truth, so those inside the intelligence community and the Deep State would decide just what they needed to know. Truth, in fact, had very little to do it.

Major Dewey Fournet recalls that he received a call from Frederick Durant at about this time. According to Fournet, Durant asked him to make a presentation to the CIA that summarized his own opinions and observations. From that briefing, he claims, the Robertson Panel was born.[5] Well, not exactly—at least not according to documents now declassified and available to us today. In fact, it can be argued that the idea for the panel already existed by the time Fournet made his presentation to the CIA, and that he was asked to make the presentation to help them decide on the direction they would take in dealing with UFOs. In December 1952, just weeks before the group actually met, Chadwell had already decided to form the scientific advisory panel.

Michael Swords, who reviewed all this history carefully, said that Robertson had apparently accompanied Chadwell and Durant to Wright-Patterson. According to Swords, Robertson accepted the assignment against his better judgement because Chadwell insisted he take it on. Robertson said that he, in turn, had to "strong-arm" four other scientists to join him in this alleged scientific evaluation— which, of course, suggests that a certain bias had already set in, not to mention pressure from the Deep State. Swords reconstructed this history using documents from a variety of sources, including those housed at the J. Allen Hynek Center for UFO Studies (CUFOS), the declassified Project Blue Book files now available on line, and the files of the National Investigations Committee on Aerial Phenomena (NICAP), also housed at CUFOS. According to Swords:

> The first guy he gets to do this [meaning serve on the committee] is Thornton Page because Page is handy. Page turns out to be the junior member . . . but he doesn't know anything about UFOs. Robertson sent him an article to read.[6]

The fact that Page doesn't know anything about UFOs doesn't seem to disqualify him. Rather, it seems to indicate that he was the right man for the job. Swords went on:

> I think Alverez [Dr. Luis Alverez] is the next guy . . . and Alverez comes in hostile . . . Robertson has to get two more people . . . I think Goudsmit [Dr. Samuel Goudsmit] is probably the last guy . . . and I'm not sure when they talk Lloyd Berkner into [it]. Goudsmit is just incredibly hostile [to the idea that UFOs are anything other than hallucination and hoax].[7]

From this, it seems that panel members were deliberately chosen to reject the idea that UFOs are alien craft or craft of any kind. In theory, it wasn't necessary for them to enter the investigation as believers, as long as they were willing to look at the evidence critically and with an unbiased attitude. But that doesn't seem to be the case here. These men all came into the meetings with preconceived notions and had no intention of being convinced of anything else regardless of the evidence. In other words, their attitudes fit with the goals of the Deep State, who wanted nothing more to suggest that UFOs might be real and therefore dangerous, and nothing to suggest they might be interstellar craft.

Under the auspices of the CIA and the Deep State, the panel met for the first time on January 14, 1953. J. Allen Hynek, who attended the meeting as the Air Force consultant to Project Blue Book and not as a panel member, later told Swords in private conversations that the members entered the committee room convinced from the start that UFOs were going to be debunked. According to Hynek, Alverez and Goudsmit were saying "nothing but hostile things and Goudsmit is saying wiseass things . . . Page is more open minded and Berkner is not there."[8]

Ruppelt, who was still the chief of Project Blue Book in 1953, provided more insight about the panel:

> When this high court was convened . . . one of three verdicts would be acceptable. 1. All UFO reports are explainable as known objects or natural phenomena; therefore, the investigations should be permanently discontinued. 2. The UFO reports do not contain enough data upon which to base a final conclusion. Project Blue Book should be continued in the hopes of obtaining better data. 3. The UFOs are interplanetary spacecraft.[9]

But the sad fact here is that the panel's conclusions were a *fait accompli* even before the first meeting began. According to Swords, the panel had been salted, not with skeptics, but with men who were hostile to the whole idea of alien visitation. They weren't interested in determining if some UFOs might be alien; they only wanted to end public discussion about them, which mirrored the goal of the Deep State. To them, flying saucers were no more real than the Easter Bunny and everyone should agree with their assessment because they were, after all, scientists. It was a blatant appeal to authority.

According to Ruppelt, the panel's first two meetings focused on his review of the work done by and the findings of the various Air Force projects—that is, Projects Sign and Grudge (see chapter 2), and Project Blue Book (see chapter 7). Swords learned a little more about the exact chronology of events in the meetings during his discussions with Hynek. During the first half day, no one was allowed into the meeting room except for a few CIA men. These included Chadwell and Philip G. Strong, who may have been quietly representing those in the Deep State. Hynek and Ruppelt cooled their heels outside waiting to present their evidence.

Ruppelt reported that his team, and those who preceded him, had analyzed 1,593 reports and found explanations for all but 429. Confidence in those explanations ranged from "known" to "possible," which meant they thought they knew what had caused a sighting but couldn't objectively prove it. This also meant that nearly a third of the sightings had no explanation, something that was unacceptable to both the panel and those in the Deep State who were monitoring the situation.[10]

Ruppelt made it clear during his presentation that most of the data they had gathered was observational. That is, they had relied on the abilities of the eyewitnesses to accurately estimate the size, distance, and speed of the objects they had seen. For instance, Ruppelt reported that they could say only that "some of the UFOs had been traveling pretty fast." He pointed out that radar documentation was available, but that too was open to the interpretation of the operators and thus was observational as well. They had to rely on the abilities of radar technicians and operators to interpret what they saw onscreen and no one had any idea of how reliable those observations might be. This was simply a way to belittle the accuracy of the data and suggest that it might not be all that reliable.

Ruppelt also said that no good physical evidence existed. Of course, he was unaware of the Roswell UFO case. In fact, in a search of the Blue Book files, only a single mention of Roswell has been found—in another case file and in the second paragraph of a four-paragraph newspaper story that suggests that the officers at Roswell had been issued a "blistering rebuke" for their claim of having "captured" a flying saucer. Walter Haut, the information officer at Roswell who had issued the press release, told me repeatedly that he had received no such rebuke and asked: "Don't you think I would remember if I received a call from the Pentagon?"[11] Ruppelt also said that most of the photographs they had seen were fakes—some crude, others more sophisticated. He also suggested that photo-graphs, no matter how good, would not prove the case. And in fact, even today, video tapes of flying saucers in motion are easy to fake, making photographic evidence even more problematic.

FILM FOOTAGE

According to Ruppelt, the last day of the Robertson Panel meetings was reserved for a review of two films purportedly taken of UFOs. Ruppelt believed these were the best evidence held by Blue Book. No one believed they had been faked, which meant that no one considered them to be hoaxes. There were other mundane explana-tions available, however, at least in the minds of those on the panel.

One film, taken in Montana in 1950, showed two brightly lit objects crossing the sky, passing behind a tower and over a rooftop. This short film is fascinating because the objects it shows never resolved themselves into anything resembling aircraft. They were just bright lights crossing a deep blue sky. Nick Mariana, who shot the film, and Virginia Raunig, who was with him, both saw the objects in the sky. While Raunig watched them, Mariana ran to his car to get his 16-mm camera.[12] According to Mariana, the two objects crossed the sky in a straight line. On the film, the objects seem to flash brightly once and then move away. In less than twenty seconds, according to Mariana's estimate, the UFOs disappeared. Raunig, on the other hand, claimed she had only seen them for five or ten seconds.

Although Raunig said she had seen the objects for only seconds, she did watch them while Mariana ran for his camera. Since the film lasts sixteen seconds, it seems that her estimate of the time is wrong. But this was exactly the sort of discrepancy that panel members used to suggest that the film provided no evidence of unusual activity. At the end of their research, they decided that the footage showed two jet fighters that may or may not have been in the area at the time, ignoring the eyewitness testimony about what they had seen.

This doesn't say much for the panel's investigative techniques, or for those of the Air Force, for that matter. Moreover, there have been claims that the film was shortened by the Air Force to remove frames that showed the disks' shape, and there is some evidence to support these claims. We'll never know. Regardless, what may have been important evidence of alien visitation is now just a short film of two bright spots that could be almost anything.[13] Various studies made by both military and civilian organizations have shown that the jet aircraft explanation doesn't work, which means that the objects on the film should have been classified as "unidentified." But that conclusion didn't satisfy either the Robertson Panel or the Deep State. The film had to be discredited if it couldn't be explained, and the aircraft theory accomplished that.

The second film reviewed by the panel was shot by Navy Warrant Officer Delbert C. Newhouse. It showed a series of objects spotted near Tremonton, Utah in July 1952. After first sighting the objects, Newhouse stopped his car and grabbed his 16-mm camera from the trunk. He and his wife both report seeing oval-shaped objects that passed over their car. They flew in no real formation, but looked more like several craft operating independently of one another. The panel decided that these objects were sea gulls milling about on mid-day thermals. Naval investigators didn't agree, believing the objects were internally lit rather than reflecting the bright sunlight. That, of course, meant they were not birds of any kind.[14]

The campaign to eliminate these films fell to those in the Deep State. Nick Mariana found himself under assault. On January 9, 1953, Major Raymond L. Kolman, who had investigated the sighting, wrote:

> Shortly after the incident, Bob Considine, a nationally syndicated newspaper columnist, denounced all who claim to have seen "flying saucers." Particular reference was made

to Mr. Mariana. This bad publicity resulted in the loss of sponsors on nine (9) of the fourteen (14) radio stations for Mr. Mariana's sports broadcasts. It was nine (9) months before these stations returned to Mr. Mariana's program and this undoubtedly resulted in considerable financial loss to him. At present, Mr. Mariana is in the final stages of a lawsuit against Mr. Considine.[15]

This seems to indicate manipulation by the Deep State. The film was classified, as was part of the investigation, but classifying the film simply wasn't good enough. Mariana had to be silenced and Considine's column seemed to have that effect. The pressure put on Considine could have consisted of threats about the loss of future access to important people, or perhaps just a suggestion that these UFO stories were causing trouble. At any rate, Considine went after Mariana for the crime of filming something unknown over Great Falls. This tactic would be used again in the future to silence witnesses who had seen something that the Deep State didn't want publicized.

THE END OF THE PANEL

Howard Robertson was given the task of writing the panel's final report. Swords, aided by his discussions with Hynek, comments on this unlikely choice:

> I can't imagine that H. P. Robertson, a guy like him, is going to sit down and late into the evening and bang out a draft of the report on his own that somehow, mysteriously, the next morning is already read by Lloyd Berkner and has already been taken by Marshall Chadwell to the Air Force Directorate of Intelligence and been approved . . . So, when they show up on Saturday, Robertson presents this draft to the rest of the committee and the rest of the committee does minor

revisions . . . There are some remarks that are out of line that they decided are not going to be included. . .

It seems an amazingly cut-and-dried deal that by the time Saturday shows up, here's this mildly to be revised draft that has already been seen by one of the other committee members who wasn't even there for the first two and a half days. It's already been seen by Chadwell and the U. S. Air Force.[16]

The implication here is that the draft document had been created sometime before the end of the Friday session and a very rough draft may have been completed before the panel even met. This means that Robertson was working from a script provided by those in the Deep State and that the outcome was a foregone conclusion. It also suggests that the CIA—and, by extrapolation, the Deep State—had decided what the panel would find and how those findings would be presented to those responsible for investigating UFOs.

Dewey Fournet—who had a chance to review the data, who had been present for some of the sessions, and who now had a forty-year perspective on the investigation—said that the scientists had no choice in their conclusions. For him and for them, the evidence simply wasn't persuasive—just the testimony of eyewitnesses, none of whom had appeared before the committee so that their observations could be examined and understood. Fournet later referred to this testimony as mere "anecdotal gossip"—a phrase that would eventually become the rallying cry of the debunking community.[17]

But to understand the Robertson Panel, we must understand what was happening at the time. UFO sightings, including radar confirmation and fighter interception, had just occurred over Washington, D. C. UFOs were flying around over the capital and it appeared that the Air Force was powerless to stop them. This was presented to the public as a threat to national security. But if the sightings were nothing more than hoaxes, mirages, misidentifications, and ambiguous eyewitness reports, then national security wasn't an issue at all. If the UFOs were all, basically, imaginary, then there was nothing to intercept, nothing to challenge, and nothing to fear. It was all just public hysteria—and therefore not the Air Force's problem.

The panel did suggest one area of concern, however. Fournet mentioned, as did Ed Ruppelt, that too many UFO reports at the wrong time could mask a Soviet attack by flooding communication channels with bogus sightings. Although hindsight shows that such an attack was impossible in 1952, those working in the lower levels of intelligence at the time didn't know the sorry state of Soviet missile and bomber development. They thought that a sudden flood of UFO reports could create havoc and cause critical messages to be lost in increased classified message traffic. A possible Soviet attack, they feared, might be lost in the chaos.[18] Thus the panel included this warning in its report:

> [A]lthough evidence of any direct threat from these sightings was wholly lacking, related dangers might well exist from: a. Misidentification of actual enemy artifacts by defense personnel. b. Overloading of emergency channels with "false" information . . . c. Subjectivity of public to mass hysteria and greater vulnerability to possible enemy psychological warfare.
>
> Although not the concern of the CIA, the first two of these problems may seriously effect [sic] the Air Defense intelligence system, and should be studied by experts, possibly under the ADC. If U.F.O.'s become discredited in a reaction to the "flying saucer" scare, or if reporting channels are saturated with false and poorly documented reports, our capability of detecting hostile activity will be reduced. Dr. Page noted that more competent screening or filtering of reported sightings at or near the source is required, and that this can be accomplished by an educational program.[19]

At first, this concern seems reasonable. But in the event of a Soviet attack, messages would not come solely through the communication centers at various levels of command. Those on the front line of the attack, meaning those at the various forward Air Force bases both in the United States and overseas who were manning the various radar fences, could communicate in a more direct way with their superiors. In other words, no one would rely on a classified message that needed to be encrypted, decrypted, and carried by hand from a message center to headquarters. In 1952, those at forward bases would have picked up a dedicated telephone line and spoken directly to their superiors, probably telling them that a coded message would follow if needed. In a critical situation, the message might even have been given in the clear.

The idea of an educational program to teach people how to spot natural and astronomical phenomena did make some sense, however. If the public was more familiar with what appeared in the sky—including meteors, Venus, and weather events—the number of questionable UFO reports could be significantly reduced. And some of the ideas offered for doing that weren't all that bad. They might even have helped eyewitnesses correctly identify "unusually illuminated objects" and bring about "a marked reduction in reports caused by misidentified cases and resultant confusion." For example, those who might once have been fooled by Venus would recognize that the planet was not a craft flying in the atmosphere. The problem lay in motive. Under the guise of education, the panel recommended "a broad educational program integrating efforts of all concerned agencies . . . with two major aims: training and 'debunking.'"[20]

Many in the UFO community saw this more as a "disinformation" campaign designed to explain away all UFO sightings so that interest in the phenomena would disappear. While most agree that to debunk myths, legends, and fantasies is a good idea, here the suggestion seems to be a propaganda effort aimed, not at clarifying misidentifications, misinterpretations, or hoaxes, but rather at convincing people there was nothing to any UFO reports at all. In other words, the goal was to debunk *all* UFO sightings with little regard to accuracy or truth. Robertson wrote:

> The "debunking" aim would result in reduction in public interest in "flying saucers" which today evokes a strong psychological reaction. This education could be accomplished by mass media such as television, motion pictures, and popular articles. Basis of such education would be actual case histories which had been puzzling at first but later explained. As in the case of conjuring tricks, there is much less stimulation if the "secret" is known. Such a program should tend to reduce the current gullibility of the public and consequently their susceptibility to clever hostile propaganda. The Panel noted that the general absence of Russian propaganda based on a subject with so many obvious possibilities for exploitation might indicate a possible Russian official policy.[21]

The interests of the Deep State are revealed in these concerns. The problem wasn't that the Soviets could mask an attack by creating a wave of UFO sighting reports; it was rather a growing interest in the public, who now wanted answers. If the public could be convinced that UFO sightings were reported only by the drunk, the illiterate, and the conspiracy-minded, then there would be no serious scientific or journalistic effort to learn more, and the Deep State would be preserved.

Many have even suggested that the information presented to the panel had been "managed" to lead to several predetermined conclusions.[22] The panel had a limited time in which to do its work. In fact, it could be argued that its charter was designed by the Deep State specifically so that there would be no time for embarrassing questions to be asked or careful examinations to be made. Moreover, when issues arose, Robertson always had a quick answer. For example, he immediately opined that the Newhouse film merely showed birds and was quite vocal in his defense of that explanation.

To prove his point, and to undermine the value of the film, he presented a film of seagulls soaring above the ground and suggested this was what Newhouse had seen. He pointed out that the birds were at the extreme range of vision and that was why no flapping of the wings could be detected. They were just bright white blobs reflecting the bright sunlight in the late morning sky. This, of course, ignored two important points. First, Newhouse was a Navy officer who had seen seagulls soaring on thermals many times in the past, both over land and out to sea. And more important, when he was interviewed by Air Force investigators, Newhouse told them that he had seen the objects at much closer range and that they were disk-shaped. By the time he stopped the car, retrieved his camera, and began to film, however, they had moved off into the distance and their shape was not readily discernable.[23]

Once Robertson and his allies had dismissed the Mariana and Newhouse films, they could begin to develop a careful presentation of the data that allowed for a biased conclusion. In fact, the panel was loaded with scientists who had already formed their conclusions before they looked at a single bit of evidence or read a single word of testimony. They overlooked or dismissed as anecdotal some of the truly extraordinary cases that had been submitted to Project Blue Book over the years. It can even be argued, based on the timing, that the final report was written before a single minute of testimony or data had been reviewed.[24] In fact, the panel was designed, not to actually review the status of UFO investigations, but rather to reduce public interest in them.

But how could the interested parties be sure that they could micro-manage the results in a way that would guarantee the desired conclusion? How could they be sure that some wild card wouldn't knock their plans off the rails and lead the panel in another direction? This seems a big risk to take, unless those managing the flow of information could totally control what the panel members learned. According to Swords, Robertson, Chadwell, and others at the CIA were just the sort of heavy thinkers to design such a plan and pull it off. When all is said and done, the only member of the panel who was even mildly unbiased was Thornton Page, and he was overwhelmed by the prestige of the other, high-powered members and the personality of Robertson himself—just as planned.[25]

The panel's ultimate purpose was supposedly to determine if UFOs posed a threat to national security. But the cases they reviewed contained little more than sighting information and certainly nothing to suggest that UFOs might be hostile or threatening. Those conclusions would come later, in a study by the Brookings Institute that examined what happens when a technologically superior society encounters a technologically inferior one. In such a case, they concluded, the inferior society ceases to exist—not because it was conquered, but because the introduction of new technologies radically alters it. The odd thing about the Robertson Panel was its suggestion that UFO investigations through Project Blue Book be expanded, and that the project lose its classified status. Robertson believed that the best way to debunk UFOs and educate the public was to make everything transparent. Besides, he knew that the really convincing UFO reports were not represented in the Blue Book files. And that was part of the Deep State's plan: Make the investigation appear transparent, but keep the real evidence highly classified and hidden under layers of security.

Dewey Fournet, who attended some of the Robertson Panel sessions, claimed years later that he believed that the panel members were honest in their evaluations of the UFO sightings.[26] He argued that the evidence presented was weak and that the only conclusions that *could* be drawn were those that *were* drawn. But Fournet had not been present at all the meetings and he did not know that the final report existed, at least in draft form, prior to the final sessions—in fact, that it may have existed even before any evidence was heard.

Fournet was out of the loop because he was not part of the Deep State.

What the evidence shows us today is that the Robertson Panel wasn't a group of impeccably credentialed and highly placed scientists taking a dispassionate look at UFOs. It was a panel designed by those much higher up in the chain of command whose specific conclusions were formed before any work was done by the panel itself. Those conclusions were clearly approved prior to the last day of the panel, and they were designed to end interest in UFOs by explaining everything in mundane terms, even if those explanations were less than solid.

In other words, the panel presented *possible* solutions and insisted that they be treated as *actual* solutions. Anything labeled as "probable" or "possible" was replaced with explanations that were assumed to be "true." UFOs were to be explained. Period.

CHAPTER 6

The Condon Committee

Those working in the Deep State believed that, with the conclusion of the Robertson Panel and its suggestion that all mystery had been removed from the UFO phenomenon, the situation would work itself out. Those on the panel—and, by extension, those in the Deep State—knew what was best for the country and seemed to assume that the majority of citizens either didn't care about UFOs or were too ignorant to understand the overall situation. The Robertson Panel had done its job by explaining the nearly inexplicable and suggesting a solution for the problem without revealing much in the way of the truth. For them, this was the ideal outcome.

In 1953, before the work of the Robertson Panel had begun to have an impact, the number of UFO reports was slightly higher than normal. But by June of that year, sightings had dropped off dramatically. By the middle of the 1950s, the strategy seemed to have worked.[1] Public interest in UFOs and flying saucers waned and almost disappeared. The number of sightings reported to the Air Force was significantly reduced, which was the goal of the Robertson Panel and of the Deep State.

Things changed as the end of the decade approached, however. In late October 1957, reports of UFOs began to increase steadily, culminating in the national publicity that followed the sightings around Levelland, Texas.[2] For several hours, multiple eyewitnesses in multiple locations—including law enforcement officers—reported seeing a large, glowing, egg-shaped UFO that stalled car engines, dimmed headlights, and filled radios with static. Although not the first to surface, the report given by Jose Alverez (sometimes spelled Alvarez) was typical of the reports given by others. Alverez claimed he was near Whitharral, Texas when he saw an egg-shaped object that he said killed his engine. Once the object was gone, the engine worked properly. Alverez then found a telephone and called law enforcement authorities to report his sighting.[3]

Ronald Martin reported that he saw a bluish-green glowing, egg-shaped object sitting on the road about four miles east of Levelland. As he approached, his car engine died and his lights went out. When Martin started to get out of the car, the object took off. Once it had disappeared, he was able to start his car's engine and the lights came back on.[4]

Levelland Sheriff Weir Clem decided, after receiving multiple reports, that he needed to get into the field to investigate. Clem, along with a deputy and other law enforcement officers traveling in another vehicle, spotted a red streak in the distance, confirming, at least for them, that something unidentified was flying around Levelland.[5] The Air Force did, reluctantly, investigate, but that investigation was conducted by a single NCO, Norman Barth, who didn't take statements from all the witnesses, and who suggested that weather-related phenomena had caused the sightings.[6] He had found what he thought was the explanation and the Air Force, never one to ignore a superficial solution, accepted it.

Decades later, the true story of what the sheriff had seen that night emerged. He had driven out to look for the object and actually got much closer than the Air Force reported. Although the official file reports that the sheriff didn't get very close to the UFO and didn't get a very good look at it, Clem, as reported in 1957, actually got within 200 feet of the glowing red object and could see that it was oval or egg-shaped. He also inspected a burned area on a ranch not far from Levelland, but this additional physical evidence was ignored because it would have ruled out the Air Force explana-tion and added another dimension to the case, one that couldn't be easily explained and one that the Deep State wanted to keep secret.[7]

According to family members, Clem was told by a military officer not to say anything about what he had seen. This "request" didn't come from Barth, the Air Force investigator sent to Levelland; it came from an officer whose name is not found in the Project Blue Book files and whose affiliation with the UFO investigation is unknown.[8] Clem's report was modified to place him farther away and to claim he said that he had seen nothing but a streak of light in the distance. By sticking to that story, Clem made the Deep State happy. But why did Clem agree to downplay his role in the night's events to something that was unimpressive? What pressure was brought to bear to get him to change his report?

The Air Force, working on instructions from the Deep State, diverted attention from the sightings, the landings, and the elec-trical interference to a discussion about the witnesses and their reliability. They claimed that only three eyewitnesses had seen the object up close, despite the fact that Donald Keyhoe, director of the National Investigations Committee on Aerial Phenomena (NICAP) claimed that nine people had seen more than just lights in the dis-tance.[9] The pressure put on some of the witnesses and the dismis-sive attitude directed at others soon convinced people that there wasn't much to the Levelland sightings, and the sightings were quickly buried, explained as a response to recent reporting about the Soviet launch of a second satellite. That news, officials claimed, put the idea of spacecraft into the heads of the public, causing them to think that the lights they saw were actually UFOs.

The Deep State was lucky in this case, because, once again, the sightings occurred in a remote part of the country, away from more sophisticated urban areas where they controlled the flow of informa-tion. Thus the Levelland sightings, as well as many others reported at that time, were overlooked. The Levelland events did, however, point to a problem for those suppressing the investigation of UFOs. The official investigation conducted by the Air Force seemed to add legitimacy to the idea of alien visitation. After all, if there was nothing to these wild stories, why was the Air Force wasting its resources investigating flying saucers?

Prompted by this perception, the Deep State decided, around 1960, that the Air Force should drop its public investigations of UFOs. This decision, suggested by an increasing fear of the information that was circulating at the time, is born out by documents found in the Project Blue Book files. In a letter to Major General Dougher at the Pentagon dated April 1, 1960, A. Francis Archer, a science advisor to Blue Book said: "[I] had tried to get Bluebook out of ATIC for ten years . . . and do not agree the loss of prestige to the UFO project a disadvantage."[10] In other words, the Deep State had seen the problem and tried to remedy it by changing the chain of command in the Blue Book hierarchy. While this does show the diminished status of the project, it also calls attention to the disadvantages of public discussion. It was awkward at best for the Air Force to investigate something they didn't want made public, so they needed to bury the topic even deeper.

In 1962, Lieutenant Colonel Robert Friend, who had led Project Blue Book, wrote to his headquarters suggesting that the project be handed over to a civilian agency that could word its reports in a way that would allow the Air Force to drop the study. Friend didn't just want the investigations hidden. He wanted them dropped completely.[11] At about the same time, Ed Trapnell, an assistant to the Secretary of the Air Force, told Dr. Robert Calkins of the Brookings Institute much the same thing, suggesting that they ask a civilian committee to look at the investigation and then conclude it the way the Air Force wanted it concluded.

The Air Force, contrary to what the news media might report or what most people might believe, was no longer interested in the investigation of UFOs, at least at the lower levels of its hierarchy.

They found themselves in a position they did not like. By regulation and expectation, they had to investigate UFO sightings. But someone in a high position in the government had determined that UFOs did not pose a threat to national security, and their continuing investigation had become a public-relations nightmare. No matter what they said, no matter how they spun the information, no matter how many cases they solved, the public continued to believe they were hiding information about alien visitation.

In fact, after the Levelland events, Richard Horner, then an Assistant Secretary of the Air Force, felt the need to say in a broadcast: "The Air Force is not hiding any UFO information. And I do not qualify this in any way."[12] Of course, his statement was untrue. Air Force regulations demanded that the sightings be investigated. If they were not easily explained, Air Force personnel were instructed to refer reporters to the Pentagon. They were only authorized to provide information to the media if an easy explanation was found. Other documents that surfaced after the Blue Book files were made public in 1976 suggest that the Air Force wanted *everything* explained. In December 1958, an officer assigned to the UFO project said that he had found "certain deficiencies" that he believed "must be corrected." He was referring to Air Force Regulation 200–2, revised on February 5, 1958, which ordered investigators "to explain or identify *all* UFO sightings."[13]

Essentially, the Air Force was ordering its officers to investigate UFO sightings and then explain them. If the sightings could be easily explained, they were authorized to offer those explanations to the public. If they couldn't, they were instructed to treat possible explanations as the real thing and offer *those* to the public. What this really meant was that the Air Force was being ordered to hide information. Horner, as a civilian in the chain of command, had to know that there were classified reports, classified studies, and classified analyses of UFOs. He was just taking his orders from higher up the food chain.

THE COMMITTEE CONVENES

The Deep State solution to this problem was to find a university that would study the question of UFOs, determine that national security was not an issue, suggest that the Air Force had done a good job during its years of investigation, and then recommend that the Air Force no longer needed to investigate. This study, undertaken by the University of Colorado, was supported by half a million dollars of taxpayer money. Edward Condon, a well-respected scientist, was chosen to lead the investigation.[14]

At first glance, this may seem an odd choice, given Condon's background. He was a scientist who favored the free exchange of ideas, theories, and information within the scientific community—even with colleagues in the Soviet bloc. He had worked briefly on the Manhattan Project but quit over what he believed to be overzealous enforcement of security regulations. He had worked in government, in private industry, and in academia. Although he had been granted security clearances and had them revoked a number of times, there is nothing in his background to suggest that he was disloyal or that he would have shared either military or industrial secrets with unauthorized personnel. Although he was investigated several times for violating security protocols, his record was cleared of most of these allegations. In the end, however, his clearances were finally revoked.

Nonetheless, the Air Force selected him to lead the committee's UFO investigation, claiming that it was his lack of a stated opinion on the subject that led to his selection. Yet in January 1967, some eighteen months before the committee's final report was due and with the investigation still under way, Condon told scientists in Corning, New York: "It is my inclination right now to recommend that the government get out of this business. My attitude right now is that there is nothing in it. But I am not supposed to reach a conclusion for another year."[15] This statement merely confirms that conclusions had been formulated before the committee had done its work—or perhaps before that work had even begun. In fact, ten days before Condon made his statement in Corning, Lieutenant Colonel Robert R. Hippler of the Science Division, Directorate of Science and Technology (part of the Washington HQ, USAF) wrote to Condon saying:

> This is an informal letter expressing some thoughts on our round-table discussion on the UFO program, and does not constitute the formal letter requested by John Coleman.
>
> There are two items which leave me a little uneasy. The first is the Wertheimer Hypothesis, and its corollary that one cannot "prove" the negative on extraterrestrial visitations. The second is an apparently obscure understanding of what the Air Force wants. Since I will discuss this second item, you will see why this is an informal letter expressing my own opinion—and hence is not binding on you.
>
> On the first item, I wish to present a slightly different approach. When we first took over the UFO program, the first order of business, even before approaching AFOSI, was to assure ourselves that the situation was as straightforward as logic indicated it should be. In other words, we too looked to see if by some chance the intelligence people have information other than what exists in Blue Book files. There were no surprises. While there exist some things which may forever remain unknowable in the universe, certainly an extraterrestrial visitation must fall in the "knowable" category. An alien would not come light years merely to pick up surreptitiously some rocks, or melt holes in reservoir ice (á la Edwards). He would have long since gone through the geologic bit, and would be fairly knowledgeable of the make-up of stars and planets. You have stated that President Truman was unaware of the Manhattan Project until he became President. In that

same time period, physicists not connected with the project were aware of the possibilities and knew that something was going on.

No one knows of a visitation. It should therefore follow there has been no visitation to date. As you are aware, if UFOs are an Air Force "sacred cow," the other services in the usual competitive spirit would not be constrained by this "sacred cow." Nor is the "fear of panic" holding anyone's tongue. No one is reticent about the horror of an ICBM attack. Words such as "end of civilization" have been used many times.

And this brings us to the second problem—the cost of these investigations. Hippler continues:

When you have looked into some sightings and examined some Blue Book records and become acquainted with the true state of affairs, you must consider the cost of the Air Force program on UFOs, and determine if the taxpayer should support this for the next decade. It will be at least that long before another independent study can be mounted to see if the Air Force can get out from under this program. If the contract is up before you have laid the proper groundwork for a proper recommendation, an extension of the contract would be less costly than another decade of operating Project Blue Book.[16]

In his response, which is not reproduced in its entirety simply because some of the content is not important here, Robert Low, a member of the Condon Committee, responded:

Maybe we will find that extraterrestrial visitations have occurred, but there's no way to demonstrate that they haven't. This is a logical problem that can't be skirted, and I'm sure, if we were to miss the point, the National Academy would set us straight . . .

We don't know what technology exists on other planets. I think one can assert, however, that, for a spaceship to get to the earth from a planet outside the solar system, it would be necessary to employ a technology far more advanced than we enjoy. Since we have no knowledge of that technology, speculation on it brings one right into science fiction, and once one has crossed that boundary the sky is the limit. He can argue anything, and the rules of scientific evidence and methodology have been abandoned. So there is no point in stepping across the boundary, except to engage in idle speculation! Such speculation isn't useful in helping to close in on an answer to the problem of whether there have been extraterrestrial visitors or not. And probability won't help.

You mention that the fear of panic is not holding anyone's tongue. That's an extremely good point; I had not thought of it. On the second page, you indicate what you believe the Air Force wants of us, and I am very glad to have your opinion. In fact, you have answered quite directly the question that I have asked—you may remember that I came back to it a couple of times—at our meeting on Thursday evening, January 12.[17]

Low then signed off, after suggesting that he and Condon should "perhaps" meet in Washington. The language in both Hippler's and Low's letters can be seen as benign, but it can also suggest an attempt by Hipple—and, by extension, the Deep State—to tell Low what they were to find and what recommendation the Air Force wanted the Committee to make.

All of this was part of the original plan that was discussed in what was called the Air Force Advisory Panel Briefing. This meeting, referred to by Low, occurred on January 12, 1967. Attendees included Hippler, Major Hector Quintanilla, who ran Project Blue

Book at the time, and a number of civilian scientists who held various positions with the Air Force, including John W. Evans, Myron B. Gilbert, John Howard, and Kenneth E. Kissell.[18] Some of these players were working from instructions supplied by their bosses safely hidden away in the Deep State. The meeting was called to determine how the investigation of UFOs should proceed.

Condon confirms this, saying:

> At this meeting we would like to discuss our progress and future plans with you, and especially we hope to benefit from your opinions on where the emphasis should be placed with respect to policy questions the Study must deal with.

He then notes that one of the problems they faced was the transitory nature of UFO sightings. Because the appearance of UFOs could not be predicted and sightings were relatively short-lived, their investigators would have no chance to make independent observations and measurements in the field before the object or phenomenon had disappeared. Problems in physics, he observed, are solved in the laboratory, not using data obtained by interviewing citizens. "I don't necessarily draw the conclusion that one should not make the effort," he argues, however, and goes on to say:

> One or two good field incidents which we ourselves can observe with a camera or spectrograph or radiometer under our own control would be very good evidence. When one considers what is implied in attempting to do this, however, the feasibility is considerably reduced.

Then in October 1967, an event occurred in Shag Harbor, Nova Scotia that gave the lie to Condon's observation. This sighting transpired over a period of time that allowed a team to get to the location, interview many first-hand witnesses, examine residue, and even obtain a photograph of the object in the air.

SHAG HARBOR

The Condon Committee learned about the Shag Harbor event from Jim Lorenzen of the Aerial Phonemenon Research Organization (APRO).[19] In an attempt to show that their system for gathering current reports was flawed, he called to let them know that something was going on in Canada that involved a UFO that might have fallen or crashed into the waters of Shag Harbor. Committee scientists, apparently led by Dr. Norman E. Levine, made a short telephonic investigation and decided that there was nothing of interest to be learned and therefore no reason for them to travel to Canada. Levine later prepared a report on the incident and the investigation by the Committee. I include it here at length because of its importance:

> He [Lorenzen] stated that the original report had come from two teenagers, and that the Navy was searching for the wreckage. No aircraft were reported missing in the area . . . A corporal from the RCMP [Royal Canadian Mounted Police] stated that the first report had come from five young people, 15–20 yr. old, who while driving near the shore had seen three or four yellow lights in a horizontal pattern comparable in size to a "fair-sized" aircraft . . . [They] then report the incident to the RCMP detachment.

> Two officers [Ron O'Bien and Ron Pound] and the corporal had arrived about 15 min. later, in time to see the light on the water. It persisted about five minutes longer. Ten minutes after it went out, two officers were at the site in a rowboat; a Coast Guard boat and six fishing boats were on the scene. They found only patches of foam 30–40 yd. wide that the fisherman thought was not normal tidal foam.

> The site of the presumed impact was in between an island and the mainland, about 200–300 yd. offshore. Apparently

no one actually saw anything enter the water (though I must point out that a number saw the object descend to the water, which is, essentially, the same thing). However two young women driving on the island reported that a horizontal pattern of three yellow lights had tilted and descended, then a yellow light had appeared on the water . . . The RCMP corporal stated that the light on the water was not on any boat, that Air Search and Rescue had no reports of missing aircraft in the area and an RCMP radar station nearby reported no Canadian or U. S. air operations in the area at the time, nor any unusual radar object . . . A search by Navy divers during the days immediately following the sighting disclosed nothing relevant.

Five days later the National Maritime Command advised the project [the Condom Committee] that the search had been terminated. The watch officer read a report from the RCMP indicating that at the time in question a 60 ft. object had been seen to explode upon impact with the water . . . A captain of a fishing boat that had been about 16 mi. from the sight of the earlier reports, reported to the project that he and his crew had seen three stationary bright red flashing lights on the water, from sundown until about 11:00 PM. The ship's radar showed four objects forming a six mile square; the three lights were associated with one of these objects. [Here Levine contradicts his claim that there were no radar reports and that no one saw the object strike the water.] At about 11:00 PM, one of the lights went straight up. The captain had judged that the radar objects were naval vessels and the ascending light a helicopter; he had attached no significance to these observations until he had heard on the radio of the sightings; he then reported the foregoing observations . . . However, since the position he reported for the objects was about 175 n. mi.

from the original site, the two situations do not appear to be related.

No further investigation by the project was considered justifiable, particularly in view of the immediate and thorough search that had been carried out by the RCMP and the Maritime Command.[20]

Levine's conclusions were inaccurate, although certainly in line with what those in the Deep State wanted.

Canadian UFO researchers Chris Styles and Don Ledger pursued the case because, to them, it deserved more than the telephonic investigation conducted by the Condon Committee. According to Styles and Ledger, the events began on the night of October 4, 1967, when witnesses reported seeing an object as large as sixty feet wide descend to the surface of the water in Shag Harbor, about a half mile from shore. There were four bright lights on it that flashed in sequence.[21] Its impact with the water seemed to be accompanied by a bright flash of light and then an explosion. Several witnesses, thinking that this might be some sort of aircraft accident, called the police at Barrington Passage. Although some talked about the event as a plane crash, others who called mentioned only the bright lights on the water. No one suggested, at that point, that a UFO had fallen into the harbor.

Corporal Victor Werbicki, the officer in charge, headed out to the shoreline with Constables Ron O'Brien and Ron Pond. Pond reported seeing the lights from his cruiser and, as the object dove toward the water, a solid shape behind them. Somehow the Condon Committee missed this vital piece of evidence.

As the three Mounties stood on the shore with other civilian witnesses, they all saw a pale-yellow light that floated about a half mile offshore. Through binoculars, they could all see that whatever floated on the surface was creating a foaming, yellow wake as it moved. Because of the location of the object, or rather the yellow wake, Coast Guard cutters and local fishing boats were summoned to attempt to identify it. Whatever it was, however, dove deeper into the water before any of the boats arrived. Those on the fishing boats did see the dense yellow foam, but that too disappeared before the Coast Guard cutter arrived. At 3:00 AM, the search of the area was suspended and set to resume at dawn.

The Rescue Coordination Center in Halifax prepared a preliminary report for transmittal to Canadian Forces Headquarters in Ottawa. The report confirmed only that something had fallen into the water in Shag Harbor. According to Styles, however, as the message headed up the Canadian chain of command that "something" was described as "no known object," prompting an alert to the Air Desk, which he described as equivalent to Project Blue Book. The Air Desk ordered Maritime Command to dispatch a mobile unit to Shag Harbor.[22] The HCMS Granby proceeded to Shag Harbor and searched the area with divers until last light on Sunday, October 8. When they failed to find anything, the search was ended and media interest in the event faded. Although the sighting seemed to indicate the presence of physical evidence—something that should have been quite important to an investigation of UFOs—the Condon Committee conducted only a telephonic investigation, which they closed with these words: "No further investigation by the project was considered justifiable, particularly in view of the immediate and thorough search that had been carried out by the RCMP and the Maritime Command."[23]

The situation, however, wasn't quite as cut and dried as the Condon Committee made it out to be. Styles and Ledger found official Canadian documents that suggested there was more to the story. The Canadian search mission was apparently larger than first thought and involved elements of the United States Navy as well. Although they were unable to locate the object that had fallen into the harbor, a picture of it in the sky surfaced, as well as multiple eyewitness accounts, including those from law enforcement officers.

The Canadian government carried out an extensive investigation that might have provided important evidence for the Committee and moved them beyond the typically transient nature of UFO sightings. Committee investigators could actually have arrived in time to see some of it for themselves.[24]

As we have seen, however, the mission of the Condon Committee was not to investigate UFOs in search of true answers, but rather to devalue the idea of alien visitation, convince the public that there was nothing out of the ordinary in UFO sightings, and close Project Blue Book, saving Air Force resources. Committee members were merely following the instructions they had been given by those in the Deep State who were actually in charge. To investigate Shag Harbor would have violated their real mission to end Project Blue Book and, by extension, public interest in UFOs.

OVERT BIAS

There are some other quite interesting, if not disturbing, aspects to all this, however. Those present at a subsequent briefing discussed the number of UFO sighting reports that had been gathered, concentrating on the Air Force but not ignoring civilian organizations.

> Briefly, he [Michael Werthelmer, cited above in Hippler's letter to Condon] has hypothesized that regardless of how many reports we receive and how many we are able to dispose of, we are almost certain to find a residue of unexplained ones. The existence of the residue, however, does not prove that anything is coming from outer space. To prove that, one needs direct evidence that some objects are really from outer space and that they are intelligently guided; the existence of a residue of unexplained sighting reports does not constitute such proof.[25]

Condon stated that he would only accept the recovery of a space-ship as evidence of alien visitation, claiming:

> I wouldn't be satisfied with anything other than actually get-ting a vehicle, with or without occupants, so under my control that I could take it and exhibit it to something like this com-mittee so that all of you saw it, or take you to a place where I had it "captured." Anything less than that I wouldn't believe.[26]

Even direct observation by military and commercial pilots or by scientists would not be sufficient, much less indirect evidence like multiple eyewitness accounts, landing traces, radar returns, pho-tographs from multiple locations, and other measurements. Wert-heimer, who had put forth the hypothesis in question, discussed some of these various possibilities at length:

> Unfortunately, I think it is becoming clear that the funda-mental question that the public wants answered is simply unanswerable. The assertion that at least some of these are actually caused by objects of intelligent extraterrestrial origin is neither proof nor disproof, nor made less likely by the exis-tence of cases in the X class [meaning those cases that have no suitable explanation, or in other words, the "unidenti-fieds" in the Project Blue Book files].[27]

This suggests that, at this point, they had no hope of (and no inter-est in) learning if UFOs were extraterrestrial in nature.

Wertheimer believed that they couldn't possibly come to any sort of conclusion about this, which is what the public expected and what it was suggested this scientific study would do. The expectation was that scientists would review the data, evaluate the evidence, investi-gate new cases, and come to some sort of a conclusion. Of course, this was not exactly what the Deep State had in mind—unless, of course, they could offer solid evidence that there had been no alien visitation. For them, that was the only acceptable outcome and they had stacked the deck to ensure they got the answer they wanted. In reality, however, all the committee was supposed to do was to say something positive about the way the Air Force had handled the UFO investigations and confirm that UFOs did not threaten national security. Wertheimer, in fact, confirmed this during the briefing:

> Here is an excerpt from a memorandum I sent to the UFO Study:
>
> *I think the Blue Book attempts have been superb—that the Blue Book personnel are badly overworked, that considering the small amount of time and staff available they have done a superb job. Chances are that a substantial proportion of the cases, though, that are now carried explained in the files would on closer examination not be very convincing after all. There are probably some also which are now unexplained which more careful analysis might find a fairly plausible explanation for. But I am also convinced that however much time we or any other group spend studying these detailed reports, there will still remain some that are unsatisfactorily explained.*[28]

In other words, the Blue Book team had done a good job with little support and few resources. If better information had been provided originally, then perhaps some of the "unidentified" cases might have been resolved to everyone's satisfaction.

This, however, was not an accurate reading of the situation. There were other resources available to investigators, even if the Condon Committee and those at Blue Book had no knowledge of them. Brigadier General Arthur Exon, one-time base commander at Wright-Patterson AFB, talked of support teams that came from outside of that base, flown in and then ferried to the scene of sightings. It is clear that this information never made it into the Project Blue Book files, however, and that the information was provided only to the Deep State.[29] Take, for example, Project Moon Dust, a classified project that had a UFO component (see chapter 8). I find only four cases in the Blue Book files marked "Moon Dust" and all of them are very poorly documented. Nonetheless, documentation from the State Department and other governmental sources proves that Moon Dust existed, that it gathered UFO data, and that team members were deployed for UFO investigations.

At the beginning of the committee's "investigation," Condon seemed to be having some fun with UFOs. He attended UFO conventions, was interviewed, and had his picture taken with some of the more outrageous characters who dot the Ufological field. But this attitude slowly began to change—almost as if he began to fear UFOs. After the summer of 1967, the general theme of the discussions was that UFOs were harmful—not that seeing them or getting close to them was harmful, but rather that the possibility that they were of extraterrestrial origin could be harmful to young minds. This had been the attitude of the Robertson Panel—one that was reinforced by the Deep State. In the committee's final report in 1969, Condon wrote:

> [W]e strongly recommend that teachers refrain from giving students credit for school work based on their reading of the presently available UFO books and magazine articles. Teachers who find their students strongly motivated in this direction should attempt to channel their interests in the direction of the serious study of astronomy and meteorology, and critical analysis of arguments for the fantastic propositions that are being supported by appeals to fallacious reasoning or false data.

This suppression of research into UFOs was part of the overall Deep State plan that had been suggested by the Robertson Panel and was now being seconded by the Condon Committee. The Deep State planned years and even decades in advance. Convince youngsters that there was nothing to UFOs, deny them credit for researching the topic—even if that research used proper scientific and research methods—and when they eventually grew up, they would not even inquire into UFOs. They would already know the answers because they had been fed to them by the Deep State.

The committee's final report claimed, as had all previous official and allegedly unbiased investigations, that UFOs posed no threat to national security, asserting:

> The history of the past 21 years has repeatedly led Air Force officers to the conclusion that none of the things seen, or thought to have been seen, which pass by the name UFO reports constituted any hazard or threat to national security.[30]

But this statement was directly contradicted by an event that occurred near Belt, Montana in March 1967. Although there were sightings all around Belt, the most important took place around Malmstrom AFB and the ballistic missile fields spread through an area of eastern Montana that was home to Echo Flight. These events had a major impact on the Deep State.

ECHO FLIGHT

The story starts early on the morning of March 16, 1967, when two missile-maintenance teams who had been working on two of Echo Flight's widely scattered launch facilities said they saw strange lights in the sky nearby. A mobile security team confirmed this, saying they had seen the lights as well. When Colonel Don Crawford came on duty, he was informed of the sightings by Captain Eric Carlson and 1st Lieutenant Walt Figel, at least according to what UFO researcher Robert Hastings was told some years later during his interviews with Figel.

At about 8:30 that same morning, as both Carlson and Figel were performing routine checks, the flight's missiles began to drop off line. Within seconds, although Figel would later suggest it was minutes, all ten missiles were rendered inoperable. This was a major national security issue and was alarming to those in the Deep State because it threatened their control. Hastings wrote:

> Immediately after the malfunctions at Echo, the launch offi-
> cers ordered two separate Security Alert Teams to drive to each
> of the launch facilities where the UFOs had been sighted . . .
> [T]he maintenance and security personnel at each site
> reported seeing UFOs hovering near the missile silos.[31]

When Hastings talked to Figel on October 20, 2008, he was told that one of the guards suggested that a UFO had shut down the missiles. Figel thought the guard was joking. When Hastings asked what the guard had seen, Figel described it as "a large, round object that was directly over the launch facility."

"[When] the missiles dropped off alert," Figel told Hastings, "I started calling the maintenance people out there on the radio . . . [I asked] 'What's going on?' . . . And the guy says: 'We got a Channel 9 No-Go. It must be a UFO hovering over the site.'" Figel, of course, didn't believe him. He said that one of the two strike teams they had dispatched thought they had seen something as well and told Figel that a large object was hovering over the site.

Maintenance teams were dispatched to bring the missiles back on line, but the process was not simple and required hours for each missile. In other words, it took a couple of days to get the entire flight operational. The events prompted an extensive investigation that involved not only the Air Force but also the contractors who had designed and built the missiles. According to the 341st Strate-gic Missile Wing Unit History, recovered by a Freedom of Informa-tion request:

> On 16 March 1967 at 0845, all sites in Echo (E) Flight, Malm-
> strom AFB, shutdown with No-Go indication of Channels 9
> and 12 on Voice Reporting Signal Assemble (VRSA). All
> LF's [launch facilities] in E Flight lost strategic alert nearly

simultaneously. No other Wing I configuration lost strategic alert at that time . . .

All 10 sites were reported to have been subject to a normal controlled shutdown . . .

The only possible means that could be identified by the team involved a situation in which a couple self test commands occurred along with a partial reset within the coupler . . . This was also quite remote for all 10 couplers would have to have been partially reset in the same manner . . .

A check with Communications maintenance verified that there was no unusual activity with EWO-1 or EWO-2 at the time of the incident.[32]

In other words, they didn't actually know why the missiles went down, although they could determine that a "30 micro sec Pulse . . . was placed on the Self Test Command (STC) line," and that "seven out of 10 separate applications of a single pulse would cause the system to shut down with a Channel 9 & 12 No-Go."

This randomly introduced electronic pulse, which might be considered an EMP (electromagnetic pulse), shouldn't have affected the missile systems at all. EMPs were well-understood at this time and the Launch Control Facility (LFC), where the pulse originated, should have been shielded from just such an intrusion, because this kind of attack had been deemed possible during any sort of atomic warfare. Nevertheless, it had shut the missiles down.

When these events were communicated to the Condon Committee, Dr. Roy Craig responded. Craig made notes on his meeting with Lieutenant Colonel Lewis Chase, Malmstrom's UFO officer:

After Colonel Chase and I exchanged pleasantries in his office, I asked him about the Echo incident. The Colonel caught his breath, and expressed surprise that I knew of it. "I can't talk about that". . . If I needed to know the cause of this incident, I could arrange through official channels, to see their report after the completion of the investigation . . . Although local newspapers carried stories of UFO sightings which would coincide in time with Echo, Colonel Chase had assured me that the incident had not involved a UFO . . . I accepted the information as factual and turned review of Major Schraff's report (on the Echo incident) over to Bob Low [Dr. Robert Low, also a member of the Condon Committee], who had received security clearance to read secret information related to the UFO study.

Low, in turn, had to interface with his Air Force Liaison in Washington, Colonel Hippler, as he informed Craig:

Roy, I called Hippler and he said he would try to get this, but he suspects it's going to be classified too high for us to look at. Says he thinks interference by pulses from nuclear explosions is probably involved.[33]

It seems they had found the cause of the shutdown, but not the ultimate source of the pulse. Hippler, speculating about that, came up with the explanation of an EMP from a nonexistent atomic blast. That the pulse shut down all the missiles made it a national security issue, which changed the level of classification and took it out of the UFO arena. Oddly, the same Unit History noted:

Rumors of Unidentified Objects (UFO) around the area of Echo Flight during the time of the fault were disproven. A Mobile Strike Team, which had checked all November Flight's LFs on the morning of 16 March 67, were questioned and stated that no unusual activity or sightings were observed.[34]

But that doesn't seem to be quite accurate. Hastings interviewed James Ortyl, an Air Policeman at Malmstrom, who told him:

I was an Airman 2nd Class [A2C] at the time. We were working the day-shift at Kilo Flight in March of 1967 . . . It was
mid-morning and three or four Air Policemen were gathered in the launch control facility dispatch office. Airman
Robert Pounders and I were facing the windows looking
out to the yard and parking lot. The others were facing us.
As we were conversing, I witnessed a shimmering, reddish-
orange object clear the main gate and in a sweeping motion
pass quickly and silently past the windows. It seemed to be
within 30 yards of the building. Stunned, I looked at Pounders and asked: "Did you see that?!" He acknowledged that
he had.[35]

Craig's notes indicate that he had the names of some of those
involved with the UFO sightings at the time of Echo's shut down,
but he never contacted any of them. There is no reason for him not
to have done so, unless he had been directed not to ask questions
by someone outside of the Condon Committee. It was, after all, his
job. This seems to indicate that some sort of pressure caused them
not to follow up on the investigation. Naturally, that influence came
from the Deep State, because such an investigation could lead back
to them if pursued with any sort of vigor.[36]

Craig also had the name of Dan Renualdi who, in March 1967,
was a member of the Site Activation Task Force (SATAF). He said
that he had been within a few feet of the object. A sergeant with
the Air Force Technical Evaluation Team also said he had seen the
flying saucer. There is no record of Craig talking to either of these
men, however, nor are there any reports in the Blue Book files to
suggest that the sightings were reported through channels, a violation of Air Force regulations. All this demonstrates that there was
a UFO reported around the time that Echo Flight went down, contrary to what the Unit History said and what Air Force personnel on
the scene reported at the time.

And there is another aspect to these events. Quite naturally, the Air Force wanted to know what had happened. In a letter dated February 1, 1997 to UFO researcher Jim Klotz, Robert Kaminski, the man who conducted the investigation for Boeing, the defense contractor responsible for the missile systems, wrote:

> Since this was a field site peculiar incident, a determination was made to send out an investigative team to survey the LCF and the LFs to determine what failures or related incidents could be found to explain the cause . . . After a week in the field the team returned and pooled their data. At the outset the team quickly noticed a lack of anything that would come close to explaining why the event occurred. There were no significant failures, engineering data, or findings that would come close to explaining how ten missiles were knocked off alert. This indeed turned out to be a rare event and not encountered before. The use of backup power systems and other technical system circuit operational redundancy strongly suggests that this kind of event is virtually impossible once the system was up and running and on line with other LCF's and LF's interconnectivity . . .

> The team met with me to report their findings and it was decided that the final report would have nothing significant in it to explain what happened at E-Flight. In other words there was no technical explanation that could explain the event . . . Meanwhile I was contacted by our representative . . . (Don Peterson) and told by him that the incident was reported as being a UFO event—that a UFO was seen by some Airmen over the LCF at the time E-Flight when down.

> Subsequently, we were notified a few days later, that a stop work order was on the way from OOAMA [Office, Ogden Air Material Area] to stop any further effort on this project. We stopped. We were also told that we were not to submit the

final engineering report. This was most unusual since all of our work required review by the customer and the submittal of a final Engineering report to OOAMA . . .

However, as I recall nothing explained this anomaly at E-Flight.[37]

Hastings, in a review of the material in 2013, wrote:

Actually, the large round object sighted by the missile guard, and reported to launch officer Lt. Walter Figel, had been hovering over one of the Echo missile silos, not the launch control facility itself. Nevertheless, Boeing engineer Kaminski's revealing testimony essentially confirms Figel's account of a UFO presence during the incident.[38]

THE COMMITTEE'S FINDINGS

After suggesting that the effect of UFOs on national security was outside the committee's purvue and agreeing that committee members would pass any such evidence on to the Air Force, Condon wrote: "We know of no reason to question the finding of the Air Force that the whole class of UFO reports so far considered does not pose a defense problem."[39] He went on to say:

It is our impression that the defense function could be performed within the framework established for intelligence and surveillance operations without the continuance of a special unit such as Project Blue Book, but this is a question for defense specialists rather than research scientists.[40]

With that, Condon fulfilled most of the requirements of the study. He added some positive comments about the way the investigation had been conducted by the Air Force, and concluded that there were no national security issues involved, although he clearly had information to the contrary. He then recommended the closing of

Project Blue Book because other military organizations could perform its investigative functions without a dedicated budget.

But to make sure the general public was not fooled by civilian UFO researchers or writers of popular literature, Condon added, rather ironically:

> It has been contended that the subject has been shrouded in official secrecy. We conclude otherwise. We have no evidence of secrecy concerning UFO reports. What has been miscalled secrecy has been no more than an intelligent policy of delay in releasing data so that the public does not become confused by premature publication of incomplete studies or reports.[41]

This too, was untrue. There are sighting reports in the Blue Book files in which the security markings have been blacked out. In some cases, a single line is drawn through the security stamps, clearly showing that there had been secret reports and classified sightings.

Condon did the job he had been hired to do. He attempted to bury questions about UFOs under a blanket of scientific jargon, biased and incomplete investigations, and supposed objectivity. The final report was structured the way Condon wanted it structured, which is to say the way the Air Force had been instructed to have it structured by the Deep State. The UFO case book that was supposed to accompany the report was scrapped because it might have led to embarrassing questions about some of those conclusions.

Condon also produced a deceptive "executive summary"—a short volume that supposedly included all the relevant information drawn from the much thicker formal report. The problem is that the executive summary, which is about all the news media and scientists outside the committee read, is not accurate. In it, Condon suggests that he had finally put the idea of UFOs as alien craft to rest, something the statistics in his main report do not confirm. Yet today, this report is held up as an example of scientific research into UFOs. To skeptics and debunkers, it proves that there is nothing to the theory that some UFOs represent alien spacecraft and alien technology. The report accomplished its mission, however. On December 17, 1969, the Air Force announced the closing of Project Blue Book. Investigating UFOs would now be left to local law enforcement or civilian UFO groups. The Air Force was no longer interested.

Or so they said.

Although the Robertson Panel had suggested in 1953 that the Air Force stop investigating UFOs, that recommendation was not accepted. Many tried to end the investigations because they believed nothing would come of them. But they failed. Others tried to end them because the Deep State wanted them ended. It was only after the Air Force and the Condon Committee conspired to ignore evidence that the official public investigation of UFOs by the Air Force ended.

But the end of public Air Force involvement was not the end of these investigations, as documents, letters, and other evidence have shown. As late as 1987, these investigations were still ongoing, but they were properly classified and tightly held—until the Freedom of Information Act (FOIA) reared its ugly head. The Air Force may have said they were done with UFOs, but clearly they were not. They just buried their inquiries more deeply.

CHAPTER 7

Project Blue Book

P roject Blue Book was the name given to the systematic study of UFOs conducted by the Air Force between 1952 and 1969. Initiated to take up investigations previously carried out under Projects Sign and Grudge (see chapter 2), Blue Book claimed to have two goals: to determine if UFOs were a threat to national security, and to analyze UFO-related data. After collecting and investigating over 12,618 UFO reports, the project concluded that most of them were misidentified natural phenomena, weather-related phenomena, military reconnaissance missions, or conventional aircraft, claiming that nothing they found had any implications for either national security or extraterrestrial activity. When the project ended, its files were archived and remained inaccessible to UFO researchers and the public until they became available, although heavily redacted, in 1976.

In the summer of 1953, after the situation created by the massive wave of sightings that included the all-important Washington National events had quieted down, Ed Ruppelt made a request for assistance for Project Blue Book:

> During the summer of 1953, UFO reports dropped off considerably . . . We had been waiting for the magic month of July to roll around again because every July there had been the sudden and unexplained peak in reporting; we wanted

to know if it would happen again. It didn't—only twenty-one reports came in, to make July the lowest month of the year. But July did bring new developments.

Project Blue Book got a badly needed shot in the arm when an unpublicized but highly important change took place; another intelligence agency began to take over all field investigations.

Ever since I'd returned to the project the orders had been to build it up—get more people—do what the [Robertson] panel recommended . . . I did the next best thing and tried to find some organization already in being which could and would help us out. I happened to be expounding my troubles one day at Air Defense Command Headquarters where I was briefing General Burgess, ADC's Director of Intelligence, and he told me about this 4602nd Air Intelligence Squadron . . . Maybe it could help—he'd see what he could work out . . .

Project Blue Book was once again back in business. Until the formal paper work went through, our plan was that whenever a UFO report worth investigating came in, we would call the 4602nd and they would get a team out right away. The team would make a thorough investigation and wire us their report. If the answer came back "Unknown," we would study the details of the sighting and with the help of Project Bear [actually the Battelle study for the Air Force called it Project Stock], try to find the answer.[1]

But there were other forces at work here. The Robertson Panel had suggested that UFOs be "demystified" and that teachers reject the work of students studying them for class projects. Now, rather than shoring up Project Blue Book's resources, the project was actually being stripped of its investigative work, which was given to the 4602nd Air Intelligence Service Squandron (AISS). New regulations written at the time required that the 4602nd investigate UFOs.

This is underscored by statements made at a commanders' conference held on June 22, 1953 that many officers assigned to the
4602nd attended. After a brief discussion of UFOs, Lieutenant Colonel Richard C. Jones, the operations officer, said:

> Investigation of unidentified flying objects is not presently part
> of the mission of this squadron. Field Units are not authorized
> to make investigation of this type unless so directed or prior
> approval is obtained from Headquarters. If ATIC gets a report
> and feels that an investigation is necessary, they will notify this
> Headquarters and we in turn will then direct the proper field
> team to make the investigation . . . If it is not going to involve
> too much time, you can go ahead and make the investigation
> based on your own judgment. Don't let this sort of thing get out
> of hand but if it will assist you in your relationships with the D/I
> [Director of Intelligence] and you feel you have the time, go
> ahead. Otherwise, notify this Headquarters for prior approval.[2]

What is interesting about this statement is that it shouldn't exist.
Nothing in the original mission of the 4602nd discussed UFOs and,
at this point, Ruppelt had not made his request for assistance to
General Burgess. There would have been no reason for the operations officer to warn his personnel about UFO investigations—
unless, of course, someone at a higher level of command, perhaps
in the office of the Secretary of the Air Force or the Secretary of
Defense, was thinking about ways to divert attention from Project
Blue Book. Clearly, some sort of inquiry had been made, and commanders at the local level were attempting to keep the 4602nd from
being dragged into UFO investigation.

This was happening at the same time that new officers were being
appointed to run Project Blue Book. Unlike Ruppelt, however, these
officers were not objective. They believed that UFOs represented
nothing more than misidentifications, illusions, delusions, lies, and
hoaxes. Jerry Clark noted this in his massive *UFO Encyclopedia.*

Capt. Charles Hardin was appointed Blue Book director in March 1954. The 4602nd assumed a larger and larger role in investigation and analysis, leaving Hardin with relatively little to do, which was fine with him, according to a private memorandum Ruppelt wrote. "He definitely doesn't believe in UFOs . . . in fact, he thinks that anyone who is even interested is crazy."[3]

More evidence of Deep State influence appeared at a third commanders' conference held in 1954. At these meetings, Captain Cybulski of the 4602nd provided a long discussion of UFOs in a document originally classified as "secret":

> The primary reason for our [4602nd] participation in this program is to solve a very perplexing problem for the Air Force and the country as a whole. To the Air Force the investigations of the UFOB is very important. In all but a few cases a satisfactory solution has been reached and the Air Force feels that adequate, thorough investigative procedures can solve the small percentage of unsolved sightings. This is where we come into the picture.[4]

Like so much else that was hidden behind the curtain of national security, this statement is quite illuminating. Cybulski is telling those assembled that the mystery had been solved and that there would have been no residue of unsolved cases if a thorough investigation had been conducted by trained investigators in the first place.

There are clear hints of Deep State manipulation in Cybulski's presentation. Buried at the end of his report is a discussion about photographs of UFOs. "The photographs go to Washington," Cybulski wrote. "In addition, one copy of each print will be forwarded to ATIC, and one to us here at headquarters."[5] The obvious question here is: Why? Given the rules and regulations in effect at the time, shouldn't everything have gone to ATIC, meaning Project Blue

Book? And who in Washington had the power to demand something like that? This anomaly subtly demonstrates that those in the seats of power in Washington had more than a passing interest in UFOs. Moreover, it demonstrates that those in the Deep State wanted to know what was happening with UFOs but that they weren't all that interested in eyewitness testimony. They wanted something more. They wanted to see if the photographs showed something more than blobs of light. This becomes clearer with Cybulski's next statement: "In almost every case where gun cameras have been used, the thing has been too small for identification and photographs haven't been of much value."[6]

The real point is that Cybulski mentioned a group in Washington that wanted the original photographs of UFOs and then made reference to gun-camera films. This is official confirmation that some sort of investigation was being conducted into actual evidence of UFOs and that gun-camera films existed, although they are virtually absent from the Blue Book files. In fact, Ruppelt implies that these films all identify mundane objects. He did suggest they had some very good film taken by a pilot who reported that he had tried to catch a UFO. But when that film was analyzed, they suggested that the object was the size of a standard weather balloon.[7] What they didn't explain was why a fighter aircraft was unable to catch a weather balloon.

Cybulski's statements, found in documents formerly classified as secret, clearly suggest that another group or organization was interested in UFOs. While it can be said that the Air Force chain of command in the Pentagon had the power to require that the information be forwarded—and it should be noted here that none of the generals at the very top were elected officials—the information being developed suggests that this group was made up of bureaucrats whose stay in Washington transcended that of elected officials. In other words, they were members of the Deep State who were interested in UFOs. That, of course, didn't mean that they wished those at the lower levels of the hierarchy to have the information necessary to understand what was going on. They wanted to control that information. By forcing it up the chain of command, they hoped to keep those lower down the ladder from putting the pieces of the puzzle together.

In February 1955, the Air Force changed the investigative techniques used to "solve" more of the sightings. Those at the top, those taking their instructions from the Deep State, had decided that there were too many sightings being labeled as "unidentified." From that point on, report categories were broadened. "Possible" solutions became "probable," and "probable" solutions were relabeled as "explained."[8] Many sightings were labeled as "insufficient data for a scientific analysis." That meant, of course, that no solution had been found, but that they didn't want to label the case as "unidentified." Some 5,000 cases ended up being classified as "insufficient data." These required no further explanation and they didn't count in the statistics for "unidentified" cases. In other words, some 5,000 Project Blue Book cases that should have been labeled as "unidentified" were not.

In April 1966, Hardin's tour as head of Project Blue Book ended and Captain George T. Gregory was brought in. Gregory was considered a hardline debunker, even more radical than Hardin, making it clear the direction that the UFO project had taken.[9] Gregory's orders were clear. They wanted no more UFO sightings labeled as "unidentified." All cases would be explained, regardless of how ridiculous the explanations might be. And this would be the project's mission for the rest of its run, with the exception of the period during which Lieutenant Colonel Robert Friend headed the team. Friend appeared to have no agenda regarding UFOs, but, during his tenure, the project suffered from a lack of funding and influence and came to be seen as a liability that needed to be dropped. Through no fault of his own, Friend presided over the project's demise.

The Air Force's change of mission is typified by the response to a UFO report made by Ray Rosi of Austin, Texas on June 24, 1967.[10] At about 3:00 AM, Rosi was driving on the north side of the Mansfield Dam when he stopped to let his dog out of the car. He was surprised by a bright, elongated, solid-looking object just above the horizon. Moments earlier, two men in a small, red sports car had passed him on the road. They had slowed down as they approached and then sped up, pulling to the side of the road about 250 feet away. Rosi thought nothing of this until he saw the UFO. In his official report, Rosi said:

> I wondered why they would be at such a place at that time of night. They parked with lights tilted up the hill and flashed their beams several times. It was a short time later that the strange object appeared on the northwest horizon. Occupants of the red auto pulled over to the other side of the road, and stopped the car again—out of my sight.[11]

After watching the men apparently send a signal, Rosi took out a big spotlight and began flashing the "only code he could think of that anyone would understand (mathematical: 3.14, *pi*)." He flashed it a few times and the object "stopped dead still."[12] The illumination faded for a second or two, then brightened. The UFO hovered for a few minutes, then finally started to move again, following its original path.

As the UFO moved, Rosi got out his binoculars. Through them, he could see a blue cigar-shaped craft. When he flashed his signal at it again, the UFO slowed and the brightness faded. Then it brightened and the craft resumed its original speed. According to Rosi, the UFO disappeared at 3:22 AM into a low cloud cover. He had the UFO in sight for about ten minutes, noting that he had timed the sighting on his electronic watch.

After the UFO disappeared, Rosi, with his dog back in the car, drove to the nearest telephone and called the Air Force. They responded, as required by regulation, by sending one officer, Lieutenant Robert Foreman, with a long questionnaire. As he was completing the form and telling Foreman about the sighting, Rosi mentioned that he had had the feeling that he was being watched. He compared it to "a youngster doing something wrong in the backyard of a home who all of a sudden felt that he was being watched." He said that it was a feeling of communication "somewhat like mental telepathy, yet not strong enough because I have never experienced or received any message by brain wave."[13]

Foreman completed his investigation, took the completed form with its complicated questions and drawings, and left. He submitted Rosi's account to Project Blue Book. Rosi, of course, was interested in the case and, when he later asked what was being done, he learned that his sighting had been stamped as "insufficient data for a scientific analysis." In other words, it was now being ignored rather than being labeled "unidentified."[14] This made Rosi so furious that he filled out another Air Force form, adding a lengthy comment to a question that asked for pertinent information that was not adequately covered elsewhere in the questionnaire:

> It is a real mystery to me why you state in your August 21 missive, "The information which we received is not sufficient for a scientific evaluation," in consideration of the fact that the very thorough report which Lieutenant Forman took and supposedly submitted to you contained far more definitive information . . . than could be elicited via your questionnaire.

Rosi wondered what additional data might be required to prompt a "scientific analysis" and where those points were covered on the form. He wrote that their handling of the case led him to believe "that the accusations of negligence heaped upon you . . . by some independent investigations in recent years may NOT [emphasis in the original] be entirely unfounded."[15]

Rosi thought that a great deal of time and effort was being expended on gathering data that were later found to be inadequate. Rather than follow up, it seemed that the Air Force had just labeled the case as "insufficient" and stuck it in a file. But the Air Force did review the case again.

According to Project Blue Book files, Rosi had a technical background. He had done research into solid-fuel rockets and written three extensive mathematical papers on the performance of three- and four-stage rockets. He was considered highly reliable. In other words, he wasn't some drunk or poorly educated hick; he was well-educated and highly intelligent. Since they couldn't dismiss him as a kook, they changed the labeling of the case to "unidentified." Rosi's report came at a time when the Air Force was attempting to shed its UFO investigations, and the very last thing they wanted was an unidentified sighting by a man with a good education and a background as a rocket scientist. They just wanted the sighting to go away. By changing their designation, they satisfied Rosi and nothing further was heard about his case in the civilian world.

By this time, however, the Condon Committee was taking care of the UFO investigations and they had their orders, issued both by the Air Force and the Deep State. Rosi's sighting was just the sort that they wanted to avoid. If the information got out to the public, some very difficult questions might be asked. The Air Force, on orders from above, successfully hid the case until nearly a decade later, when the files were declassified and civilian researchers had a chance to review them.

The last officer officially in charge of Project Blue Book was Hector Quintanilla, who was interested primarily in maintaining the status quo—which is to say that he saw his mission as providing solutions for sightings rather than actually investigating them. He believed the answers to UFO sightings were terrestrial and embraced any explanation that seemed reasonable, with only a few exceptions. But he did seem to try to find proper solutions, for example in the

Socorro UFO landing, witnessed by police officer Lonnie Zamora. Quintanilla made a real effort on this case because he believed the solution was an experimental craft from White Sands. He failed to find any solution at all, however—a failure that is reflected in both the Project Blue Book files and in his own manuscript, which was later privately published.

BEYOND BLUE BOOK

In 1957, another project was created—one that even had a classified name and a classified mission (see chapter 8). That mission was to recover returning space debris of foreign manufacture or unknown origin. "Unknown origin" included the possibility of a craft of alien creation. Project Moon Dust, as it was called, had a UFO component, and it seemed that the important cases ended up there, rather than at Blue Book.

J. Allen Hynek, who was a scientific consultant to Project Blue Book for decades, often said that the really convincing UFO cases never made it into the Blue Book system. He knew, from his own experience, that some of the reports that should have gone to Blue Book according to Air Force regulation simply never got there. He suspected that there was another reporting system, but he couldn't prove it. If his suspicions were correct, this amounts to a Deep State conspiracy to hide UFO information for their own protection.

Brigadier General Arthur Exon, who was base commander at Wright-Patterson Air Force Base in the mid-1960s, seems to confirm this. A base commander is similar to the mayor of a city. In fact, in today's Army, each facility has a unit known as the "mayor's cell." But the base commander is not necessarily the highest-ranking officer on the base. He is responsible for the facilities and for the support of various base operations like security, repair, and upkeep. Exon claims that, while he was base commander, he periodically received instructions to prepare aircraft assigned to Wright-Patterson for missions outside the local area. Those planes could be sent almost anywhere in the world, given the capabilities of military aircraft and the global reach of the Air Force. According to Exon:

> I know that while I was there . . . I had charge of all of the administrative airplanes and had to sign priority airplanes to the members who would go out and investigate reported sightings . . . I remember several out in Wyoming and Montana and that area in the '60s, '64 and '65 . . . I knew there were certain teams of people, they're representing headquarters USAF as well as the organizations there at Wright-Pat, FTD and so on . . . When a crew came back it was their own business. Nobody asked any questions . . .
>
> The way this happened to me is that I would get a call and say that the crew or team was leaving . . . there was such and such a time and they wanted an airplane and pilots to take X number of people to wherever . . . They might be gone two or three days or might be gone a week. They would come back and that would be the end of it.[16]

Asked about the overall control of these teams, Exon said: "I always thought they were part of that unholy crew in Washington that started keeping the lid on this thing."[17] In other words, he was talking about some sort of organization that controlled information and the overall direction of the UFO programs. He was talking about the Deep State.

In a follow-up interview conducted by Don Schmitt on June 18, 1990 and recorded on audio tape, Exon clarified what he had meant. Asked if these teams of eight to fifteen people were stationed at Wright-Patterson, he said:

> They would come from Washington, D. C. They'd ask for an airplane tomorrow morning and that would give the guys a

chance to get there [Wright-Patterson] by commercial airline
. . . Sometimes they'd be gone for three days and sometimes
they would be gone for a week. I know they went to Montana
and Wyoming and the northwest states a number of times in
a year and a half . . . They went to Arizona once or twice.[18]

In the interview with me, he added: "Our contact was a man, a telephone number. He'd call and he'd set the airplane up. I just knew there was an investigative team."[19]

These teams were made up of eight to fifteen individuals at a time when Project Blue Book had only three military men and a single secretary assigned to it. The Blue Book team was stationed at Wright-Patterson, but the other teams were assigned elsewhere, and there is no reason to assume that all members of a particular team were assigned to the same base. They came together as needed and, once the investigation was over, they dispersed to their home stations. The teams, whoever they were, flew into Dayton, Ohio on commercial flights and then drove out to the base. If a reporter attempted to trace their movements after the team was deployed, the trail led back to Wright-Patterson—and then just disappeared. And this is what happened on May 19, 1990, when Exon received instructions to support an operation that was run through the Foreign Technology Division (FTD), the parent organization to Project Blue Book at Wright-Patterson.

What all this boils down to is an attempt to cover the activity. It also all strongly suggests that there were other people involved in the investigation of UFOs who were not members of the Project Blue Book team. Hynek hints that the more convincing reports were sent elsewhere and Exon suggests that investigative teams that were not part of Blue Book were stationed elsewhere and called when needed. This is the very essence of a Deep State operation, carried out by a group of high-ranking unelected officials who had the power to control the flow of UFO investigations and information.

But Exon, because of who he was, provided more than just a suggestion of high-ranking officials operating outside normal channels. He named names. In an interview with me on May 19, 1990, he claimed: "Well, I know that at the time the sightings happened [in Roswell] it went to General Ramey . . . and he along with the people out at Roswell decided to change the story while they got their act together and got the information into the Pentagon and into the President."[20] He described the composition of the teams working inside the Deep State like this:

> One of my officers who did some research, who worked for me at Wright-Patterson, who had done some research on this as part of his school came up with a deal that there was great concern at that time and there was fear that people would panic if the sketchy information that they had . . . got out . . . and that it probably wouldn't be released until everybody who was involved in it, including the thirteen people I'm talking about and their immediate staff who made up the investigative team, had passed away. So, they wouldn't divulge information or information wouldn't come out that they may or may not have been involved while they were still alive.
>
> That's the logical thing and I know most of those people were around. I did know that they're numbers one and two people at the top of the staff included the Secretary of Defense and the Chief of Staff and the intelligence circle around the President's office, I never heard of any elected officials [involved] . . .
>
> I just know there was a top intelligence echelon represented and the President's office was represented and the Secretary of Defense's office was represented and these people stayed on it in key positions even though they might have moved out to investigate all sightings and . . . get information and bring it into the central repository wherever that was.[21]

In his interview with Schmitt on June 18th, Exon provided more information on the Deep State operation, giving names rather than just positions in the government or the military:

> I can't remember how it came up . . . Forrestal, Truman, [General Carl] Spaatz, [Stuart] Symington, I'm sure there were more guys next to Spaatz, like intelligence guys or some information type close to him at the Pentagon and to Forr-estal, CIA, and I know it was just more than military . . . In there someplace, and maybe it was the command post guy or somebody in operations . . . in a confidential meeting was telling them about Blue Book and ah, there were supposed to be thirteen, and I remember it . . . that were named in that outfit and were sworn to secrecy.[22]

His observation that the people he named remained in place in those key positions from administration to administration is cru-cial here. This is the very definition of the Deep State. Those in power retain their power, regardless of circumstances. They remain in place for decades.

Exon also mentioned Project Blue Book during these discussions, suggesting that Blue Book might not be the end of the investiga-tive chain. These people were clearly briefed about Blue Book and, although Exon seemed to believe they had a role in the project, there is no evidence to back that up. Instead, his comments seem to suggest another level of security above and beyond Blue Book. This was confirmed by Brigadier General C. H. Bolender.

On October 20, 1969, some seventeen years after the Robertson Panel ended its superficial investigation of UFOs, Bolender wrote about Project Blue Book and its investigations in a memo that was partially in response to questions about what the University of Col-orado was doing and how that might affect national security if Blue Book were ended.

In paragraph four of his memo, Bolender wrote:

> As early as 1953, the Robertson Panel concluded "that the evidence presented on Unidentified Flying Objects shows no indication that these phenomena constitute a direct physical threat to national security" . . . In spite of this finding, the Air Force continued to maintain a special reporting system. There is still, however, no evidence that Project Blue Book reports have served any intelligence function. Moreover, reports of unidentified flying objects which could affect national security are made in accordance with JANAP 146 [Joint Army, Navy, Air Force Publication] or Air Force Manual 55–11, and are not part of the Blue Book system.[23]

In other words, the suspicions of Hynek and Exon were correct. There was, and still is, a system for reporting UFO incidents to another group, one that has not been identified.

The Air Force, by its very nature, is charged with the protection of the United States, and UFOs flying through our airspace without permission or communicating with ground stations threatens that security. What they have done, however, is to ignore civilian interests and abdicate their responsibility to inform the public. All the data collected, all the information derived, now remains safely buried deep in the military bureaucracy and the Deep State.

CHAPTER 8

Project Moon Dust

P roject Moon Dust was a cover project whose aim was to recover objects and debris from spacecraft that survived re-entry through the atmosphere and to exploit Soviet hardware that fell into American hands. Contrary to what has been reported in the past, however, the 4602nd Air Intelligence Service Squadron (AISS) was not part of Project Moon Dust and apparently had no reporting requirement for it. In fact, the creation of the 4602nd preceded the creation of Moon Dust by about five years.

According to Project Blue Book files and Unit Histories, the 4602nd was activated and organized at Peterson Field, Ent Air Force Base in Colorado Springs under the authority of the Air Defense Command (ADC), General Order Number 20 (ADC GO #20), dated February 28, 1952. The unit had an authorized strength of thirty-four officers and ninety-seven enlisted personnel. (A reorganization was directed by the ADC on October 17,1952 by ADC GO #47.) The original mission of the unit, which was classified as secret, was to gather intelligence in a variety of areas. This mission included the collection of positive air intelligence by overt means from downed enemy air crews, enemy material and enemy documents, and bomb-damage assessment information.[1] These were fairly routine intelligence-gathering activities designed to fill specific needs like the interrogation of enemy pilots and aircrews, and the examination of enemy equipment related to the Korean War. This mission was later expanded in scope and training.

The history of Project Moon Dust has been difficult to determine because of all the clandestine maneuverings, the secret nature of the investigations of the best UFO reports, and the desire of the Deep State to keep the best information and evidence hidden from the general public. Some believe that Moon Dust began in 1952 with the activation of the 4602nd AISS, while others attribute its start to a Draft Collection document created in 1961. But both these theories are wrong. The best evidence currently available is that Moon Dust began during the last months of 1957, perhaps in response to the Soviets launching the first of their satellites. The enabling document—Message #54322—is dated December 23, 1957. There is no other documentation that pre-dates this 1957 memo.

The memo discusses a new project whose mission was "to collect and analyze raw intelligence reports from the field on fallen space debris and objects of unknown origin." Written about ninety days after the launch of Sputnik I, it addressed the possibility that there could be unplanned reentries as these satellite orbits decayed, which could provide opportunities for recovery and analysis of debris if there were teams prepared to do it. By 1960, Moon Dust information was being fed periodically into the Project Blue Book system, as shown on several of the project cards.

There is some indication that, in the very beginning, there was coordination between Projects Blue Book and Moon Dust. Several cases found in the Blue Book files reference Moon Dust. All of the cases that I was able to review, however, reported sightings of short duration that had conventional explanations, leading me to wonder what happened to the other cases that were obviously reported to the Moon Dust teams. The cases I reviewed don't reveal much of anything important, other than naming Project Moon Dust as their source.

One came from Ramey Air Force Base, Puerto Rico on September 15, 1960. The Blue Book file, which noted one of the addressees on the message as Moon Dust, said:

> Round object with a tail, size reports vary from the size of a pea to half dollar, color reports vary from bluish-white to dusky red. Tail aprox [sic] 3–5 times the size of the object. No sound. Object reported to have broken up into several fireballs. One report stated that object finally fell into ocean.
>
> It is possible that this object was a very slow meteor. However it is more probably a reentry of the 1960 Epsilon vehicle, parts of which reentered during Sep and Oct 1960. Epsilon had an inclination of 64 [degrees], therefore the heading would be about 26 degrees.[2]

Another sighting whose source was listed as Moon Dust took place on September 23, 1960 at Bitburg AB, Germany:

> Luminous streak, like shooting star, colors red and yellow. Object left a trail. Object appeared very suddenly and was red in color, gradually changing to bright yellow. Appeared much larger than meteor . . . Path momentarily broken and when reappeared was red in color, no smoke but numerous sparks.
>
> Description conforms to satellite reentry as to direction, color and breaking up. 1960 Lambda II (rocket body) reentered this date. Case evaluated as satellite reentry based upon general description, although duration of sighting was omitted.[3]

This seems to be a reasonable explanation, especially since there was documentation to back up the solution. A few days later, on September 26, an object that was yellowish-green and described as a "falling star or object" was seen northeast of Bermuda.

A better Moon Dust case came from Thule, Greenland, where a teletype message reported:

> Bright comet like object presumably MOONDUST sighted at Thule AB Greenland . . . on 24 Sep 60. Estimated elevation less than ten degrees. Direction: Appeared from south east and disappeared into the west . . . Observed time 5 seconds."[4]

This was written off as a possible meteor.

What all this suggests is that Project Moon Dust was in operation prior to the Draft Collection document dated November 1961. Some of its information was being shared with Project Blue Book, but only from cases that had little overall importance and certainly no national security impact. The real question is how knowledge of the project was leaked to the public if Moon Dust was a classified mission and the Deep State was controlling access to its data. According to what we now know, Moon Dust was discovered—or compromised, in the world of intelligence gathering—by accident. A skeptical UFO researcher, the late Robert Todd, filed a FOIA request for a number of documents from the Department of State, which led him to the Air Force. These documents made reference to Moon Dust and it was clear from their context that some of them referred to UFOs. With that in hand, Todd made additional FOIA requests and gathered more information.[5]

Following suit, Cliff Stone, a retired Army Sergeant First Class (SFC), and I both submitted FOIA requests and received a dozen or so microfiche that contained dozens of documents, some nothing more than foreign newspaper articles. The documents were all from the Department of State and all referenced UFOs in some fashion. After the information had been gathered, however, it was forwarded with the Moon Dust identifier attached. Most of the UFO information in the classified Moon Dust messages is little better than most found in the Project Blue Book files. The real point is that the Deep State had moved UFO investigating and reporting from the Air Force into another channel that was not open to public scrutiny. Because the message traffic was classified, and because the project itself was classified, virtually no information leaked out to private civilian UFO groups. Only after Todd received the documents from his FOIA request did Moon Dust become known to the public.

The Deep State and the Air Force were not quick to verify the information made public about Moon Dust. Stone wrote that, in December 1989, he asked the Air Force for information on both Project Moon Dust and Operation Blue Fly, which seems to have provided logistical support for the project. In January 1990, an Air Force officer responded that they had no information about Moon Dust.[6] Several months later, they sent another letter saying they had two documents that were responsive to Stone's request, but that they were properly classified.[7] Neither of these answers was adequate, but they do demonstrate one of the problems with FOIA requests. The answers to them come slowly and are sometimes not responsive to the specific issues addressed by the request.

Stone, unhappy with the responses he received from the Air Force, eventually contacted United States Senator Jeff Bingaman of New Mexico, who in turn wrote to the Air Force. Their reply, from Lieutenant Colonel John E. Madison of the Congressional Inquiry Division, Office of Legislative Liaison, said:

> There is no agency, nor has there ever been, at Fort Belvoir, Virginia, which would deal with UFOs or have any information about the incident in Roswell. In addition, there is no Project Moon Dust or Operation Blue Fly. Those missions have never existed.[8]

There are many problems with this reply, not the least of which is that the 4602nd, which clearly had a UFO mission, was, at the time of Stone's request, stationed at Fort Belvoir.

Various official files, from Project Blue Book to the Department of State, prove that Madison was also in error when he stated categorically that there had never been either a Project Moon Dust or an Operation Blue Fly. That denial was just another attempt to divert attention. Bingaman, who had copies of Moon Dust documents that had a clear and verifiable provenance, knew that Madison had not provided accurate information. Anyone could follow the paper trail and see the truth for themselves. He wrote back to the Air Force, challenging their response, but this time included documents that proved that Moon Dust did exist. Colonel George M. Mattingley, Jr., Madison's superior, replied:

> This is in reply to your inquiry on behalf of Mr. Clifford E. Stone on the accuracy of the information previously provided to your office. Upon further review of the case (which was aided by the several attachments to Mr. Stone's letter), we wish to amend our last statements contained in the previous response to your inquiry.[9]

The Air Force—and, by extension, the Deep State—had been caught in what could be called, at best, a mistake and, at worst, a blatant lie. Madison could certainly have found information on Moon Dust and should have been able to learn something about it that he could have passed along to Bingaman.

In the wake of Madison's erroneous letter, Mattingley, wanting to provide as much information as possible while still maintaing the cloak of national security, wrote:

> In 1953, during the Korean War, the Air Defense Command organized intelligence teams to deploy, recover, or exploit at the scene of downed enemy personnel, equipment, and aircraft. The unit with responsibility for maintaining these teams was located at Fort Belvoir, Virginia. As the occasion

never arose to use these air defense teams, the mission was assigned to Headquarters, United States Air Force in 1957 and expanded to include the following peace-time functions: a) Unidentified Flying Objects (UFOs), to investigate reliably reported UFOs within the United States; b) Project MOON DUST, to recover objects and debris from space vehicles that survived re-entry from space to earth; c) Operation BLUE FLY, to expeditiously retrieve downed Soviet Bloc equipment . . . These teams were eventually disbanded because of a lack of activity; Project MOON DUST teams and Operation BLUE FLY missions were similarly discontinued. The Air Force has no information that any UFOs were ever confirmed downed in the United States.[10]

Mattingley revealed here that Moon Dust was discussed at high levels, and that teams were requested. From his statement, we can infer that Moon Dust began no earlier than 1957 as an Air Force mission, and some of the units that supported it were organized in the 1950s.

There is some evidence, however, that Colonel Mattingley's response to Senator Bingaman was in error as well. He suggested that the teams had never been deployed and that the mission had been abandoned because of lack of activity. But some of the Department of State documents recovered through FOIA show this to be untrue. Documents supplied by the Department of State to me and to others, including Robert Todd and Cliff Stone, enumerated Moon Dust–related events. Moreover, although some of these reports cover the period of operation for Project Blue Book, they never made it into Blue Book files. Remember that Hynek, the scientific consultant to Blue Book, said that the really interesting cases somehow never reached their files. This is more evidence that he was right in that criticism. Although some cases have obvious terrestrial explanations, others are more mysterious, as is shown by this list of sightings pulled from Department of State documents and other sources:

January 22, 1965—Rajasthan, India.

January 11, 1967—Agadir, Morocco. An object fell into the sea.

March 28, 1967—Kasba Tadia, Morocco. An 8.5 mm in diameter object landed on the roof of a house and then took off again.

August 17, 1967—Sudan. Cube-shaped satellite weighing about three tons was found fifty miles from Kutum.

March 25, 1968—Katmandu, Nepal. Four objects were found.

August 7, 1970—Lai, Chad. Eighteen-inch in diameter sphere weighing 20 to 25 pounds. It appeared to have been in two halves, welded together and resembled a pressurized fuel tank.

April 7, 1972—New Zealand. Space Defense Center reported that two objects had "deorbited" and fell to the ground.

October 20, 1973—New Zealand. A cylindrical object two feet long and seven inches in diameter was found.

May 6, 1978—Bermejo, Bolivia. An egg-shaped object made of metal and nearly five feet in diameter was found.

October 23, 1978—Ashburton, New Zealand. Two spheres were located.

It is obvious that some of these objects were not of extraterrestrial origin but were debris that had fallen off aircraft or returning space objects manufactured here. Even these reports are interesting, however, because they demonstrate that the U. S. government, using various entities and agencies, had been working to recover these materials for analysis for decades, going back to at least 1965. The final reports of these events and the existence of these materials has been classified and released only after long battles with these government agencies, usually under FOIA requirements.

One of the most interesting cases concerned an object that fell near the Bermejo River in the Taija Province of Bolivia on May 6, 1978. According to a document sent from the American Embassy in La Paz to the Department of State:

1. The Bolivian newspapers carried this morning an article concerning an unidentified object that apparently recently fell from the sky. The paper quotes a "Latin" correspondent's story from the Argentine city of Salta. The object was discovered near the Bolivian city of Bermejo and was described as egg-shaped, metal and about four meters in diameter.

2. The Bolivian Air Force plans to investigate to determine what the object might be and from where it came. I have expressed our interest and willingness to help. They will advise.

3. Request department check with appropriate agencies to see if they can shed some light on what this object might be. The general region has more than its share of reports of UFOs this past week. Requests a reply ASAP.[11]

This is interesting because it suggests a real interest in these sorts of things and the mention of "more than its share of" UFOs suggests that there is good reason for this interest. Something strange found in the jungle shouldn't have come to the attention of the American ambassador, but it did—which suggests that they may have been looking out for these sorts of things. It suggests a Deep State interest that had expanded beyond the borders of the United States and hints at a worldwide phenomenon.

Why this was considered important becomes clearer in light of a CIA document dated May 15, 1978:

> Many people in this part of the country [Bolivia] claim they saw an object which resembled a soccer ball falling behind the mountains on the Argentine-Bolivian border, causing an explosion that shook the earth. This took place on May 6. Around that time some people in San Luis and Mendoza provinces reported seeing a flying saucer squadron flying in formation. The news from Salta confirms that the artificial satellite fell on Taire Mountain in Bolivia, where it has already been located by authorities. The same sources said that the area where the artificial satellite fell has been declared an emergency zone by the Bolivian Government.[12]

The next day, the CIA added more information about the sightings and the object that fell in a document headed "Conflict on Details of Fallen Object":

> We have received another phone call from our audience requesting confirmation of reports that an unidentified object fell on Bolivian territory near the Argentine border. We can only say that the Argentine and Uruguayan radio stations are reporting on this even more frequently, saying that Bolivian authorities have urgently requested assistance from the U. S. National Aeronautics and Space Administration [NASA] in order to determine the nature of that which crashed on a hill in Bolivian territory. Just a few minutes ago Radio El Espectador of Montevideo announced that there was uncertainty as to the truth of these reports. Argentine sources indicated that the border with Bolivia had been closed but that it might soon be reopened. They also reported that an unidentified object had fallen on Bolivian soil near the Argentine border and that local Bolivian authorities had requested aid from

the U. S. National Aeronautics and Space Administration to investigate the case.

A La Paz newspaper said today that there is great interest in learning about the nature of the fallen object, adding that local authorities for security reasons had cordoned off 200 km around the spot where the object fell. The object is said to be a mechanical device with a diameter of about 4 meters which has already been brought to Tarija. There is interest in determining the accuracy of these reports which have spread quickly throughout the continent, particularly in Bolivia and its neighboring countries. Is it a satellite, a meteorite, or a false alarm?[13]

On May 24, another message was sent from the American Embassy in La Paz. This one, from the Defense Attaché, was directed to several military agencies, including the Department of the Air Force, the North American Aerospace Defense Command (NORAD), and the Department of State:

This office has tried to verify the stories put forth in the local press. The Chief of Staff of the Bolivian Air Force told DATT/AIRA [Defense Attache/Air Attache] this date that planes from the BAF have flown over the area where the object was supposed to have landed and in their search they drew a blank. Additionally, DATT/AIRA talked this date with the Commander of the Bolivian Army and informed DATT that the Army's search party directed to go into the area to find the object had found nothing. The Army has concluded that there may or may not be an object, but to date nothing has been found.[14]

Leonard Stringfield, in his 1980 book *The UFO Crash/Retrieval Syndrome, Status Report II: New Sources, New Data,* noted:

The case of the mysterious flying object crashing into the mountains bordering Argentina and Bolivia, May 8, 1978

[sic], is well known by researchers. Was it a meteorite, part of a satellite or spacecraft? Rumors say nothing was ever found after extensive search on the precipitous slopes by Bolivian and Argentine military teams and by NASA.

In June 1979, I [Stringfield] received a stack of clippings from Argentine newspapers with stories that claim otherwise. The sender, Nicholas M. Ojeda of Rosario, Argentina, stated in his letter, ". . . As you know, our country is one of the most visited areas in the world by OVNIs [UFOs] as we call them in Latin America. Last year, May 8, we had a very significant case in the Salta Province in the north of the country. A long object crashed into the mountains. Although some people think it was a meteor or part of a satellite, this case is not closed yet. There is a report of a group of investigators who vanished mysteriously in the area. I really think something big happened in Salta. NASA investigated, but there was not news of it. I have to tell you that in La Paz, Bolivia, a huge USAF Hercules C-130 carried "something" from the area where the UFO crashed. What was it?

When this question and the news of the cargo plane being there was put to Bob Barry's former C.I.A. contact, he confirmed the flight and admitted, "I was aboard the plane." He offered no answer to, "what was aboard?"[15]

Antonio Huneeus, a science journalist who is fluent in Spanish, provided additional, clarifying information about the case. Given his contacts in South America, his accounts of what happened there can be considered among the very best and the most reliable. In the Winter 1994 issue of *UFO Universe* and later in the 2011 issue of *Open Minds,* Huneeus wrote:

At 4:30 PM on May 6, 1978, a UFO—whether natural, man-made or unknown origin—crashed in South America on the hill at El Taire near the Bermejo River, which divides Bolivia's remote Tarija Department with the province of Salta in Argentina. The crash was first felt as a shattering explosion—a sonic boom that was heard within a range of 120 miles and which shattered windows of villages 30 miles from the target site . . .

It was reported that the explosion had shaken the village of Mecoya . . . The sonic boom, on the other hand, was heard over a radius of 150 km inside Argentina . . . Patrols of the 20th Detachment of the "Gendarmeria" (Border Police) of Oran were dispatched towards the rugged terrain around the river Bermejo, where it was believed the object had crashed. The town of Aguas Blanca in the Department of Santa Victoria in Salta rapidly brought a swarm of reporters following the patrols. An increasing number of eyewitness accounts followed the reporters . . . It [the object] was sometimes described as a "fireball" the size of a soccer ball. For the most part, however, people described the UFO as an artificial-looking shiny space object.

A number of eyewitnesses were interviewed by a variety of people, including military representatives of Bolivia and Argentina, reporters from several countries, and eventually American officers who may have been working at the request of NASA and who were certainly operating under the banner of Moon Dust. It is also likely that they were providing information to those in the Deep State about this incident.

The highest-ranking military official on the scene was Corporal Natalio Farfan Ruiz, who told reporters:

I don't know what would have happened if the UFO had fallen on their houses. Can you imagine? . . . It was around 4:30 when a cylinder shook the Earth . . . I believed the end of the world was coming.[16]

Huneeus reported that engineer Velez Orozco had seen the cylindrical object as well. He thought it was four meters (about fifteen feet) in diameter and had a conical shape in front. As communications from the area continued, two Americas arrived for an inspection or investigation. According to Huneeus:

> Clarin and other news media from the continent reported that two "NASA experts," Colonel Robert Simmons and Major John Heise, arrived in Tarija. Though the officers were allegedly "on vacation," their mission was actually to take the object, or parts of it, to a USAF Hercules C-130 cargo plane waiting at La Paz to carry pieces back to the United States.
>
> Naturally, the American Embassy in La Paz vehemently denied this story. Ernesto Uribe, chief of the Embassy's Information Service, was quoted in the press as saying that no satellite had been found . . .
>
> However, according to recently declassified documents [governmental files that were declassified in 1994], it appears that Simmons and Heise were from the Defense Attache Office in La Paz, and that they did fly to Tarija with Bolivian Air Force officers as part of the "Moon Dust" project.[17]

While there is good documentation in the files of various countries that something was seen and reported, there is no documentation of any sort about what caused the high level of interest. The newspaper articles, some of which were found through FOIA requests for Moon Dust information, are based on eyewitness accounts without benefit of other evidence or independent investigation. Stringfield's report was based on a source that was identified only as "Bob Barry's former CIA contact," which does not allow for any additional verification and does nothing to validate the event. However, the mention of the CIA does take us into the Deep State and underscores their interest in such things.

Some important details were apparently not reported at the time of the sighting. Huneeus wrote that a Bolivian UFO researcher, Jorge Arias Gonsalvez, had told the Argentinian UFO Congress in Santa Fe that government sources had told him that "a large dark object, 80 or 100 meters long" had been seen and that "two peasants and herds of sheep and goats were found dead by the Commission some 60 meters away from the crater." Bob Pratt, an American UFO researcher who had traveled into the remote area and interviewed many of the witnesses in the months that followed the incident, told Huneeus that he at first had trouble getting into the area, but eventually reached the site:

> A lot of misinformation has been published about this incident. I am certain, however, that the area was not cordoned off by the military, that no object was recovered by NASA or anyone else, that no Hercules picked up anything and there was no news blackout . . . the "crash" area is in such rugged, remote territory that it would have been difficult for anyone to retrieve anything without the use of a large helicopter such as a CH-47, and had such an operation taken place, the people living in the area would have known about it. In the four weeks I spent in the area, including a total of seven days at the "crash" site itself, I never found anyone who had ever seen a helicopter or any stranger in the area, other than me and a few Argentine and Bolivian newsmen who tried to reach the crash site immediately after the incident occurred . . .
>
> I believe something crashed into the mountain and was buried under the landslide it created. But the six people I know who had personally inspected the site could find no debris of any kind. Whatever struck there is probably going to remain buried there.

MORE MOON DUST MISSIONS

In July 1968, a document from the Department of State that was originally sent to the 1127th Air Activities Group at Fort Belvoir and labeled as "Moon Dust (U)" mentioned a different recovery. Although heavily redacted on orders from those in the Deep State, the message references the arrival of a film that the Foreign Technology Division (FTD) was waiting to process. Results of the examination would determine whether a technical team would be dispatched to determine the identity of the "object." Since the message stated that the film was to remain "unclassified," it is ironic that some of the message was redacted. Notes at the bottom of the message read:

> By ref a, (redacted) advised sequence (redacted) in obtaining MOON DUST specimens, advised film of nose cone photographed by DATT on 19 July being forwarded unprocessed to DIACO-2B, and requested copies of prints of film for (redacted) as well as guidance as to what DATT can tell (redacted) as to identity of object photographed. By ref b. (redacted) requested permission to retransmit ref a. (redacted). By ref c, FTD requested courier these items back to (redacted) and further requested (redacted) to attempt to obtain results of (redacted). By ref e, (redacted) stresses need to protect our knowledge of (redacted) this matter, and state we cannot approach (redacted) on any of the objects which (redacted) had in their possession. MSG above coordinated with DIACO-D in draft.[18]

The fact that most of the details of this case are hidden, however, isn't what's important. What's important is the reference to the possibility of dispatching a technical team. This confirms that these teams existed and could be sent into various areas for analysis of space debris. Moreover, it suggests that Mattingly's claim that teams were never deployed is, at best, inaccurate. Teams did deploy.

On July 19, 1968, the embassy in Katmandu sent a message that dealt with a number of Moon Dust activities. This message details recovered debris and also discusses the possibility of "sending experts," although the need for "a technical team" is ultimately rejected. Once again, this underscores the fact that teams were being deployed under Project Moon Dust, as discussed in the November 1961 document. On July 30, 1968, another Moon Dust message noted: "No new developments here except (redacted) first secretary visited (redacted) on unsuccessful fishing expedition for info on space objects."[19]

Although Colonel Mattingley wrote that Project Moon Dust ended because of lack of activity, a search of various government agencies proves that Moon Dust teams were, in fact, used. While not all its missions were related to UFOs, that was an important part of their charge. Requests were made and teams were deployed, although there is no documentation currently available that shows how many times these teams were used and we have very little information about what they may have recovered.

Other information shows that Project Moon Dust was never actually discontinued. Robert Todd wrote to the Air Force when he learned that the code name of the project had been changed. In a reply dated July 1, 1987, he was informed that the "nickname Project Moon Dust no longer officially exists." According to Colonel Phillip E. Thompson, an intelligence deputy chief of staff:

> It [Moon Dust] has been replaced by another name that is not releaseable [sic]. FTD's duties are listed in a classified passage in a classified regulation that is being withheld because it is currently and properly classified.[20]

The Air Force had used this trick in the past and continues to use it today. They announced that there had been a final report for Project Sign, implying that the project had been discontinued. But Project Sign had simply been renamed Project Grudge (see chapter 2). Later, they announced that Project Grudge had been terminated, but instead they just changed the name to Project Blue Book and continued to investigate (see chapter 7). Here, they claimed that Project Moon Dust had been terminated when, in fact, it was simply operating under another name that was, of course, classified.

Project Moon Dust established the standard operating procedure (SOP) for the Air Force in the recovery of returning space debris and objects of unknown origin. Tell the public one thing and do something completely different. Say the project has ended, then change the name and march on. But it also demonstrates that an interest in UFOs had been in existence since the 1940s and that this interest continued long past the end of Project Blue Book in 1969. Indeed, this interest clearly continues today. While Project Moon Dust no longer exists by that name, it was replaced by another project. Without knowing the code name, there is no way for us to learn anything more about it or to penetrate any further into the machinations of the Deep State. All we know is that it exists and that it is classified. Yet we are told that there is nothing to UFOs, that they are not alien spacecraft, and that they pose no threat to the United States.

CHAPTER 9

Secret Space Programs

I n the last half century, there have been many instances of rocket research that has been shrouded in secrecy. Dozens of satellites have been launched whose purpose remains unknown. Satellites are gathering data from all the around the globe, some of which could not be collected in any other way. Seemingly innocent weather satellites may be tracking and recording everything from storm patterns to military movements, or locating and documenting "lost" cities and civilizations. And because these satellites are an important part of our intelligence-gathering capability, they are important to the Deep State.

Satellites launched late at night from Vandenberg AFB and other locations. Shuttle missions that have carried out "experiments" in secret. Closely guarded technologies that can track and document UFOs. These are all indications that there are secret dimensions to the U. S. space program. A somewhat reverse bit of evidence for this appeared in the late 1980s when the *New York Times* reported that Vandenberg Air Force Base had ended a program that included a "secret cadre of thirty-two" astronauts because they thought it "too dangerous." According to their sources, the Challenger shuttle disaster had sparked the closure. But how does hiding information about UFOs or a secret space program increase the power of the Deep State and help to keep them in place?

We have already seen many instances in which the influence of the Deep State has been evident—from the Robertson Panel in 1953, to the Condon Committee in 1969, to its collaboration with the Air Force in their UFO inquiries. And we have seen evidence of their participation in and control over several secret studies and investigations. In fact, there is no question that the Deep State has been running the show ever since Kenneth Arnold reported strange objects near Mt. Rainier and a mysterious craft fell at Roswell some two weeks later. What isn't quite as clear is why they would be involved in a secret space program.

Military doctrine dictates that you take the high ground. You force your enemy to come to you. World War II had proven the value of air superiority in any sort of ground fight. And the ultimate high ground is space. He who controls space, controls the planet. Although science fiction tells of aliens who come to Earth for any number of reasons, these creatures always land and engage the human race in some sort of land warfare. In fact, all they really need to do is stay in orbit and throw rocks at us! The destructive power of large space rocks that have fallen to Earth is awesome. When an asteroid estimated to be about 250 to 300 feet in diameter exploded over the Tunguska region of Siberia in 1908, the devastation covered hundreds of square miles, flattening entire forests and setting widespread fires. An attack like this would be nearly unstoppable, especially if we had no way to respond—no way to confront alien invaders in space.

Evidence for a secret space program was reinforced in 2008 when something fell near Needles, California. Around 3:00 AM, a cylinder-shaped object with a turquoise glow fell out of the sky and landed, or crashed, just west of the Colorado River in Nevada. When George Knapp of Las Vegas CBS TV investigated the story, he learned from eyewitnesses that five helicopters had flown into the Needles area within minutes of the object hitting the ground.[1]

As part of his investigation, Knapp interviewed a man he called "Bob on the River." Bob, who lived on a houseboat and didn't want to be identified, said that, when he saw the object fly overhead, it appeared to be on fire. He didn't see it crash, but he heard the impact. He told Knapp that it had "smacked into the sand," meaning that it had hit near the river. Although Bob tried to call for help, he couldn't because his satellite phone failed. Not long after the crash, he heard helicopters and saw five of them flying in a loose formation toward the crash site. Oddly, one of them fell out of formation to circle Bob's houseboat and then rejoined the others. Bob thought they might have been Hueys, but it is more likely, given the date, that they were Black Hawks. Once the helicopters located the crash site, a huge craft known as a Sky Crane was brought in to retrieve the downed object. Although none of the witnesses saw any of the helicopters land, we can assume that they must have in order rig the object for lifting.

If Bob had been the only witness, he might have been dismissed as deluded. But there is more to the story. Frank Costigan, a retired police chief who had also worked security at Los Angeles Airport (LAX) and was much more credible than Bob, said that he had seen the object as it flew over him. According to Costigan, the object was bright enough to light up the ground as it passed. It flashed a number of colors, including turquoise, blue, and green, and then disappeared behind some low hills. When it didn't reappear, Costigan assumed it had crashed somewhere just beyond those hills. In a strange coincidence, David Hayes, the owner of KTOX radio in Needles, reported seeing a strange assortment of vehicles get off the highway as he was on his way to work not long after the object had fallen. Thinking there might be a connection, he drew a picture of the lead vehicle, which looked like a large SUV with a dome on top. Hayes thought the vehicle might have been carrying a remote-control drone. One of the vehicles broke off and followed Hayes to the radio station. It parked briefly outside the KTOX building and seemed to be conducting some sort of surveillance. Hayes said that it had a real "Men in Black" vibe.

When I talked to Knapp in Las Vegas, he told me:

> Out of the blue the [television] station got a call from a friend in Laughlin [Nevada] who said the Laughlin Airport had been inundated on the night of the crash with so-called Janet planes. That's the airline that flies workers to the top-secret Area 51. Costigan says the airport could not confirm this because no one is on duty after 6 p.m., not even [in] the [control] tower.[2]

Knapp was intrigued by all this. "The black vehicles have left Needles," he noted, and "Bob, the houseboat guy, can't be found either . . . The point is that something definitely happened."[3]

Knapp continued his investigation into both the events. He learned that similar vehicles—sometimes black, sometimes not—were often seen in the Needles area. Accompanied by a camera crew, he spotted one of the convoys and joined the rear of the formation as it drove down the road. When one of them eventually pulled over, Knapp followed. Several armed men who said they were federal agents got out and a brief encounter ensued. The men never said which agency they were from, but one of them flashed an official-looking ID. Knapp, who didn't get a good look at it, asked to see it again. Eventually, everyone returned to their vehicles.

Not long after that, Knapp received a telephone call from a friend in the Department of Energy who told him he was lucky that the confrontation had ended so peacefully, observing that Knapp and his crew could have been detained. Knapp later learned that the agents and their black vehicles had nothing to do with the UFO crash that started his investigation. Instead, they were engaged in another very real and very secret mission.

When I met Knapp at the 6th Annual UFO Crash Conference in Las Vegas, he told me and others that he knew the real name of Bob, the "houseboat guy." When he showed me the whole interview, which had never aired on television, it was clear that Bob had seen something real. Just because his lifestyle was somewhat odd didn't mean that he hadn't seen something fall out of the sky. Other witnesses had seen what he saw. The helicopters Bob described had been on the scene in less than twenty minutes. That meant that someone, somewhere, had been monitoring the progress of the object as it moved over the area. Someone, somewhere, knew what it was, knew that it was down, and wanted to retrieve it.

Knapp didn't seem to believe, however, that the object was of alien origin. In fact, he told me that, based on what he had seen and later learned, the object was a failed experimental craft. And since this all happened not far from Area 51 and Edwards Air Force Base, his conclusion is not without merit. Nor is it a reach too far to assume that this craft, whatever it was, wasn't necessarily built to operate within the atmosphere. It may have been designed to reach the atmosphere's upper limits, or even possibly to enter space. This all suggests some sort of Deep State connection. Because no further information has ever emerged about the object, these events serve to illustrate the secrecy that surrounds the Deep State's need to produce a spacecraft to perpetuate their power.

AREA 51

Area 51 is made up of military installations that are shrouded in secrecy. It is here that the next generation of military aircraft are being developed. For instance, the SR-71, which can brush the edge of space and fly at over Mach 3, was developed at Area 51. Built on 1950s technology and modified into an "air breathing" craft, the SR-71 is the next thing to a spacecraft. Doubtless there are now other aircraft that are half a century more advanced than the SR-71 that are still classified and still hidden by the Deep State. Clearly, what goes on at Area 51 is a matter of national security. The last thing the military wants is to reveal these secret projects before the hardware is operational as a weapons system that can be used in future wars.

Area 51 is also where recovered alien spacecraft are allegedly housed. Bob Lazar, an alleged engineer who worked at Area 51, told George Knapp in 1989 that he had helped to reverse engineer one of nine flying saucers that were kept in hidden hangars at the S-4 facility on the Area 51 complex. These saucers were of extraterrestrial origin, which accounts for the intense secrecy. Lazar's reputation has been challenged by some in the UFO community, however. Stanton Friedman reports that Lazar's claims of advanced degrees could not be corroborated and suggests that Lazar was not who he claimed to be.[4] Lazar did, however, produce a W-2 that showed he had worked at Area 51 for a short period of time, placing him in a position to be able to see and talk to others who were working there.

If what Lazar says is true, it suggests that a secret space program exists that has taken some of its capabilities from recovered alien craft. A reverse-engineered spacecraft could potentially enable technological leaps that would never be reported in scientific publications, or in patent claims, or in observations by pilots on American military bases. Such a program could put the United States years, or even decades, ahead of conventional research by providing a blueprint for building such a craft. And, of course, secrecy would be required to protect what was learned. The Deep State would clearly want to hide any advanced knowledge of space travel that they acquired. And secrecy is paramount at Area 51.

The entire perimeter of Area 51 is fenced and guarded by both military and civilian personnel. Signs warn that deadly force is authorized and that those even approaching the perimeter will be stopped and either turned back or arrested. The area surrounding the base is under government control, and the one piece of high ground some miles away has been annexed by the government so that no one can use it as a vantage point. Until recently, the government wouldn't even admit that the base existed at all—and then they only admitted it because of a lawsuit. And these precautions are certainly justified by the need for heightened secrecy to protect the next generation of military aircraft and weapons.

Nick Redfern reported on the *Mysterious Universe* web site that the activities occurring at Area 51 have been corroborated by several sources:

> [T]he theory is that although NASA's manned space program is largely no more, there exists—maybe deep within the heart of the military—a secret group that is running a clandestine space program. We might even be talking about highly classified return missions to the Moon, and possibly even secret flights to Mars.[5]

Redfern wasn't just speculating here. Remember the article from the *New York Times* that reported on the end of a program that involved thirty-two astronauts? That information came from Gary McKinnon, who, while hacking into various government computers searching specifically for information about UFOs, blundered into confirmation of a secret space program.[6]

One of the first things McKinnon found was a list headed "Non-Terrestrial Officers." McKinnon said that he didn't think the list identified alien officers, but rather officers who were serving somewhere other than on Earth:

> I found a list of fleet-to-fleet transfers, and a list of ship names. I looked them up. They were U. S. Navy ships. What I saw made me believe they have some kind of spaceship, off-planet.[7]

And that wasn't all McKinnon claimed. In an interview published in *Wired* magazine, he claimed to have seen additional evidence:

> A NASA photographic expert said that there was a Building 8 at Johnson Space Flight Center where they regularly airbrushed out images of UFOs from high-resolution satellite imaging . . . I was able to briefly see one of these pictures. It was a silvery, cigar-shaped object with geodesic spheres on either side. There was no visible seams or riveting. There was no reference to size.[8]

Matthew Bevan, another hacker looking for information about crashed UFOs held at Wright-Patterson Air Force Base, stumbled onto information about a top-secret project to build what were basically flying saucers. Under interrogation after his hacking was discovered, Bevan claimed that the files he saw "clearly referred to a working prototype of an anti-gravity craft that utilized a heavy element to power it."[9] He also claimed to have found emails about an anti-gravity propulsion system.

This takes us back to Bob Lazar, who had talked about a new element that didn't appeared on the Periodic Table—Element 115, named Moscovium. Scientists have actually been able to create this element, but its half-life is too short for it to be produced in quantity, and that makes it useless for powering any sort of craft. First synthesized in 2003 by a team of Russian and American scientists, its most stable known isotope is Moscovium-290, which has a half-life of less than a second. To be fair to Lazar, he never claimed this element could be used as a fuel, only that it existed.[10]

During his interrogation, Bevan referred to what he called "Hangar 18" as "a hoarding place for alien technology."[11] *Hangar 18* was a science-fiction film produced in the 1980s about the crash of an alien craft that had hit an American spaceship. According to Bevan, his questioners kept returning to the name, indicating that there was a nugget of truth in what he was saying. The man representing American interests during Bevan's interrogation even suggested that his motives for hacking into those computer systems was to learn about UFOs and Hangar 18. When asked if Hangar 18 existed, he said: "I can neither confirm nor deny as I'm not in possession of that information."

Bevan was eventually arrested for hacking into computers at both NASA and Wright-Patterson. The case collapsed, however, when the judge said that a jail sentence was out of the question and that any fine imposed would be minimal. Neither NASA nor the U. S. government wanted to divulge any of the classified information that Bevan might have found. Bevan's conclusion after the episode was: "I know what I read. America has a secret space plane."[12]

My point here is that now two computer hackers claimed to have found classified files that suggested some kind of secret space program. Their claims could even suggest that what Lazar saw wasn't an alien spaceship, but rather an experimental craft constructed by American scientists for the purpose of space travel, and that some sort of reverse engineering had contributed to the construction of that craft. Either conclusion supports the existence of a secret space program conducted by the Deep State. The name of that program is Solar Warden. And with Solar Warden, we leave the realm of the somewhat plausible and enter the realm of the truly implausible.

SOLAR WARDEN

In 1984, all available UFO research, information, and theories were reportedly organized to produce a program that isn't just an American enterprise, but includes other nations. Japan, Russia, the United Nations, and the European Space Agency are also involved. The purpose of Solar Warden is to control the entire solar system with the goal of "terraforming" planets and some of the larger moons and establishing bases on both the moon and Mars.[13] The ships that support Solar Warden are described as eight cigar-shaped mother ships

200 yards long, which may explain the photograph that McKinnon claimed to have seen. In addition to these mother ships, the project boasts forty-three smaller craft and some 300 sailors. Others have even suggested that a Solar Warden space fleet exists whose command structure falls under the U. S. Naval Network and Space Operations Command (NNSOC). The project is funded by black budgets to which other nations contribute. Its craft are tested at and operate from Area 51 and other secret military installations that have yet to be compromised. Some are on remote Pacific islands where access can be easily controlled.

The problem with this speculative information is that it can be traced back to McKinnon, but not beyond. Very little testimony and documentation are available from other sources to support the existence of Solar Warden—as is often with the case when chasing Deep State and black projects.

One off-the-record source has told me that he has been into deep space on occasion, but not as part of the publicly acknowledged space program. He wasn't based in Houston or Florida, but rather on a large base whose secret facilities were heavily guarded and hidden from those whose jobs were much more mundane. It is possible that he was referring to the White Sands Missile Range and Holloman Air Force Base in New Mexico. We know that missile and rocket testing has taken place in that area and that maps of New Mexico show a spaceport that was designated as an emergency landing site for the space shuttle. This area has also been the site of much atomic research and development, and is where the first atomic bomb was detonated. My source claims to have made flights into space and into orbit—first to repair satellites and later deeper into space. He would not confirm that he had visited bases on the moon or on Mars, but he hinted that such places exist, saying he had either flown over them or seen film and photographs of them.

Other anonymous sources have provided additional details about Solar Warden. One tells how one of the forty-three scout ships was lost in an accident in Mars orbit during an attempted resupply mission. One claims that every planet in the solar system except Mercury has been visited, although I would have thought that Venus would also be ignored given its prohibitive surface temperatures. One claims that Solar Warden missions have landed on Pluto and on many of the bigger moons of the larger planets. Of course, anonymous sources are always suspect. If their claims are true, why would they not provide the information to verify them? Why not provide documentation to prove their case? But remember: This is the way the Deep State operates. Never tell anyone anything if you can avoid it, and certainly don't write anything down that could come back to haunt you.

We do have *some* testimony to at least *partially* verify the existence of Solar Warden. Moreover, Solar Warden could represent a contingency plan designed to take advantage of our growing technical ability to move into space. The moon landings of more than a half century ago were marvels of engineering, but so much more has been learned and so many of the technical problems we faced then have been eliminated that a new trip to the moon wouldn't be as difficult as it was in 1969. Solar Warden may just be a way of exploiting space flight as new techniques are developed. And the project could exist as a plan to be implemented later. Others have suggested that it may have been developed, not to control the solar system, but rather as a way to ensure that hostile nations can't initiate an attack on the United States. Any of these explanations takes Solar Warden out of the realm of science fiction places it solidly in the realm of plausibility.

SCIENCE FACT VERSUS SCIENCE FICTION

While Solar Warden may be a deeply hidden space program with peaceful intentions, there are some who suggest that an actual secret space force exists that is engaged with other space-faring races in a war fought around Earth and on the surface of Mars and other planets. And these claims lead us from the implausible directly to the impossible.

One man who has hit the lecture circuits in recent years claims that, as a seventeen-year-old, he was abducted from his bed and inducted into some sort of multi-species force that was fighting on Mars and in other places. He claims to have served for twenty years, after which he was discharged. Through some sort of time manipulation or distortion, he returned to his bed as a seventeen-year-old just fifteen minutes after he was abducted. So no one knew he was missing, he was ready for school the next morning, his friends saw him the next day, and no report was filed with law enforcement authorities.

Of course, the problem with such claims is that there is no way to verify them. Those making them provide interesting explanations for why there are no other witnesses, why there is no documentation, and why they can not provide any sort of other evidence. They just tell an interesting story, filled with all sorts of impressive, though sometimes unbelievable, details. And we are left with no way to verify anything.

On the other hand, there is some evidence that, when examined dispassionately, seems to indicate that a secret space force actually exists. We know that there have been secret missions launched—in most cases, to place spy satellites or other black satellites into orbit. We know that there are objects in orbit whose purpose has not been disclosed and that these black projects are funded by black budgets for which there is little or no accountability. And we know that the overall goal of these programs is to put people into space for a hidden purpose.

All this is suggestive of Deep State involvement in a secret space mission. In fact, McKinnon suggests that some of these missions are already deployed. But while some of his claims are plausible, some seem to be little more than science fiction—at least at the moment.

The idea of interplanetary travel has been around for more than a century and, given the state of our technology, it may be possible. We have sent probes throughout the solar system; we have photographed all the planets to learn what they are like and what they can offer us; we have sent missions into deep space beyond the reach of solar gravity; and we receive information broadcast from outside the solar system. These projects have not been carried out in secret, and they all demonstrate our ability to accomplish amazing things.

Putting a live crew on another planet is another matter, however. That would require a pioneering spirit, an extremely brave crew, and a budget greater than any single nation could provide. This means that a project like Solar Warden, which is described as a cooperative effort of many countries, may well be within the realm of possibility tomorrow. This closely held ongoing project, which encompasses many scientific disciplines and includes many nations, may be just the answer. If just some of what McKinnon reports is accurate, we may be on the threshold of some incredible journeys.

When I was growing up, I saw a number of science-fiction movies that told tales of space flight and landings on the moon. *Forbidden Planet* suggested that these events were centuries in the future. That movie was made in 1956. Thirteen years later, the idea of men landing on the moon was no longer science fiction. It was science fact.

So, although I don't accept the idea that there are already fleets of spaceships operating under the aegis of Solar Warden, I *do* accept the idea that such things aren't that far in our future. The science fiction of today is the science fact of tomorrow. At some point, we will know the truth about the Deep State's role in this secret space program.

PART III

UFOS AND THE AIR FORCE

CHAPTER 10

Enter AFOSI

I n June 1947, there was no United States Air Force and by extension, no Air Force Office of Special Investigations. But in September 1947, the National Security Act established the Air Force as a separate branch of the military, with the same status as the Army and the Navy. On August 1, 1948, a little less than a year after the Air Force was established, the Air Force Office of Special Investigations (AFOSI) was created. The new Secretary of the Air Force, W. Stuart Symington, modeled the agency after the FBI, appointing Special Agent Joseph F. Carroll, previously an assistant to J. Edgar Hoover, as its first commander. AFOSI's publicly stated mission was to provide the newly established Air Force with the ability to conduct internal inquiries and to investigate criminal activity.[1] But it wasn't long before that mission was expanded to include the investigation of UFO phenomena, and attitudes toward those investigations underwent a subtle change.

Previously, the Army Air Forces (AAF) and the Counterintelligence Corps (CIC) held responsibility for the investigation of flying saucer reports. Inquiries from that era—known publicly as Project Saucer and officially as Project Sign—contain hundreds of references to CIC agents involved in those investigations. But AFOSI's role in these inquiries became more aggressive and more negative, and their findings were kept more secret.

Take the case of William Rhodes, a self-styled inventor described by friends and colleagues as a genius, who took two photographs of an object over Phoenix, Arizona on July 7, 1947. The pictures showed a heel-shaped object that somewhat resembled the nine crescent-shaped craft that Kenneth Arnold had reported two weeks earlier. Various official investigations were launched and on July 14, two months before the establishment of the Air Force as a separate branch, CIC special agent Lynn C. Aldrich reported: "On July 8, 1947, this agent obtained pictures of unidentifiable objects . . ."[2] On August 29, George Fugate, Jr., another CIC special agent, interviewed Rhodes in person, accompanied by an FBI agent named Brower who kept his association with the Bureau quiet.[3] Their interview was comprehensive but resulted in no identification of the object that Rhodes had photographed and little additional information.

On May 11 the following year, however, after the Air Force had broken off as a separate service, Rhodes was interviewed again by Lieutenant Colonel James C. Beam and Alfred Loedding, who had both been assigned to Project Sign. They wrote:

> Although, Mr. Rhodes is currently employed as a piano player in a night club, his primary interest is in a small but quite complete laboratory behind his home . . . in subsequent correspondence to the reporter of this incident [Rhodes], the observer refers to himself as Chief of Staff of Panoramic Research Laboratory.[4]

What none of these reports mention is that Rhodes had worked for the Navy at the beginning of World War II, and had been assigned work normally done by scientists with post-graduate degrees. Nor did they mention that he held several patents that produced some income for him, making his occupation as a piano player more of a hobby than a vocation.

On August 17, just weeks after the establishment of AFOSI, Special Agent Thomas F. Doyle began an all-out assault on Rhodes' reputation, citing evidence from various sources, including the Better Business Bureau, the Chamber of Commerce, and even the Credit Bureau. In one of the attachments to his report, Doyle noted that Rhodes had falsely referred to himself as "doctor" and had grandly named his laboratory "to impress people with his importance."[5]

This attempt to smear Rhodes is typical of investigations that occurred after the creation of AFOSI. Based on the "negative information" they gathered, they concluded that his photographs were fake and the entire case was labeled a hoax. And that is where the official case remains today, regardless of evidence that Rhodes was a highly intelligent man whose abrasive personality was his worst enemy.[6] The whole tone of UFO investigations changed when General Vandenberg rejected the EOTS, and that attitude made its way into the offices of AFOSI.

Although AFOSI's original mission seemed to be directed specifically at criminal activity, other tangential functions were soon added. While the agency still actively worked to solve crimes, it also protected secrets, warned of threats to ongoing Air Force missions, exploited intelligence opportunities, and today works to counter cyber crime.[7] There is nothing in its charter to suggest responsibility for investigating flying saucers, although there is a clear history of them conducting these investigations.

In fact, within days of the creation of AFOSI, its agents were involved in investigating a series of UFO sightings. According to an Inspector General Special Investigative Report dated September 9, 1948:

> At 1020, 8 August 1948, this headquarters was advised by letter, dated 6 August 1948, originating at Hq, Air Materiel Command, Dayton, Ohio, to conduct an investigation pertaining to an aerial phenomena [sic] reported by various people with the 6th OSI District.[8]

This investigation was related to the Chiles-Whitted sighting that was one of the precipitating events leading to the Estimate discussed in chapter 2. The two pilots reported seeing a cigar-shaped craft with square windows flash by their aircraft. No other witnesses on the aircraft came forward, with the exception of one passenger who reported seeing a streak of light but couldn't contribute much to the descriptions of the object.[9]

There was a possible witness at Robins Air Force Base, however. Walter C. Massey was working as a fire guard as the engines of a C-47 were started. Sometime between 1:40 and 1:50 AM, he spotted an object coming from the north. He watched it for about twenty seconds, until it disappeared to the southwest.[10]

> The first thing I saw was a stream of fire and I was undecided as to what it could be, but as it got overhead, it was a fairly clear outline and appeared to be a cylindrical-shaped object with a long stream of fire coming out of the tail end. I am sure it would not be a jet since I have observed P-84s in flight at night.[11]

During the investigation, Walter E. Cassidy, of AFOSI's 6th District, questioned a number of other officers attempting to pin down an accurate time for the sighting. Given that Massey had been standing fire guard during an engine start and run-up, there were documents that could be examined. The time frame given by Massey seemed to be corroborated by that documentation and matched the time frame given by Chiles and Whitted. All the witnesses agreed that the object was traveling in a northerly direction. Although both pilots reported turbulence as the object passed, neither reported any buffeting of the aircraft. This "fact" only entered the report much later.

Although the sighting was marked as "unidentified" for a brief period, in his September 9 report, Cassidy wrote:

> On 12 August 1948, S/A Montgomery, 111th CIC Det, contact personnel at the Atlanta Naval Air Station and adjoining municipality regarding a reported aerial phenomena (sic). It

was generally agreed that the phenomena resembled a shooting star, despite the fact that course and altitude did not correspond to the characteristics of such an aerial phenomena.

During the period, 24–27 Aug 1948, Special Investigator Morris interviewed seven (7) residents of Atlanta, GA regarding reported aerial phenomena. It concluded that objects observed were not aircraft, but probably of meteoric nature.

Allen Hynek, the Air Force scientific consultant who reviewed the case file, commented: "[N]o astronomical explanation" was possible "if we accept the report at face value."[12]

But that wasn't all that Hynek said about the case. He wondered if Massey had gotten the time wrong and didn't actually see the object at the same time as Chiles and Whitted. Given the different time zones, this wasn't an unreasonable question. Hynek thought that, if the sightings had been made at the same time, the object must have been a very bright, extraordinary meteor known as a "bolide," whose "train" might have given the "subjective impression of a ship with lighted windows."[13]

We now know that such a conclusion isn't as unrealistic as it seemed in 1948. During the Zond IV spacecraft reentry in March 1968, witnesses on the ground reported seeing something similar. They provided drawings of cigar-shaped objects with square windows and a flame shooting from the rear. These were, in fact, remnants of the Zond IV spacecraft breaking up on reentry. Informed by twenty years of technological advance, these witnesses understood what they had seen. But the brief appearance of glowing pieces that burned out quickly could easily have given the "subjective impression" of a cigar-shaped spacecraft in 1948.[14]

What's important here is not that a plausible solution was offered for the Chiles-Whitted and Massey sightings, but that AFOSI agents treated the witnesses as unreliable, just as the CIC agents had treated Rhodes, rather than reporting what they had learned without editorial comment. But these "facts"—along with editorial comments—were sent up the chain of command and provided to those at Project Sign.

It was not long after the Chiles-Whitted sighting that Project Sign produced the Estimate of the Situation discussed earlier. In it, they concluded that, according to various former military officers, later including Captain Ed Ruppelt, flying saucers were interplanetary craft. The Air Force Chief of Staff at the time, General Hoyt S. Vandenberg, did not accept these conclusions, however, and suggested that the evidence presented was not sufficient to prove the case for alien visitation. The Estimate was rejected as flawed and those involved in creating it, with a few low-ranking exceptions, found themselves looking for new jobs. Almost all were transferred to other Air Force missions. Sign was gutted and those remaining could read between the lines. If General Vandenberg didn't believe that UFOs were extraterrestrial, then those serving under him had to believe the same thing.[15] These attitudes led to an environment in which fifty feet of 16-mm film of a UFO taken over Louisville, Kentucky that was confirmed by several eyewitness reports could be ignored by the Air Force and every other government agency involved.

In 1950, *Louisville Times* staff photographer Al Hixenbaugh filmed a bright object flying over Louisville. According to the newspaper, the Army knew about the film and "they indicated an eagerness to examine the pictures."[16] Attempts to secure the film were stalled, however. Although Dr. George Valley, an Air Force Advisory Member, requested that the Air Force obtain a copy, his efforts were blocked. General Cabell also believed the Air Force should have a copy, but wanted to obtain it secretly. No one agreed with him. The CIA and FBI declined to participate in any sort of investigation, and a memo attributed to the FBI suggested that it would be nice if "OSI could arrange to get a copy in some kind of a covert manner."[17]

Eventually, the request was made to AFOSI. Hixenbaugh reports that he met with members of military intelligence (who were undoubtedly agents of AFOSI), but that they wouldn't tell him what would happen to the film if the Air Force took it. All this really demonstrates the attitude of the military and intelligence communities toward UFO investigation, especially after Vandenberg had made his opinion known. Ultimately, film footage taken by a professional photographer was ignored and the buck was passed from one agency to the next, finally ending up with AFOSI. In 1950, AFOSI didn't want to dirty its hands with UFOs, even if there was film documentation of them.

Or rather, they didn't want to get their hands dirty *publicly*. But attitudes shifted subtly again in early 1951, when a young airman stationed at Canon Air Force Base in northeastern New Mexico sighted a UFO. He described the craft as no more than fifty feet high, and hovering close to the ground no more than 100 yards away. He said it was disk-shaped, about twenty feet in diameter, and about twelve feet thick. The craft was a dull gray and appeared to have been through a difficult flight. He watched the object for about a minute as it hovered with a rocking motion, and then it lifted straight up and disappeared. He got a very good look at it. The airman mentioned his experience to a friend, cautioning him to say nothing to anyone else about it. He recalls being surprised that his friend didn't make a wiseass comment or two about seeing flying saucers.

A day or two later, the airman was called to the squadron commander's office, where he found two men in civilian clothes whom his squadron commander declined to introduce, saying only that they wanted to talk to him and that he was to answer all their questions as honestly as possible. The men escorted the airman to a private place, where they flashed IDs that identified them as special agents. He later concluded that they were members of AFOSI. I speculate that they may have been dispatched by AFOSI District #17, which is in Albuquerque and would have had jurisdiction for the sighting at Canon AFB.

The agents' demeanor wasn't overly intimidating. They were polite, but it was clear that they intended to get the answers they wanted. The airman repeated his story of the sighting, giving all the details he could remember and confirming that he had had the time to get a good look at the object. He told them that he'd heard no sound and that there had been no lights on the object, although its outline was sharp and well-defined, suggesting that it wasn't a mirage but something real. As he described the sighting, he noticed that only one of the men asked questions while the other took notes. When he asked if he had seen some kind of experimental aircraft, he was told not to speculate. When he asked if the sighting would be reported up the chain of command, his question went unanswered.

When the interrogation was over, the agent who had been asking the questions emphasized that the sighting was classified and that he was not to tell anyone about what he had seen under penalty of law. Revealing classified information, he warned, could result in both a hefty fine and imprisonment. This airman spoke to me only on the condition that I would not reveal his name, which, of course, makes his story problematic. The case does not appear in the Project Blue Book files and I have found no reference to it in the Unit Histories or in other documentation at Canon AFB. I don't know the name of his friend and the squadron commander in question died in 2008, before I knew of this event.

It is important to note that the two agents who warned about disclosing classified information didn't provide any insight into who had classified that information, how highly it was classified, or how they had learned about the sighting. The obvious assumption is that the airman's friend told someone who told someone, until eventually AFOSI got involved. But this question has never been adequately answered.

At 8:12 PM on July 14, 1952, another event occurred that nearly duplicated the Chiles-Whitted report from 1948. In what is now known as the Nash-Fortenberry sighting, William B. Nash and

William H. Fortenberry reported seeing eight flying saucers while piloting a DC-4 carrying dozens of passengers. They both reported seeing six red dots that, to them as combat veterans of World War II, looked like tracers coming at them from enemy machine guns and anti-aircraft emplacements. These dots quickly resolved into disk-shaped objects that Nash described as "clearly outlined and evidently circular . . . The edges were well defined . . . not fuzzy in the least."[18] Nash said that they were about 100 feet in diameter and twelve to fifteen feet thick. He added:

> [W]e could observe they were holding a narrow echelon formation—a stepped-up line tilted slightly to our right with the leader at the lowest point and each following craft slightly higher . . . Abruptly, the leader began to slow. The second and third object wavered slightly and almost overran the leader.[19]

Some ten years later, in an article published in the NICAP *UFO Investigator*, Nash wrote:

> Flying in line, at approximately 2000 feet, the UFO formation started under the airliner. Then the six discs abruptly flipped on edge, their glow briefly diminishing and made a sharp angle turn to the west. As the discs flipped back to their original flat position, two other identical discs flew under the DC-4 and joined the rest. Then all eight UFOs accelerated to tremendous speed and disappeared.[20]

Nash and Fortenberry radioed a report to the CAA (forerunner to the FAA) immediately after the sighting, suggesting that it be forwarded to the Air Force. The Blue Book files confirm that they "made a report to Air Force authorities on landing." At 7:00 AM the next morning, Nash recalls:

> [W]e were telephoned by the Air Force to come in for questioning. There were five men, one in uniform; the others

showed us ID cards and badges of Special Investigators,
USAF. In separate rooms, we were questioned for one hour
and forty-five minutes—then about a half hour together. We
made sketches and drew the track of the objects on charts . . .
the tracks matched [and] the accounts matched . . . all conversation [was] recorded on a stenotype machine.[21]

Unlike the Chiles-Whitted sighting, they were told that their sighting had been "confirmed to Air Force intelligence by seven ground
witnesses, including a Navy lieutenant commander."[22]

After months of investigation, the sighting was eventually labeled
as "unidentified." Although Harvard astronomer Donald Menzel
tried to provide several different explanations—including fire flies
caught between the cockpit windowpanes—he never succeeded.
AFOSI did, however, investigate, and, although their interrogation
of the pilots was extensive, it did not seem to be adversarial. They
were just gathering information that was going to be sent on to ATIC
for further analysis. In a letter from Nash to Dr. Menzel, however, he
suggests that pressure was applied to keep the sighting quiet:

Your definite statement that the Air Force did not silence
[name redacted]. How could you *know* [emphasis in origi-
nal] if not closely associated with the A.F.? You said, "I can
say authoritatively that they (A.F.) did nothing of the sort."
(silence [name redacted])[23]

This indicates that some attempt was made by the Air Force to keep
the details of the sighting from the public.

The letter also provides a subtle indication that AFOSI and Major
John Sharp, identified as an AFOSI officer, attempted to suppress
information about a sighting that Menzel had found interesting
because the pilots had seen the UFOs *below* their aircraft, setting the
UFOs off against the background of the terrain below them. And
what about those other witnesses on the ground who saw virtually

the same thing? A message in the Blue Book files reads: "Request also cy [copy] of the ground observers if any. This is a great priority." Add this to Nash's claim in the NICAP *UFO Investigator* in 1962 that ground witnesses had been located, and it seems strange that the only mention of these witnesses is a query to receive copies of the interrogations, if any exist. Apparently, this investigative avenue was never followed up.

AFOSI's official involvement in UFO investigation ended on August 26, 1953, when Air Force Regulation 200-2, which dealt specifically with the subject, was published. This document provided for investigative assistance from the 4602nd Air Intelligence Service Squadron (AISS), but makes no mention of AFOSI. Ruppelt suggests that, as 1953 progressed, the UFO project was simply overwhelmed. There were too many sightings and they simply didn't have the time or the staff to investigate even the most interesting cases. He finally requested assistance from up the chain of command, hoping to have more personnel assigned to the UFO project. It was then that General Burgess told him about the 4602nd:

> Inside of two weeks General Burgess had called General Garland, they'd discussed the problem, and I was back in Colorado Springs setting up a program with Colonel White's 4602nd.
>
> The 4602nd's primary function is to interrogate captured enemy airmen during wartime; in peacetime all that they can do is participate in simulated problems. Investigating UFO reports would supplement these problems and add a factor of realism that would be invaluable in their training.[24]

Relevant portions of the regulation under which the 4602nd operated read as follows:

> 6. ZI [Zone of the Interior, the United States]. The Air Defense Command has a direct interest in facts pertaining to UFOs

reported in the ZI and had, in the 4602d Air Intelligence Squadron (AISS), the capability to investigate these reports . . .

    a. All Air Force activities are authorized to conduct such preliminary investigation as may be required for reporting purposes, however, investigations should not be carried beyond this point, unless such action is requested by the 4602d AISS . . .

    c. Direct communication between echelons of the 4602d AISS and Air Force activities is authorized.

9. Release of Facts: Headquarters USAF will release summaries of evaluated data which will inform the public on this subject. In response to local inquiries, it is permissible to in form (sic) news media representatives on UFOBs when the object is positively identified as a familiar object . . . except that the following type warrants protection and should not be revealed: Names of principles (sic), intercept and investigation procedures, and classified radar data. For those objects which are not explainable, only the fact that ATIC will analyze the data is worthy of release, due to many unknowns involved.[25]

What this regulation did was to effectively take AFOSI out of UFO investigations. While the main effort would remain with Project Blue Book, the 4602nd could be dispatched to fill any gaps. There is no mention of AFOSI and their mission did not require them to participate in these investigations. The problem is that AFOSI did, in fact, continue to investigate UFOs.

THE 4602ND STEPS IN

In 1957, the 4602nd was replaced by the 1006th AISS, which in turn evolved into the 1127th Field Activities Group in 1960. Despite these name changes, however, their mission remained the same:

. . . to conduct collection operations and develop and maintain force and unit training programs, operational plans, and
combat human intelligence (HUMINT) collection forces to
fulfill ACS/I HUMINT responsibilities to HQ USAF, USAF
Commands, and DOD in cold, limited and general war.

There was no change in this mission during the period of July 1
through December 31, 1967 and Group functions also remained
unchanged.

This appeared to take the 1127th out of the UFO investigation
business and return it to other Air Force intelligence functions. Air
Force Regulation 80-17 spelled out the requirements for the investigations, ordering that each base commander maintain a UFO investigative capability. That simply meant that some officer, probably
a lieutenant, would be tasked with UFO investigation if a sighting
was reported in their area of responsibility. This suggests that, by
the time the new regulation went into effect in 1962, attitudes had
changed, at least in the eyes of most officers. It seems, however, that
AFOSI was still involved.

And in fact, there are many cases in which eyewitnesses to UFO
sightings mention that men in civilian clothes—"men in black"—
were involved in their interrogations. This was the case when retired
Air Force Captain David D. Schindele provided information suggesting that UFOs had been involved in an incident while he was
stationed at Minot AFB in 1966. He was off duty when the sightings
were reported and didn't see anything himself, but what occurred
in the aftermath of those sightings and how those events affected
him is important.

According to what Schindele told a Citizen Hearing in Washington in 2013, he was made aware of a UFO sighting about three miles
west of Mohall, North Dakota:

I drove to the airbase to attend the morning Predeparture
Briefing at [455th Strategic Missile] Wing Headquarters,

where all 15 missile crews would normally meet each day prior to "pulling alert duty" at their respective Launch Control Facilities. During the briefing, it was mentioned that some missiles at November Flight had gone "off alert" during the night, but no further information was provided. I immediately connected this to the news item that I had heard earlier in the morning regarding a possible UFO sighting near the town of Mohall.[26]

Schindele said the missiles had been disabled, but no additional information had been given to the missile crews. He reported that those at that briefing were aware of the sighting and were all speculating about the possibility that the UFO and the missile failure were connected. After all, there were more than a dozen people involved in the incident, as well as the maintenance crews and others who had to retarget and realign the missiles.

Schindele said that their normal procedure when they arrived at the LCF (launch control facility) was to inspect the grounds and the building, but on this particular morning he went in to debrief the security personnel instead. The site manager, a tech sergeant (E-6), asked Schindele if he had been briefed on what had happened. When he said he hadn't, the sergeant then told him about the UFO sighting. According to Schindele:

> We then proceeded toward the windows on the west side of the day room where he described to me the large object with flashing lights that had been hovering just outside the fence that night, and he spread his arms out in front of him to indicate its size. Based on his description, I estimated that the object may have been 80 to 100 feet wide and about 100 feet from the building, maybe a bit closer . . .
>
> He then said that the object, while hovering close to the ground, then glided to the right toward the North end of the building out of sight. The object then came into view from

the security section of the facility, and hovered just behind and slightly to the right of the main gate, concealed partly by the large garage located within the fenced area to the right of the gate . . .

Security personnel confirmed everything that the Site Manager had related to me. My commander and I then proceeded to take the elevator down to the Launch Control Center to relieve the two-man officer crew below. After entering the capsule, our eyes were immediately transfixed on the Launch Control Console, which showed that all missiles were off alert and unlaunchable.

The outgoing crew briefed us on the wild events that transpired overnight, and indicated that the missiles malfunctioned at the time the object was hovering directly above the capsule and next to the main gate. We speculated on the possibility of an EMF pulse that might have created the situation. We had no doubt, however, that the 10 outlying nuclear tipped missiles of November Flight had been compromised, tampered with, and put out of commission by the object that had paid a visit. Normally, it was quite unusual to have even one missile down.[27]

Just as at Malmstrom AFB, an entire flight of Minuteman missiles had been rendered inoperative by an outside force (see chapter 6). And if an outside force could take down a flight of missiles, it could take down the entire wing and U. S. missile strategy would become useless.

Schindele tried to get additional information from the Flight Security Controller, but the controller said he had been instructed not to discuss the situation:

My commander told me that he had received a call while I was on a scheduled rest break below ground, and he was told that

we were never to discuss the incident. When I asked where
the directive came from, he said the OSI.[28]

"Everyone had been silenced," Schindele said. "The incident was
never discussed and I never heard a word of any other incident
from people I associated with. I never spoke a word about my incident for almost 40 years."[29]

If Schindele was a stand-alone witness, his testimony could be
ignored, even though he said that he had run across others who
knew of these events:

> They fear losing their Air Force pensions or losing their per-
> sonal integrity in keeping a secret, or of being ridiculed . . .
> [T]here is the late Captain Val Smith of my squadron who was
> mentioned in official documents released via the Freedom
> of Information Act. He was interviewed by the late Dr. Allen
> Hynek . . . who wrote an article in the *Saturday Evening Post* . . .
> which described the incident that Smith was involved with on
> 25 August 1966.[30]

Those officers who were involved were warned repeatedly about
revealing classified information. If missiles were being disabled by
an outside force, that was clearly a matter of national security, and
there were legal and financial consequences for talking about the
incidents with those who had no need to know.

Former Air Force captain Bruce Fenstermacher was another officer who provided information to the Citizen Hearing in May 2013.
A Minuteman III combat Crew Commander assigned to the 400th
Strategic Missile Squadron at F. E. Warren AFB from 1974 until
1977, Fenstermacher said that they had been monitoring the VHF
radio communications between the security NCO on the ground
and the Security Alert Team (SAT) that was doing routine checks on
the missile silos. At about 2:00 AM, the security NCO asked SAT to
pull over and look around. He wanted to know what they could see.

The team spotted a pulsating white light in the sky, with other colors visible between the pulsations. Fenstermacher said:

> I got on the direct line to the FSC and asked him what was going on. His reply was that right above the LCF there was a silent object with a very bright pulsating light. Between the pulsations he could see a blue light and a red light. I asked for specifics and he said that it was shaped like a fat cigar and was about 80 to 100 feet above him and appeared to be 40 to 50 feet long . . . While we were talking, he reported that it was slowly and quietly moving away to the east.[31]

They ordered SAT to head to the launch control facility where the object was hovering. It took them some time to respond and, by the time they arrived, the object had moved farther east, so Fenstermacher ordered them to that location:

> Shortly after the object went to the first LF we reported the incident to the SAC command post at F. E. Warren. The NCO that took the call laughed at the report and said to call him back when the thing "ate the SAT" and hung up. As well as logging all the activity in the official log, my deputy also started taking personal notes dealing with what transpired.

> At our hourly 400th SMS crew check in for flights Poppa, Quebec, Romeo, Sierra, and Tango [which are the designations of other missile sites] we told the other crew members about our object and received laughter and an attitude of general disbelief. Right after the group communication, the crew from Quebec called—they were the team we had dropped off on our way to Romeo—and stated that earlier the morning they had a similar object about a couple of their LFs. When asked what direction it was headed they said that it appeared to be heading towards our area . . . We asked what happened when they reported the incident the answer

was, "Are you crazy? We didn't report it. We would have been laughed at. . . ."

We contacted the F. E. Warren SAC Command Post a few more times and finally asked if this incident had been entered into the log. They said it had not. I asked for the officer in charge and stated that if they did not enter I would wake up the base commander and report it directly to him . . . Shortly after that we got a call from a senior NCO at the Command Post asking for specific details about the incident . . .

Upon our return to the 400th SMS we discussed the incident with our flight commander. The next morning we were called in to the 400th SMS commander's office. He asked us about the incident and when he learned about our personal notes he asked to look at them. Once in his hands he tore them up and said we were never to talk about this again and required us to sign documents that seemed to say we would not talk about it. We reluctantly signed them.

At our next couple of departure meetings an officer in uniform (not a crew uniform and not someone we recognized) briefed all crews that this incident was classified and officially never happened and that no one should talk about it.[32]

And, in fact, there is still no evidence that these events were ever logged.

It is clear from Fenstermacher that the UFO did not interfere with the missiles in any way and that there were no reports of electromagnetic effects on any of the other equipment. What is important here, however, is the reaction of his fellow Air Force officers and the command structure. The culture inside the Air Force suppressed any sharing of information about UFO activity simply by wrapping it in a cloak of ridicule. This accomplished two things. It prevented the crews from talking to one another about UFOs and destroyed the paper trail so that those who attempted to verify the information would be unable to find any documentation.

All these cases, from the Rhodes photographs to the interference with ballistic missiles, are quite strong. They are based on the testimony of multiple eyewitnesses, photographic evidence, radar tracks, and the interaction of UFOs with the environment. They are supported by documentation in the Blue Book files, by on-the-record statements from many of the principals, and, ironically, by an interesting lack of reports in the Blue Book files where they should have been. Witnesses were told not to talk about their experiences and, in some cases, were asked to sign nondisclosure agreements by anonymous government officials, some of them representing AFOSI.

All this demonstrates that, from the very beginning, the intelligence communities—and often AFOSI—have been investigating UFO sightings and related matters, and have been intimidating witnesses with threats of fines and jail time. These investigations and these threats seem to remove the question of UFOs from the arena of national security into the arena of protecting individuals and policies. Clearly those individuals are well-positioned in the Deep State.

CHAPTER 11

Alien Abductions

The first reliable case of alien abduction reported in the United States occurred in 1961, when Betty and Barney Hill claimed they had been taken aboard an alien craft in rural New Hampshire. An earlier incident, reported in 1957 by Coral Lorenzen, involved a Brazilian farmer/attorney named Antonio Villas-Boas who claimed that he had been captured and taken aboard an alien craft for a reproductive experiment that was crude by 1950s standards.[1] Lorenzen and the Aerial Phenomenon Research Organization (APRO) did not report on Villas-Boas, however, until after the Hill case became public.

The Hill case stands out because it was confirmed in an Air Force report by radar at Pease Air Force Base in New Hampshire. That report, however, was plagued with controversy. According to John Luttrell, the radar return seen by operators at about the time the Hills reported the UFO was a shimmering image that resembled an air mass on the screen. In other words, it could have been a temperature inversion. This claim was later rejected by skeptics, however, and replaced with a theory that what the radar had detected was an object that was apparently closer to Pease.[2] While it may have been the same object seen by the Hills, the connection is doubtful given what we know today.

Under hypnotic regression, both Barney and Betty Hill told a tale of alien abduction, although Betty first recovered some of the memories through her dreams.[3] Betty recalled that they had seen a bright star that seemed to be following them as they drove along a rural road in Lancaster, New Hampshire. They stopped several times and, at one of these stops, Barney used his binoculars. He could see red, amber, green, and blue lights rotating around an object that looked like an aircraft without wings. He could hear no sound and, when he got back into the car, he was frightened.[4]

As they continued along the road, Betty, using the binoculars, saw a double row of windows on the craft. She demanded that Barney stop. He drove on for a few minutes and finally stopped in the middle of the road. Barney left the engine running and got out of the car, taking the binoculars with him. He saw a large disk-shaped object, which he told Betty looked like "a plane or something."

Although badly frightened, he walked across the road toward the object, stopping about fifty feet away from it as it hovered above the trees. Through the binoculars, he could clearly see a double row of windows behind which stood six beings. He later said that the one he thought of as the leader wore a black jacket. As he watched, five of these beings turned and seemed to manipulate some controls. The UFO began a slow descent and something, possibly landing gear, was lowered from the belly of the craft.

Barney stared at the "leader" and suddenly realized that he was going to be captured. Jerking the binoculars from his eyes, he whirled and ran back to the car to warn his wife. He threw the binoculars into the backseat, jumped behind the wheel, slammed the car into gear, and roared off as fast as he could. He yelled for Betty to watch the object, but it had disappeared.

As he calmed down, Barney slowed the car and then they both heard a series of strange electronic beeps. The beeps were repeated, and they both seemed to become drowsy. The next thing they recalled seeing was a sign that told them they were seventeen miles from home, where they arrived at about 5:00 in the morning. Six days after the sighting, Betty sent a letter to Don Keyhoe at the National

Investigations Committee on Aerial Phenomenon (NICAP) describing what they had seen. She also considered finding a reputable psychiatrist to perform hypnotic regression on Barney, because he was having trouble remembering what had happened during the encounter.

In December 1963, some two years after the sighting, Barney, complaining of stomach trouble, made an appointment with Dr. Benjamin Simon, a well-respected doctor and a highly qualified neurosurgeon. Simon suspected that Barney's illness might be psychosomatic and eventually used hypnosis on both him and Betty.[5] Under hypnosis, the Hills told of running into a road block after they had seen the UFO. As they approached, the car's engine died. Several strange beings that Betty described as having Mongoloid features with broad, flat faces and very large noses surrounded the car. Barney said that the leader had very large, almond-shaped eyes that seemed to wrap around the side of his head. His mouth was a slit with a vertical line on each side and his skin had a blue-gray cast to it.

Betty, whose story was always more robust than Barney's, told of undergoing a physical examination and described strange instruments touching her in various places. Samples of her skin, fingernails, and hair were taken, and a long needle was pushed into her navel. As that happened, she screamed at one of the creatures and the "leader" passed a hand over her eyes, stopping her pain and calming her.

During her time on the ship, Betty communicated with the apparent leader through telepathy. She asked him where he came from and he showed her a star chart, asking her to locate Earth on it. When she was unable to identify the sun, he said that the map would do her no good if she couldn't even find her own solar system. After this discussion, both Barney and Betty were escorted from the ship. They heard a second series of beeps and woke up on the road heading toward home.

During her sessions with Dr. Simon, Betty discussed the star map, which she had re-created in a drawing. Marjorie Fish, a brilliant woman, used the best astronomical information available to create a series of three-dimensional models of our section of the galaxy, looking for a pattern that matched what Betty had seen on the map. She concluded that the aliens had come from a double star system known as Zeta I, Zeta II Reticuli.[6] The star charts used by Fish have since been updated, with some stars having their distances from Earth altered. Astronomical data at that time suggested that a double star would host no planets. That argument has since been negated by discoveries of other double and even triple star systems that do support planets. When it was discovered that a large, Jupiter-like planet does, in fact, orbit Zeta II Reticuli, this added weight to Fish's conclusion by confirming that at least one planet orbited around a sun-like star in this binary star system. The announcement of this newly discovered planet was retracted four days later, however, and all data about it was removed from official databases, suggesting some behind-the-scenes manipulation.

Was radar confirmation of a UFO by the Air Force suppressed when the Air Force changed their story? Were the Deep State and AFOSI protecting this data and hiding it from the public because it would add a note of needed credibility to the Hills' story? Clearly, the striking of the announcement of a planet found orbiting one of the stars in the Zeta Reticuli system is somewhat suspicious. Although the original announcement may have been premature and a more complete analysis of the data may have indicated that the planet did not exist, it still seems a bit strange. Coincidence? Possibly. But more than a little suspicious.

In fact, it seems reasonable to suggest that the Deep State was behind the changes of this important data. After all, who controls the money for research grants? Who has the power to see that academic tenure is granted or denied? If one planet in a star system nearly forty light years away is removed from a list, who gets hurt? Make it go away and your university position, your research grants, and your life as a whole are just a little better.

DEVIL'S DEN

Although the abduction that occurred at Devil's Den doesn't suffer from the problems associated with the Hill case, it does demonstrate that AFOSI and the Air Force had an interest in alien abduction and UFOs long after Project Blue Book was closed in 1969.

At the time of the incident, Terry Lovelace was an enlisted man in the Air Force.[7] He and another Air Force enlisted man—identified throughout discussions of the case only as "Toby"—had planned a camping trip in the recreational area known as Devil's Den. They hiked into the location, set up their camp, and eventually ended up staring into a night sky filled with stars so bright that they appeared to be much closer than usual. Lovelace said that he saw the splash of the Milky Way brighter than he had ever seen it.

Toby spotted three bright lights near the horizon that didn't look like stars or aircraft or anything with which he was familiar. He pointed them out to Lovelace and they watched as they seemed to grow, meaning that they were coming closer. The lights finally stopped overhead and resolved into a triangular craft. The airmen described the three lights as bright enough to light up the meadow where they were camped.

Then a bright blue beam like that of a laser flashed from the center of the craft and hit the campfire. White beams emitted from the corners of the craft looked as if they were flashing through fog. According to Lovelace, the blue light "darted about the campsite" and had a hypnotic quality to it. When it disappeared, both men stayed where they were until Toby said something like: "Show's over." They then crawled into their tent, both so tired that they fell asleep immediately.

According to Lovelace, he was later awakened by lights and a low-pitched hum all around. The flashes of light were so bright that they lit up the interior of the tent. Lovelace climbed to his knees and, as he did, realized that he hurt all over. Toby, who was also awake and on his knees, opened the tent flap and saw flashing green and yellow lights. He wondered if they were the lights of an emergency vehicle, and if the hum outside the tent was that of a generator used by game poachers. Lovelace later said that, although he was awake, he felt as if he was in a fog. He reached for a flashlight, but, before he could turn it on, Toby grabbed it and said: "They're still out there." Toby was clearly worried about something that Lovelace didn't completely understand. There was motion outside the tent, shadows moving around, and the noise made him think that there might be as many as a dozen people in the area.

Lovelace finally pushed his way to the tent flap and saw something that he thought was much larger than a flying saucer. He described it as "absolutely huge" and sitting motionless in mid-air about thirty feet above the ground.

> We could see two sides clearly. There were randomly dis-bursed square panels of light on each side. It reminded me of a five-story office building at night . . . Along the very top was a row of larger windows that slanted outward. They were all lit. I saw faint shadows and movement behind these larger panels.

There were little figures walking around outside the tent and Lovelace remembers wondering what children were doing there. Toby quietly pointed out that they weren't children.

Although both men were frightened, they continued to watch. The small beings eventually walked into one of the lights coming from the craft and then disappeared, apparently transported up into the huge object. The craft then began to rise "like a hot air balloon." It climbed steadily until it was little more than three points of light in the distance, then slowly faded from sight.

When the craft was gone, neither man was sure what had happened. They just agreed that they needed to get out of there, so they hiked back to their car and drove home. On the way, they both felt terribly thirsty and Lovelace later said that images like still photographs flipped through his mind, providing a glimpse of an event that he couldn't remember, but in which he had been hurt. When he arrived home, his wife was concerned and thought he didn't look well. He had a temperature of 104 degrees, which is moving toward dangerous. She put him in a cool bath and, when she took his temperature again, it had dropped only two degrees. Unsatisfied and apparently worried, she insisted that he go to the clinic.

Staff at the clinic drew blood and ran other tests, apparently looking for signs of radiation poisoning. The doctor sent Lovelace's wife home to retrieve everything he had been wearing—boots, socks, clothes. He also gave her a big bag with a biohazard symbol on it and instructed her to bring back everything that he had brought home with him as well. They were clearly worried about radiation contamination. Lovelace's commanding officer visited him, asked a few routine questions, and then left. Lovelace believes that the CO then alerted the security police. Whether he did this as part of standard protocol or prompted by other concerns, the point is that the security police were called in.

After Lovelace had been in the hospital for about forty-eight hours, two men dressed in business suits who said they were part of AFOSI entered the room. They seemed to be a bit overbearing, telling the nurse to hold off on sedating Lovelace because they had some questions for him and requesting that she shut the door on her way out. When Lovelace asked that they turn out the lights because they hurt his eyes, they seemed to believe that they couldn't ask their questions in the relative dark of a hospital room. They said that they needed to see what they were doing. In the interest of fairness, watching the reactions of a subject being questioned could be an important part of any interrogation.

The older of the two agents, identified as Special Agent Gregory, read Lovelace his rights as outlined in the Uniform Code of Military Justice, the governing legal document of the U. S. military. Gregory, who said he was in charge of the case, then pulled out several documents, telling Lovelace that they were consent forms that waived his rights and promised access to a civilian attorney if he wanted to hire one. Alternatively, he could have access to a member of the Judge Advocate General's office, known as JAG. Lovelace, apparently somewhat confused and with nothing to hide, signed and initialed the documents where indicated and Gregory put them in his briefcase. When Lovelace closed his eyes to block out the brightness of the room, Gregory demanded that he "pay attention."

The description that Lovelace gives of the interrogation suggests that it was meant to intimidate him, and possibly to trip him up for some reason. Gregory pointed out that the wildlife preserve where he and Toby had camped was federal land, and asked if they had spent the night there. When Lovelace said they had not, Gregory seemed to accuse him of lying. When Lovelace explained that he had misunderstood the question, Gregory nodded and he and the other AFOSI agent left the room. When Gregory returned, he told Lovelace that they had been trespassing on federal land when they set up camp on the wildlife preserve.

Then Gregory got to the meat of the interrogation. He asked about the strange stars they had seen, and said something about them going into their tent to fall asleep. To underscore the gravity of the situation, he then asked if Lovelace and Toby had a marijuana plot on the preserve and wondered why they had left their equipment behind. Gregory apparently thought the whole thing was more than a little odd. He wanted to know how long the airmen had watched the stars, what they were doing on the nature preserve in the first place, and if Lovelace had taken any pictures. The agent seemed to believe that he knew the answers to his many questions before he asked them. When he didn't get the answers he wanted, he asked the questions again with an attitude of disbelief. He clearly thought that Lovelace was lying about what he and Toby had been doing out there that night. He wanted to know why Lovelace had brought along a camera with a "telescopic" lens on it and said he wanted the camera, the film, and any prints of pictures that might have been taken during the brief camping trip.

Lovelace suggested that his wife could bring all that to the hospital, but Gregory said that wasn't necessary. They had already "raided" his house and taken the camera, film, and prints as evidence—even those that had no relation to the events of the camping trip. When Lovelace protested, Gregory pointed out that he had signed a waiver that allowed them to search his property and confiscate various items. They had what they needed.

After Gregory had made it clear that AFOSI was in charge, the other agent returned. Assured that Lovelace was sufficiently cowed, they got to the point of the interrogation. Gregory began with a map that Toby had drawn to help them find their way to Devil's Den, seeming to suspect some sinister motive for creating the map. The agents questioned Lovelace about his photography hobby, his wish to take artful pictures out in the wild, and the fact he had a small darkroom in his house. Then the nurse returned and told the agents that the doctor had ordered her to take care of Lovelace. Before he left, Gregory informed Lovelace that he was being reassigned, and that he was to remain on base unless he had permission from either his commanding officer or from Gregory to leave. He was not to contact Toby and he was not to talk about the lights in the sky to anyone, even his wife.

Gregory also told Lovelace that, according to Toby, they had been drinking at the campsite and that the burns they suffered had been from the sun and from "naturally occurring radiation in the limestone bluffs," claiming that they had been lying on top of a uranium deposit. The red spots on his body were from chigger bites, the agent said, because they hadn't used enough DEET. Lovelace knew that this was all nonsense, but he was smart enough to say that he understood. He just wanted Gregory to leave.

When Lovelace left the hospital a couple of days later, he was given a large number of pills with instructions to take three after each meal and told that a nurse would come each day to make sure that he took them. He asked a nurse he knew what they were, but she either didn't know or had been told not to tell him. As a trained EMT, Lovelace had a working knowledge of various medications and a copy of the *Physician's Desk Reference*, but he couldn't find the pills he had been given anywhere in it. All he knew was that the pills had been sent from Wright-Patterson Air Force Base. After taking them for several days, he noticed that his short-term memory wasn't as sharp as it had been, so he stopped taking them, flushing each day's pills so the nurse would get the proper count when she arrived. When he stopped taking the medication, his memory improved.

Lovelace was transferred from his position as an EMT to another squadron where he was given a "make work" project—paint thirty plywood sheets and, when he was finished, sand them down to bare wood again. Before he had finished this task, he was ordered to report to his commanding officer. He was then escorted to another location, where he met with the AFOSI men again.

Gregory and the other agent, whose name Lovelace couldn't remember, entered the room and asked him once again about any film he might have shot on the camping trip, but it was clear that Gregory no longer cared about that. He handed Lovelace several documents, saying they were the waiver forms he had signed before. Then he read the documents into a tape recorder. But the civility that Gregory exhibited at the beginning of the interview soon evaporated. He began to demand answers and ordered that Lovelace give him specific information, making it clear that Lovelace had disobeyed lawful orders that Gregory had given him.

When Lovelace asked if they thought that he had seen something secret, he received no answer. When a major tapped on the door to the room and was allowed to enter, the dynamics of the situation changed. The major was now in charge and his attitude was different. He seemed more kind and more interested in Lovelace's comfort than in the questions being asked. After building a rapport with Lovelace and suggesting that hypnosis might help him remember what had happened, the major said that he would be given an injection to help him relax. He told Lovelace not to worry and assured him he had done it a hundred times before. Given the nature of the interrogation and the involvement of AFOSI, I have to wonder whether the major was referring to a hundred other cases in which witnesses, or victims, had seen UFOs. If so, this suggests that AFOSI was involved in UFO research long after the Air Force had closed its only official investigation. To be fair, chemical regression may have been used in many other types of investigations as well. But the major's remark is evidence that chemical regression was part of AFOSI's arsenal when dealing with UFO situations.

Lovelace wondered the same thing. Nonetheless, he agreed to the regression. While under the influence of the drug, he could hear what was being said and he was able to remember it. First, the major attempted to move Lovelace back to the meadow and the night that he and Toby had seen the strange lights. Lovelace answered: "We were parked in the right spot." This seemed a strange thing for him to say and the major caught it immediately. He asked Lovelace how they knew where to go and Lovelace replied that he didn't know, that "they had told Toby." When pressed on that point, he said that the space people had told him during the abduction. That made Gregory's questions about the hand-drawn map more important. According to Lovelace: "We found the correct spot to camp. It was on the edge of the meadow. We couldn't go to a public campsite. We had to be up high on the plateau because that's where they land."

Lovelace then said that he had been taken twice that night, but that Toby had only been taken once. He claimed that the aliens took blood and sperm and that there was no way to resist them. "They had us," he said.

During the interrogation, Lovelace said that it wasn't the first time something like this had happened to him. As a child, he had been abducted by what he called the "monkey men." He called them that because they had looked like monkeys and worn masks. Then he said that he knew they weren't monkeys, but that they were "gray people." He described their UFO as a huge triangle hundreds of feet on a side. The craft wasn't shiny, but seemed to have a matte finish of dark gray or black. It had lights on each corner and one that ran from the bottom to the top. The craft never touched down, just hovered about thirty feet above the ground. As the interrogation continued, Lovelace remembered more about his interaction with these aliens and said that they had intruded on his life many times in the past.

Then Lovelace remembered that there were human crew members on the craft as well—perhaps fifty or sixty—but that they ignored both Toby and him. These crew members wore tan flight suits with orange rank insignia on the shoulders. Gregory, who was still in the room and witnessing the interrogation, reacted to that information, saying: "Son of a bitch." At that point, they diverted the conversation and the major told Lovelace that he would forget all about the humans on the ship.

Then Lovelace began describing something that he called aquariums—big "fish tanks" that held something "lizard-like" in pink water. He was taken to a big room where there were people waiting who may not have been part of the crew. According to Lovelace, they were nude and holding their clothes. As the interrogation continued, he described tall aliens and a woman who talked to him telepathically. He said that she wasn't pretty, but that he liked her. She told him that she was half human and half alien, and that the aliens came from a world that has two suns and a couple of moons. It was never dark there, she said, but it was very beautiful.

The major again redirected the discussion back to the meadow where the aliens had taken the airmen into the ship. Lovelace said that he was given a painful examination. One alien seemed to be in charge, he said, and the little gray aliens with him were like "worker bees." Lovelace tried to communicate with them, but although he wasn't anesthetized, he couldn't. Everything in the examination room was white porcelain and there were instruments hanging from the ceiling. Lovelace thought they were studying human anatomy, but that they had no empathy. They were only interested in collecting data and didn't care what sort of trauma they might have caused him.

Eventually, Lovelace and Toby were taken from the craft and returned, not to their campsite, but momentarily to their car. The aliens then carried them back to their tent and, once inside, Lovelace again lost consciousness. When he came to, Toby was on his knees looking outside the tent. They then fled the campsite and rushed to get home.

The major then returned to a normal interrogation, asking again about photographs. Lovelace said that neither he nor Toby had taken any pictures, and that he had told Gregory the truth about that and everything else. There was nothing more for him to tell. After receiving a post-hypnotic suggestion to forget all that had been dredged up during the regression session, Lovelace was free to return to his regular duties. It was the last encounter that Lovelace ever had with AFOSI.

What is important here is that AFOSI monitored Lovelace, attempted to intimidate him, and tried to prevent him from getting together with Toby. The only time that Lovelace and Toby met after they were released from the hospital happened when Toby was clearing the base for his new duty assignment. The meeting was brief, but resulted in an immediate response from base security at the direction of AFOSI.

Could there be more to this story? Lovelace reported humans on the spacecraft. He reported humans in uniform who ignored him, but who seemed to be working with the alien beings. All this seems to lead back to the Deep State and AFOSI covering up the true nature of UFO phenomenon. AFOSI purportedly does not participate in UFO investigations unless they relate to a threat to national security. But if the Air Force position is that there is nothing to UFO sightings and that they are not the result of alien visitation, how could these sightings be a threat to national security? The fact that this question has never been answered suggests that AFOSI—and, by extension, the Deep State—knows more about this than they are letting on.

MILABS

MILABs (military abductions) are abductions to which components of the U. S. military have some sort of connection. Some believe this connection may not be voluntary. Others think there is, in fact, no alien component to it—that the military uses mind-altering drugs and other forms of mind control to prompt reports of alien abduction to cover up what the military—and, by extension, the Deep State—is actually doing. Terry Lovelace hinted at military abductions when he mentioned that there were humans on the alien ship who were dressed in tan uniforms and wearing orange insignia of rank. But it was Martin Cannon who first suggested publicly that the military was fomenting reports of alien abduction to cover up actual terrestrial events. Cannon predicated his theory on the fact that some of the alien experimentation reportedly carried out on humans was crude even by terrestrial standards. In other words, he argued that there wasn't anything being reported as alien abduction that couldn't be replicated by Earth-based science, and that much of it seemed to be crude by 20th-century standards.[8]

Part of Cannon's theory was based on the idea that aliens seemed to have an improbable level of insight into human activities, noting that Budd Hopkins had reported on a multiple-witness case in which all the participants reported missing time. They all reported encountering strange "hikers" on a wilderness trail, though each witness described the hikers differently. Why, Hopkins asked, did all these witnesses talk about hikers? He suggested it was "a screen memory"—a memory that had been implanted to explain the abductions as something more normal or mundane. The goal was to fool witnesses into seeing something that wasn't there as a way of hiding what had really been there.

Cannon went further, however. He wondered how an alien race visiting Earth would have the information necessary to suggest hikers—or if they would even know what hikers were. Instead, Cannon asked why the default position to explain these events was alien activity and not something based more in terrestrial events. He presented evidence, including studies in referreed scientific journals, that suggested that various government agencies operating as part of the Deep State—including the CIA, the Office of Naval Research (ONR), and, I would add, AFOSI—had not only experimented with mind control that would allow them to create screen memories, but may also have used those memories to create reports of alien abductions.

Then Cannon took his argument one step further by claiming that those same agencies were hiding their own research behind these reports. If UFO researchers and others were looking for abduction scenarios, then the Deep State would supply them and discredit them by claiming that "serious" researchers would not waste their time investigating them. Terry Lovelace, for instance, reported that his AFOSI interrogators seemed to know quite a bit about what had happened to him at Devil's Den, and that their questions and reactions seemed to suggest that they had some sort of inside information. Gregory knew things that he couldn't have known unless he had another source of information.

Karla Turner was among the first to embrace Cannon's theory that some abductions were the result of military activities.[9] Her journey began in 1988 when, like Barney and Betty Hill, she and her husband entered counseling because they were feeling stressed. During that time, she read two books about alien abduction that prompted a childhood memory of seeing an odd light in the sky, and she began to dream about UFOs.[10] Having learned hypnotic relaxation techniques from her therapist, she took the risk of regressing her husband. During the regression, he also remembered several childhood encounters with alien beings. A few days later, Karla began hearing strange noises in the house and remembered a childhood nightmare in which an insect-like creature told her it was her mother. This stirred up other memories.

Together, Karla and her husband underwent hypnotic regression that uncovered more accounts of childhood abduction that involved her entire family. Not long after these sessions, she was again awakened by sounds in the house. The next morning, she found small puncture wounds on her wrist and three white circles on her stomach. Additional marks appeared on her body through 1988 and into 1989. To make matters worse, she began to experience other paranormal manifestations. Strange cars parked near her house and black helicopters hovered overhead. Karla came to believe that, for some reason, the military was monitoring her.

Karla sought out others who were having similar experiences. She began to share information with others, including her belief that she had had telepathic contact with aliens and that the aliens and humans were working together. And not just one race of aliens. There were insects like the one she had encountered as a child, as well as reptoids, blue humanoids, and even dwarves, not to mention the grays that have been reported so often. Karla made contact with many other women who told her about hybrid nursey rooms and rooms that held what looked like replicas of ten or twenty people. To her, what she learned suggested that the aliens were not there to help humans, but to pursue their own agendas.

Karla finally began to suspect that there was something else going on as well. She believed that something we now know as the Deep State had taken over reports of UFO phenomena and were using them for their own purposes. She didn't fully understand why the military would be involved, only that it was. It seemed strange that military personnel would abduct people to interrogate them and even stranger if those in the military were working with the aliens. Karla died in 1996 before she could complete her research. But a Dutch scientist had reached some of the same conclusions, and he began to study MILABs.

Dr. Helmet Lammer, the MUFON representative in Austria, also became interested in MILABs.[11] Two things concerned him. First, if MILABs were real, they could be evidence that there was, in fact, a national security element involved in alien visitation. In other words, they constituted proof that UFOs were actually alien. Second, he suspected that, if the military—and, by extension, the Deep State—were using mind control to abduct people, they might be doing it to gather information about aliens and their purpose in visiting Earth. Lammer suggested that, if either of these points was correct, those advocating for Congressional hearings would be thwarted. The Deep State would protect itself from public disclosure and scrutiny.

Lammer reported on a number of MILAB victims, including Leah Haley and Katharina Wilson, noting that Wilson in particular experienced something that seemed more closely associated with mind control than with alien abduction. Wilson told of a childhood memory in which she was a part of some kind of mind-control experiment. This suggests that the Deep State may be learning how to control the population without actually revealing who they are or what they are doing.

And there are other indications that military abductions do actually occur. Lammer reported that one of the first things victims notice is surveillance by black helicopters. But this sounds more like Deep State activity than alien visitation. Aliens wouldn't be flying helicopters, nor would they be keeping close track of those who had been abducted. Moreover, many of those who report being abducted also report that they were given some sort of injection and claim that they were under the mental control of their captors. But surely aliens advanced enough to visit Earth would not have to rely on injections to control their captives. Some abductees even say that they were examined by human doctors.

Just as important is the fact that MILABs only seem to be reported in North America, and there were virtually no reports of them prior to the 1980s. This suggests that there is a connection between the Deep State as it exists in the United States and at least one part of the abduction phenomenon. The question is whether there is also a connection between the visiting aliens and the military. Is the military attempting to learn about aliens by subjecting those who claim abduction to another form of it? Are they taking people out of their homes and examining them without permission in order to learn what is happening? Although Terry Lovelace was something of an exception because he was a member of the Air Force and thereby subject to military rules that forced him to remain silent, his story establishes a link between AFOSI and the Deep State, demonstrating that there is more to UFO phenomena than just sightings of craft in the sky. This tells us that there is much more going on behind the scenes.

CHAPTER 12

Rendlesham Forest

It seems that from the moment the Rendlesham Forest events were first publicly reported in December 1980, there has been a great deal of confusion about what happened and who was involved.[1] Some of that confusion derives from how the story was leaked to the civilian world, and some of it comes from those who claimed participation in the events.[2] Much of the confusion, however, was introduced by AFOSI as they attempted to investigate the sightings while keeping the details out of public view.

In the early morning hours of December 27, the first night of what turned out to be three nights of sightings, both security and law enforcement teams at RAF Bentwaters, a base occupied by the U. S. Air Force, became involved in investigating something that occurred in the woods just outside the base perimeter.[3] Although there had been hints of strange events around the base both before and after that date, most of the accounts seem to be centered on what turned out to be the third night of intense activity. But let's begin at the beginning.

DAY ONE

SSGT Bud Steffens, who was fairly new to the base at Bentwaters, may have been the first to see the strange lights. He pointed them out to A1C John Burroughs, who was riding with him that night.

Steffens had seen blue and red lights that seemed to be descending into Rendlesham Forest, and he asked Burroughs what he thought they might be and whether he had ever seen anything like that.[4] When Burroughs looked into the woods, he saw saw green, red, blue, and white lights in the tree line that were bright enough to light up the forest. Steffens and Burroughs decided to drive into the forest, although this was in violation of the Status of Forces Agreement, which did not allow military personnel to carry their weapons off base. They stopped just off the road and saw a large glowing white light deeper in the woods.

After watching for several minutes and discussing what they should do next, the two men decided to report what they had seen. Rather than using their radio, which was monitored by both the military and civilians in the area, they drove back to the base to make their report. Once there, Burroughs ran to the phone to call SGT McCabe, who noted that the time was around midnight. Burroughs told McCabe that something had landed in the woods, but McCabe's check of the various radar facilities didn't confirm this. Although McCabe was suspicious of the report, he asked to speak with Steffens, who said that he had seen the same thing.

SSGT Jim Penniston, the noncommissioned office in charge (NCOIC) learned of the sightings when the information was gathered by the Center for Security Control (CSC). Penniston was told by SSGT Dave Coffey that he needed to drive over to East Gate to investigate the telephone report from Burroughs and Steffens. Penniston was somewhat reluctant to go, but Coffey insisted, claiming it was "an emergency." Penniston finally said: "I'm on my way."[5]

Penniston reports that it took about four minutes for him to get to East Gate.[6] When he arrived, Burroughs and Steffens were standing outside their vehicle. According to Penniston, Burroughs was slightly agitated, while Steffens seemed somewhat calmer. They pointed out the lights down in the forest and Penniston confirms that he could see red, orange, yellow, and blue lights like those often seen at aircraft accidents that are produced by burning titanium and jet fuel. Then he saw a blinking red light in the middle of the display at ground level that seemed to rule out any sort of military aircraft accident. Penniston, however, would keep coming back to the possibility of an aircraft accident. When Penniston asked whether they had seen an explosion, Steffens replied that there had been no explosion and Burroughs said that the object had "landed," not crashed. When Penniston wondered whether it might have been a helicopter, Burroughs finally said that he thought it was a UFO.

The three made calls, again avoiding the radios. Penniston, who was still thinking in terms of an aircraft accident, asked to speak with MSGT Chandler and was told that they were all on the line, meaning that the top NCOs and the shift supervisor, Lieutenant Fred "Skip" Buran, were all listening in. This suggests, of course, that those on duty that night in both security and law enforcement were taking the incident seriously. During this call, another check was made with the radar facilities and, to Penniston's surprise, there *was* radar confirmation of something in the area. Given that everyone was still thinking in terms of an aircraft accident, they were given what was known as "first responders" permission to head out into the forest. Penniston was told to take two men with him, one of whom should be law enforcement. Since Steffens made it clear that he was not interested in going, Burroughs followed Penniston into the woods, along with an airman named Cabansag. The three climbed into a jeep, left East Gate, and drove as far into the forest as they could. When they left the jeep, Penniston used the radio to inform those in the command centers and monitoring the situation that there was a fire. He said that a small aircraft might have crashed, but Burroughs interrupted to repeat that the craft had landed, not crashed, and that it wasn't an aircraft.

Taking a camera and flashlights with them, the three ventured deeper into the forest. After they had walked several hundred yards, their radios began to act up, so Penniston and Burroughs proceeded closer to the light display, leaving Cabansag behind to relay information by radio. They walked across an open field and entered the tree line. Both later reported that the air was alive with some sort of energy that caused a distinct crackling and a tingling sensation. The farther they walked, the more difficult progress became, as if they were struggling through chest-deep water. As they continued on, they could see the bright light shining through the trees and Penniston noticed that something was causing animals to flee the area.

Penniston climbed a berm, ran down the other side, and then climbed a second. As he reached the top, he spotted the source of the light—an object that he said was surrounded by a bubble of light. As he approached, there was an explosion of light, but there was no accompanying sound or flying debris. He put up a hand to block the bright light. From his vantage point on top of the berm, he could see a triangular-shaped craft hovering just above the ground. Burroughs, who had also climbed the berm, was standing as if in a trance, encased in the light. After that burst of light, Burroughs remembered very little.

Penniston began to communicate what he had seen, but got no response over the radio, although he continued to try as he walked closer to the craft. He began taking pictures as he neared the object. When he got close enough to see symbols on it, he put away the camera and drew the symbols in his notebook. He approached until he was close enough to touch the craft. He later described it as smooth, almost as if made from black glass, with no seams or imperfections. The symbols on it, however, were rough like sandpaper. As he touched the craft, the lights on it brightened and he was temporarily blinded. When he removed his hand, the lights dimmed. Then the craft began to lift off and seemed to move in slow motion as it reached the tops of the trees. Once it had cleared the trees, it accelerated at tremendous speed.

Penniston rejoined Burroughs, who was still in a state of shock on top of the berm. All they could see were lights on the horizon. They walked back through the field where the craft had landed and found holes pressed into the hard, frozen ground. There was damage to the trees where the craft had maneuvered. When they returned to the base, they thought they had been gone for only a short time. But in reality, about three hours had passed. It was nearly 5:00 AM by the time Penniston looked at his watch again.

It is important to point out here that, according to standard procedures, a number of logs were kept on this incident, including the police blotter held by the law enforcement unit on the base. But later, when Lieutenant Colonel (later Colonel) Charles Halt attempted to retrieve the various logs, they had disappeared. Some documentation remained, however. The Suffolk Police blog noted: "We have had a call from the L. E. at Bentwaters in reference to the U.F.O. reported last night. We have found a place where a craft of some sort seems to have landed."[7]

In fact, when Halt came on duty that morning and was told that Penniston and Burroughs had been chasing UFOs, he ordered that the incident be recorded on the blotters. He also ordered that an incident report be made as well. Yet none of that documentation is available today. Clearly, someone removed it from the base.

DAY TWO

There is some confusion about the subsequent events at Rendlesham Forest. In my interviews with both Penniston and Burroughs, they disagreed about whether the events occurred over two days or three. Halt eventually straightened this out for me.[8] According to him, another incident occurred the next night while different military personnel were on duty. The information collected and the response given, however, weren't nearly as detailed. According to Halt, Lori Buoen was on guard duty at the base's East Gate. She remembers that Colonel Ted Conrad took Christmas dinner to those from D-Flight as part of the tradition of officers serving enlisted personnel on holidays. According to a personal interview conducted by Halt, Buoen was looking north over Rendlesham Forest when she saw a large orange-red ball of light rotating about a mile from the guard shack. It appeared to be flying to the north above the trees and slowly descending into the forest. Some suggest that this was nothing more than the searchlights from the Orford Ness Lighthouse, but the light Buoen was watching was in front of her and above the trees, where there was nothing but darkness.

And that wasn't the only sighting that occurred that night. Halt reports that Lieutenant Bonnie Tamplin, who was a member of the security police force, went down into the forest in an attempt to identify the lights being reported. As she got deeper into the woods, her engine died and some kind of blue light flew through her vehicle. According to the report, she lost her composure and "was so upset that they sent her home." Master Sergeant Bobby Ball also had an experience that night that was so upsetting that he had to seek medical assistance for the stress, indicating, at the very least, the *something* strange was going on.

Not long after these events, Tamplin was transferred from the base. Clearly, that transfer resulted from her reactions that night, but it isn't known whether the transfer occurred because of the stress of the situation or because someone didn't want her talking to other members of D-Flight about what she'd seen. Either way, she was out of the loop.

DAY THREE

The events of the third night at Rendlesham Forest were the events that initially leaked out to the public. Halt reports that he and many other officers were attending a family dinner party when the on-duty Flight Lieutenant "came bursting in with his M-16 and said to me, 'I've got to talk to you privately, right now.'"[9] When Halt and the lieutenant, accompanied by Colonel Ted Conrad, found a private place to talk, the lieutenant reported seeing something outside East Gate. "It's back," he blurted, meaning the UFO was back. Conrad suggested that Halt go out to see what was happening.

Halt, who had talked with Penniston about his sighting, realized that the security forces were being distracted by the lights in the forest and went to talk with the Disaster Preparedness Officer. He wanted a Geiger counter and a reliable NCO to calibrate it. That reliable NCO turned out to be Sergeant Nevels. Just after midnight, Halt and his party arrived on the scene with a number of vehicles and other equipment, including "light-alls"—large free-standing lights used in the field for any activity that required a great deal of light. Halt ordered the lights erected, but they seemed to have trouble getting everything to work properly. Halt had ordered those at East Gate to wait for him. When he arrived there, he met up with Nevels and Master Sergeant Bobby Ball, the on-duty flight chief who was again involved. Burroughs, who was not on duty that night, was there as well and wanted to accompany Halt and his party.

One of the things that makes this night different is that Halt carried a small tape recorder with him and made taped notes about what he was seeing and doing throughout the night. Other voices can be heard on the tape as well, and it provides some documentation of the night's events.[10] One of the first voices heard, at 1:48 AM, said:

> We're hearing strange sounds out of the farmer's barnyard animals. They're very, very active, making awful lot of noise . . . You just saw a light?

Another voice responds:

> Right on this position. Here, straight ahead in between the trees . . . there it is again. Watch. Straight ahead off my flashlight, sir. There it is.

Halt acknowledges that he sees it too and asks: "What is it?" Someone replies: "We don't know, sir."

Halt then describes what he is seeing:

> It's a strange, small red light. Looks to be maybe a quarter to half mile, maybe further out. I'm gonna switch off. The light is gone now. It was approximately 120 degrees from our site. Is it back again?

"Yes, sir," a voice informs him. Then someone says:

> Well, douse the flashlights then. Let's go back to the edge of the clearing so we can get a better look at it . . . The light's still there and all the barnyard animals have gone quiet now . . . still getting a reading on the [Geiger counter] meter . . . Everything else is deadly calm. There is no doubt about it. There's some type of strange flashing red light ahead.

Someone else corrects this statement, saying, "Sir, it's yellow." Then Halt says that he saw a yellow tinge in it too, and says that it appeared to be moving toward them and that pieces of it were shooting off, adding: "This is weird."

When another voice says: "Two lights . . . one to the right and one light to the left," Halt orders everyone to keep their flashlights off and says: "There's something very, very strange . . . Pieces falling off it again." Another voice confirms this: "Yeah. Strange. Let's approach to the edge of the woods . . . we're looking at the thing." This statement is important because it describes, not just lights in the forest, but a "thing," which suggests that the object had returned.

The description of the situation continues:

> It looks like an eye winking at you. Still moving from side to side. And when you put the star[light] scope on it, it's like this thing has a hollow center . . . And it flashes so bright in the star[light] scope that it almost burns your eye . . . now

we have multiple sightings of up to five lights with a similar shape and all but they seem to be steady now . . . We've just crossed a creek and we're getting what kind of readings [Geiger counter] now . . . we're seeing strange lights in the sky.

The next time check on the tape is at 2:44 AM, when Halt says:

We're at the far side of the second farmer's field and made [a] sighting again about 110 degrees. This looks like it's clear off the coast. It's right on the horizon. Moves about and flashes from time to time. Still steady or red in color.

About twenty-one minutes later, he adds:

We see strange strobe-like flashes . . . well, they're sporadic, but there's definitely some kind of phenomenon . . . At about ten degrees, horizon, directly to the north, we've got two strange objects . . . half-moon shape, dancing about with colored lights on them. That . . . guess to be about five to ten miles out, maybe less. The half-moons are now turning full circles, as though there was an eclipse or something there, for a minute or two.

Ten minutes later, at 3:15 AM, Halt says: "Now we've got an object about ten degrees directly south, ten degrees off the horizon. And the ones to the north are moving. One's moving away from us." Someone corroborates Halt's observation, saying clearly: "It's moving out fast." "This one on the right's heading away too," another voice confirms. A third man notes:

They're both heading north. Okay, here he comes from the south. He's coming toward us now. Now we're observing what appears to be a beam coming down to the ground. This is unreal.

Fifteen minutes later, Halt confirms:

> [T]he objects are still in the sky although the one to the south
> looks like it's losing a little bit of altitude. We're going around
> and heading back toward the house. The object to the south
> is still beaming down lights to the ground.

Thirty minutes later, he says:

> One object still hovering over Woodbridge base at about five
> or ten degrees off the horizon. Still moving erratic, and simi-
> lar lights and beaming down.

If this incredible audio tape of eyewitnesses talking about strange lights in the forest near the base were the end of it, this would still be an intriguing case. After all, it isn't often that an Air Force officer makes a recording as he's chasing unidentified lights and objects through the woods near a NATO airbase that contains nuclear weapons. But that wasn't the end of it. About two weeks after that night, Halt sent a letter to the Royal Air Force Commander detailing the events of the day.

1. Early in the morning of 27 Dec 80 (approximately 0300L [three in the morning, local time], two USAF security police patrolmen saw unusual lights outside the back gate at RAF Woodbridge. Thinking an aircraft might have crashed or been forced down, they called for permission to go outside the gate to investigate. The on duty flight chief responded and allowed three patrolmen to proceed on foot. The individuals reported seeing a strange glowing object in the forest. The object was described as being metallic in appearance and triangular in shape, approximately two to three meters across the base and approximately two meters high. It illuminated the entire forest with a white light. The object itself had a pulsating red light on top and a bank(s) of blue lights

underneath. The object was hovering or on legs. As the patrolmen approached the object, it maneuvered through the trees and disappeared. At this time the animals on a nearby farm went into a frenzy. The object was briefly sighted approximately an hour later near the back gate.

2. The next day, three depressions 2" deep and 7" in diameter were found where the object had been sighted on the ground. The following night (29 Dec 80) the area was checked for radiation. Beta/Gamma readings of 0.1 milliroentgens were recorded with peak readings in the three depressions and near the center of the triangle formed by the depressions. A nearby tree had moderate (.05–.07) readings on the side of the tree toward the depressions.

3. Later in the night a red sun-like light was seen through the trees. It moved about and pulsated. At one point it appeared to throw off glowing particles and then broke into five separate white objects and then disappeared. Immediately thereafter, three star-like objects were noticed in the sky, two objects to the north and one to the south, all of which were about 10 [degrees] off the horizon. The objects moved rapidly in sharp angular movements and displayed red, green and blue lights. The objects to the north appeared to be elliptical through an 8–12 power lens. They then turned to full circles. The objects to the north remained in the sky for an hour or more. The object to the south was visible for two or three hours and beamed down a stream of light from time to time. Numerous individuals, including the undersigned [Lieutenant Colonel Halt], witnessed the activities in paragraphs 2 and 3.[11]

There is no doubt that these events took place. In fact, no one disputes that. The reports of the sightings and the evidence given by Halt in both his recordings and his letter, as well as the observations of other Air Force personnel out there that night, all confirm this.

AFOSI OR THE DEEP STATE?

While the events at Rendlesham Forest are supported by multiple
witnesses who watched the lights over a three-day period, there
is another reason why this case is important. Everyone who was
involved, with a singular and interesting exception, was interrogated by AFOSI. According to Penniston, an aircraft from Langley
Air Force Base arrived not long after the events on the third day
had ended. Penniston's claim was corroborated by a conversation
Halt had with late British UFO researcher and magazine publisher
Graham Birdsall:

> During the height of the UFO activity off Base, an unmarked
> aircraft made an unscheduled landing at RAF Woodbridge, I
> was puzzled when the aircraft came to a stop at the end of the
> runway, rather than into the parking slot. I set off in a jeep
> and drove towards the aircraft. As I approached, I saw numer-
> ous figures in white coveralls emerging from the aircraft and
> making their way towards the adjoining forest. Armed guards
> were positioned close to the Galaxy [an Air Force huge cargo
> plane]. These wore no insignia to identify unit or rank. I
> spoke to one of the guards, who told me as I did not have
> proper clearance I would have to leave the scene—which I
> did. Following the plane's arrival, unmarked helicopters were
> also seen over the landing site during the following days.
>
> I would deny this conversation—You have to keep in mind
> this was a foreign country to us. We had no authority here
> whatsoever, but I can assure you if it were in the US, we'd
> have had the place cordoned off with military police . . . I
> believe there is a conspiracy covering UFOs up and agents
> also attend various conferences too. I believe there are agen-
> cies within my Government and at least one in your govern-
> ment who are actively working towards that. Its [sic] simple,
> if you do talk you could disappear—it's that serious.[12]

Here an Air Force officer is describing an incident that clearly involved UFOs that was manipulated by the Deep State. For the aircraft from Langley to land on that military facility, there had to be coordination at the highest levels. Had the aircraft not been authorized to land, it would have been surrounded by security and military forces to prevent its occupants from disembarking. Instead, the aircraft was guarded by our own security forces, and one of the highest-ranking officers on the base was turned away because he didn't have a need to know.

But this was just the beginning of the Deep State's involvement and AFOSI's cover-up. While Halt and some of the others assigned to the base were asking questions, the officers and enlisted personnel who had been involved in the events were now being ordered to speak with AFOSI—and to others in civilian garb who may have been associated with AFOSI or another federal agency. This was never made clear. Penniston himself has noted that some confusion in his account of what happened while he was in Rendlesham Forest can be attributed to these agents. On the morning of December 29, Penniston was scheduled for a meeting with AFOSI at 9:00 AM. When he arrived, he was met by an AFOSI agent he had seen on the base. In 2010, he said:

> Any inconsistencies in my account can easily be attributed to the meddling of the inept debriefing and the drug-induced attempted extraction of information by the U.S. agents at the AFOSI building, or quite possibly by the phenomenon itself.[13]

That comment is interesting, because Halt also told me later that he had talked with an AFOSI agent he knew who was assigned to the base. That conversation seemed to be about the interrogation of the enlisted personnel.[14]

Penniston was taken to a room where two agents he didn't recognize rose from their chairs and introduced themselves as agents interested in the weekend's events. At the time, he wondered whether they were from AFOSI and later wrote that they didn't act like the AFOSI agents he knew. Were these two men actually working for those in the Deep State? That question has never been resolved.

The agents told Penniston that they wanted all the details he could remember, no matter how bizarre they might seem to be, saying that they understood things that he did not. They gave Penniston a yellow legal pad and a pencil and told him to write out his statement. This worried Penniston because he knew that, if he wrote everything out, it could end his military career. When he expressed his concerns, he was told:

> Don't worry about that. This is a confidential investigation and we have no ties to the USAF. The statement won't ever be viewed by anyone at the base.

This response indicated that the investigation had been moved out of AFOSI and into the Deep State. Someone outside the Air Force who had the authority to give orders to Air Force personnel at the base—and probably at the Pentagon as well—had taken an interest in the UFO landing and that person or persons intended to gather as much first-hand information as possible.

When the two agents left the room, Penniston wrote out a lengthy statement that covered everything he could remember about the sighting in "meticulous detail," including his descriptions of the symbols he had seen. But he didn't mention that he had approached to within inches of the craft or that he had touched the symbols. He did mention the photos that he had taken, which would become important evidence. When he finished writing, Penniston gave the pad to one of the agents, who took it and told him to stay where he was. Both agents returned after about twenty minutes with a typed version of the statement, which they gave to him for review. Penniston said that it did not reflect what he had written and that it left out important facts, including the date of the events. It suggested that he had only approached to within about sixty yards of the object, and put other words into his mouth as well.

Although he protested that the statement did not reflect what he had written, the agents said that they knew that, but that it said what they wanted him to say. He was told it was an official investigation and that, if he was asked about anything, he should not stray beyond the cover story given in the statement, which they now wanted him to sign. They also asked him to produce a drawing of what he had seen and provided paper and colored pencils for him to use. Once they had that drawing and a map showing the route Penniston had taken into the woods, they seemed to be pleased with how they had managed the situation.

Penniston was then told that he and Burroughs were to meet with Halt at 1:30 PM. When that meeting ended, he and Burroughs were sent to the Wing Commander's Office, and his statement and drawings were put into an envelope to be given to the base commander—that is, Halt's immediate supervisor. All of this, of course, shows that the investigation was being stage-managed and that inaccurate information was being supplied to various high-ranking officers at the base.

Nor was this the end of the interrogations. There are even hints that some of the eyewitnesses were subjected to chemical regression, either to gather additional information or to suppress observations they had made.

> Once Penniston and Burroughs left Halt's office, they went directly to the Wing Commander's office. I then briefed the Wing Commander, Colonel [Gordon] Williams, quoting the sanitized version passed to me by the agents. He was attentive, listened closely and never said a word—just an occasional nod of understanding. Even upon finishing my report, Colonel Williams never asked one question or asked us to clarify anything. *Of course, he didn't* [emphasis in original]. He was most

likely aware of the AFOSI investigation—*if that's who the agents were* [emphasis in the original]—and this may also have been a test to make sure I was complying with the agent's demands. It was apparent that the agency men—whoever they were . . . had already spoken with Col. Williams, as they must have done with Col. Halt and possibly also with Col. Conrad. At the end of this debrief with the Wing Commander, his only comment was that he appreciated all that we had done and thanked us for a good job well done.[15]

Although Penniston was told that this would by the last of the briefings and that there would be no more questions, that didn't work out as promised. There was always another meeting, always other questions, and always one last briefing, if not with AFOSI, then with other agencies or with someone in his chain of command.

It was nearly a decade and a half before Penniston submitted to hypnotic regression performed by a civilian during a therapy session. During that session, he remembered that he had undergone a seven-hour interrogation in the AFOSI building the day after the events that was *not* part of the interrogation that took place before he talked with Halt. This explains why the agents were able to tell him that they had a great deal of additional information. Penniston later remarked:

I am sure that information could have all been extracted under drugs or in other parts of the interrogation . . . When I was taken into the building for debriefing and sodium pentothal, the agents revealed nothing.[16]

Nor was Penniston the only one subjected to these interrogation techniques. Burroughs underwent something similar. Halt, however, denies that he underwent the same sort of interrogation that the enlisted personnel did. He told me that he knew the AFOSI officers and that he spoke to them without them using enhanced memory techniques.[17] It is curious, however, that Penniston had no memory of any of this until he underwent hypnotic regression years later. It may be that Halt, not having sought that sort of help, had never had those memory blocks broken. Or it may be that, as a high-ranking officer, he was exempt from such techniques. Several other witnesses to the events of those nights have confirmed, however, that they were subjected to lengthy interrogations that used a variety of methods.

And then there is the matter of Lieutenant Tamplin, who was transferred from the base not long after her experiences in Rendlesham Forest. Was she transferred to keep her from talking about what she had seen or done that night? Or was her transer just a convenient way of keeping the witnesses from comparing notes? Although I have concentrated here on Penniston's experiences on the first night and touched on those of John Burroughs on both the first and third nights, there were many others involved. Quite a few members of law enforcement and security were there on all three nights, and many of them have been interviewed about their experiences. This is important to remember, because it is not just three or four members of the Air Force who were involved, but many more.

AFOSI and the Deep State clearly went to extreme lengths to hide information about of the events at Rendlesham Forest and produce a narrative that didn't accurately reflect what had actually happened there, which was certainly something extremely unusual. It wasn't just strange lights that were seen in the forest; it was something much more substantial. It is obvious that this sighting threatened the Deep State and that their agents worked very hard to hide it and sow confusion when reports began to leak out to the public. It also went to extraordinary lengths to discredit the witnesses. Why was all this effort necessary if what was seen was nothing more than misidentified lights in the forest?

CHAPTER 13

The Campaign against UFO Researchers

A FOSI and the Deep State were also directly involved in attempts to derail research that was being done in the civilian world. There is evidence that they spied on certain UFO researchers and organizations and also spread disinformation in the guise of insider data that was handed out to those who cooperated with them. They even attempted to direct research into areas that were dead ends. To understand all this, you have to understand the conspiracy that developed near Kirtland AFB in Albuquerque, New Mexico in the late 1970s.

THE BENNEWITZ CAPER

It all began when businessman and physicist Paul Bennewitz began picking up bizarre messages that he believed were communications from alien creatures who had come to Earth from other planets. He believed that he had seen spacecraft over the Manzano Mountains outside of Albuquerque, where a nuclear weapons facility and a test site were housed. He photographed and filmed some of these lights or objects, and made recordings of their transmissions.[1]

Puzzled by all this, Bennewitz told colleagues and friends about what he had seen, filmed, and heard. Some believed he was deluded, but when he contacted officials at Kirtland AFB, they became worried about what he might actually have discovered by accident. In fact, there were no aliens communicating with one another as Bennewitz suspected. But there *were* low-frequency nets being used to broadcast communications to American submarines in far-off areas and deep underwater. Officials at Kirtland were afraid that Bennewitz might inadvertently tip off Soviet intelligence about this highly classified method of communication, and this made Bennewitz' claims a national security issue.

On October 24, 1980, Bennewitz contacted the chief of Kirtland Air Force security, Major Ernest Edwards, who directed him to an NCO associated with AFOSI named Richard Doty. That meeting resulted in a long report in which Bennewitz stated that he had been studying UFOs for about fifteen months and claimed to have tapes that showed high levels of electrical magnetism being emitted from the Manzano/Coyote Canyon area. He also claimed to have films of unidentified objects flying over that same location. The official report concluded:

> After analyzing the data collected by Dr. [Bennewitz did not have a doctorate degree] BENNEWITZ, Mr. MILLER, a GS-15 [a government service employee who was the Chief Scientific Advisor for Air Force Test and Evaluation Center at Kirtland] related the evidence clearly shows that some type of unidentified aerial objects were caught on film; however, no conclusions could be made whether the objects pose a threat to Manzano/Coyote Canyon areas. Mr. MILLER felt the electronical [sic] recording tapes were inconclusive and could have been gathered from several conventional sources. No sightings, other than these, have been reported in the area.[2]

Bennewitz was invited out to Kirtland to present his evidence to a small group of officers and scientists. Apparently, this meeting didn't go well, because Doty told Bennewitz a week later that AFOSI was no longer interested in his sightings and recordings.[3]

The problem could have ended there, but it didn't. Bennewitz, apparently unhappy with these results, communicated with New Mexico senator Harrison Schmitt, who asked AFOSI what they planned to do about Bennewitz's rather bizarre allegations. Schmitt, learning that no investigation was planned, called Brigadier General William Brooksher to ask him about it. While Schmitt was convinced by that conversation that there was no reason to continue the investigation, Bennewitz was not, so he reached out to New Mexico's other senator, Peter Domenici. Domenici talked first with Agent Doty and then with Bennewitz himself and promptly lost interest. Clearly Doty said something that suggested that Bennewitz was either off target or had stumbled onto a highly classified project that could be compromised. Either way, Domenici was convinced that further pursuit was problematic. Doty, a representative of AFOSI, had managed to derail Bennewitz's inquiry.

At about this same time or perhaps a little earlier, writer and UFO researcher William Moore was busy promoting his book about the Roswell UFO crash. He agreed to appear on a radio show in Albuquerque and, on his way out of the studio, was told by the receptionist that he had a telephone call from someone who identified himself as Kirtland personnel. Intrigued, Moore arranged to meet at a nearby restaurant with the caller, who turned out to be Richard Doty. This put AFOSI smack in the middle of another investigation about UFOs.[4]

When they met, Doty claimed to have great inside knowledge of UFOs. He admitted that he had interviewed Bennewitz about his UFO discoveries and declared that he wanted them investigated. Bennewitz believed that the proper agency to take on this investigation would be the Air Force, given the history of Project Blue Book.

Moore claims that he was then recruited to assist AFOSI in their ongoing investigations of Bennewitz and UFOs, and that Doty promised that, in return, he would be given access to highly classified information about UFOs that would turn the world on its head. Not only had alien bodies been recovered near Roswell, as Moore believed at the time, but, in 1949, an alien creature had been captured and housed at Los Alamos until it died in 1952. Moore said:

> In early September, 1980, I was approached by a well-placed individual within the intelligence community who claimed to be directly connected to a high-level government project dealing with UFOs. This individual, who subsequently came to be known as "the Falcon," told me that he spoke for a small group of similar individuals who were uncomfortable with the government's continuing cover-up of the truth and indicated that he and his group would like to help me with my research into the subject in the hope and expectation that I might be able to help them find a way to change the prevailing policy and get the facts to the public without breaking any laws in the process. I knew I was being recruited, but at that point I had no idea for what. In any case, I was told that if I was interested in cooperating with their group, I would be further contacted by a liaison man and that future meetings between me and "the Falcon" would be arranged by this person. The liaison person who subsequently made contact with me was AFOSI agent Richard Doty—a man who has since become quite controversial in his own right and who many people have mistakenly assumed is "the Falcon" himself.[5]

As Moore explained at MUFON's annual symposium held in Las Vegas in 1989:

> As for myself, I made a decision a number of years ago as a result of having suddenly found myself face-to-face with an

opportunity to learn more about what our government knows about UFOs. I believed then, and I continue to believe now, that it is possible to uncover answers by searching carefully and completely for them in the right places. Finding those answers and thus ending my so-called career as a UFOlogist poses no problems at all for me. As a writer, I am interested in a variety of subjects, many of them non-UFO related. Should I go as far as I feel I can with the UFO question, I have plenty of other fish to fry—many of which are just as interesting and every bit as challenging.

In any case, it was "Falcon" who sought me out in September of 1980, and it was Richard Doty, then with AFOSI at Kirtland AFB, who soon came into play as the middle-man in that process. Shortly thereafter, it became apparent to me that my supplying information to the government, through Doty, on the activities of Paul Bennewitz, APRO, and, to a lesser extent, several other individuals, was to be a part of this equation. I also discovered that, whatever it was Bennewitz was involved with, he was the subject of considerable interest on the part of not one but several government agencies, and that they were actively trying to defuse him by pumping as much disinformation through him as he could possibly absorb. Being a very small part of that process gave me, I thought, something of an advantage. It became my intention to play that advantage for all the information I could get out of it.[6]

Note here that Moore suggests that he was operating as an agent of AFOSI, albeit an unpaid civilian informant.

Not only had Moore been recruited to spy on Bennewitz, he was apparently asked to surveille other unnamed individuals and APRO as well. The latter would have been simple for him, because he had been appointed to their Board of Directors. APRO, of course, was interested in UFOs, and it had a more liberal policy about them that included research into sightings of alien creatures and alien abduction. Moreover, Moore also suggests that other agencies were involved in this convoluted plot. The information Moore gathered was being sent to Doty and also to other unnamed agencies, which certainly included the CIA and the NSA. And that moves us beyond AFOSI and into the Deep State.

While it can be argued that AFOSI had a legitimate reason to investigate Bennewitz, spying on APRO and other unnamed individuals was not part of its responsibility. In his speech in Las Vegas, Moore confirmed these points, telling the assembled UFO researchers:

> During this time, the only awareness I had of Bennewitz and his work was what I was obtaining through APRO. I still had not met the man, and in fact was only mildy (sic) interested in the case—this based largely upon both Jim and Coral Lorenzen's assessment of Bennewitz as a dedicated researcher, but, unfortunately, one who was, as Jim put it, "prone to make great leaps of logic on the basis of incomplete data." Both Jim and Coral felt that Bennewitz had already decided what he was going to find before he went looking for it. Still, although I didn't come to know about it until a few months later, there apparently was something going on involving UFOs near Manzano, particularly during August, September and October of 1980, and several agencies of the U. S. government, including the Air Force Office of Special Investigation, seemed more than just casually interested in it.[7]

Under this working arrangement, Moore began to pass disinformation to Bennewitz. According to an interview with Jerry Clark in 1990, one of these documents, which became known as the Aquarius Telex, was something Doty claimed to have gotten right off the teletype, meaning right out of the classified communications center at Kirtland. Doty showed it to Moore, but didn't let him have a copy of it at that point. The telex would become important later in understanding how AFOSI operated in this disinformation campaign.

The Aquarius Telex was allegedly sent from AFOSI headquarters at Bolling Air Force Base near Washington, D. C. to the 17th District AFOSI Office at Kirtland. Dated November 17, 1980, it contained an analysis of negatives from a UFO film that had originally been classified as "secret." The telex was given to Moore by Doty to be passed along to Bennewitz, which puts AFOSI, once again, in the middle of a UFO investigation—or rather in the middle of a disinformation campaign about a UFO investigation. This alleged secret message was written in all capital letters:

> USAF NO LONGER PUBLICALLY ACTIVE IN UFO RESEARCH, HOWEVER USAF STILL HAS INTEREST IN ALL UFO SIGHTINGS OVER USAF INSTALLATIONS/ TEST RANGES, SEVERAL OTHER GOVERNMENT AGENCIES, LED BY NASA, ACTIVELY INVESTIGATES [sic] LEGITIMATE SIGHTINGS THROUGH COVERT COVER . . . ONE SUCH COVER IS UFO REPORTING CENTER, US COAST AND GEODETIC SURVEY, ROCKVILLE, MD 20852. NASA FILTERS RESULTS OF SIGHTINGS TO APPROPRIATE MILITARY DEPARTMENTS WITH INTEREST IN THAT PARTICULAR SIGHTING. THE OFFICIAL US GOVERNMENT POLICY AND RESULTS OF PROJECT AQUARIUS IS [sic] OUTSIDE OFFICIAL INTELLIGENCE CHANNELS AND WITH RESTRICTED ACCESS TO "MJ TWELVE"[8] [The reference to MJ-12 will become important later].

This clearly establishes the connection between AFOSI, Doty, and Moore, because Moore received the document from Doty. It also establishes AFOSI as an agency of disinformation connected to UFO investigations because, as it turns out, the document was a retype of a legitimate classified message with the mention of MJ-12 added to prompt an investigation into a mythical committee that was allegedly created to oversee the Roswell UFO crash research. The Aquarius Telex, which begins this particular disinformation campaign, marks not only Bennewitz and Moore as its targets, but APRO and other UFO researchers as well. And this is what Moore was claiming in his 1989 MUFON speech.

Later, when Doty provided a copy of the telex for Moore to give to Bennewitz, Moore noticed that changes had been made to it. NSA had been changed to NASA, and mention of the U. S. Coast and Geodetic Survey had been added. This led Moore to speculate that what he was seeing had been retyped from a real classified message. Worried that AFOSI would close down his access to inside information if he refused to cooperate, Moore agreed to slip the message to Bennewitz, but then held on to it for several weeks. Finally, under pressure from Doty—and, indirectly, from AFOSI—he handed the telex over to Bennewitz.[9]

According to Moore, there were three copies of the Aquarius Telex in existence by September, 1982. Moore had given one to Bennewitz and he held the other two—one in his safe and the other in his briefcase. He later claimed that his briefcase was stolen and that the copy in it ended up in the hands of a New York attorney named Peter Gersten. There is no evidence, however, that Gersten had a hand in the theft.

After questions about the authenticity of the Aquarius Telex began to circulate inside the UFO community, the late Richard Hall, of the Fund for UFO Research (FUFOR), confronted Moore about it in 1989. According to Hall, Moore admitted that he had retyped the memo and pasted on the headings, because the original was too poor to read. He said that he had not added anything to the text, but was just trying to improve the document so that it would be useful as an illustration of MJ-12's activities and tend to validate the information that was leaking out to the public. But Moore never offered access to the original telex to prove this version of his story.[10]

Later, he denied that he had retyped the document. All that is irrelevant, however, because nearly everyone agrees that the Aquarius Telex is a fake. When MJ-12 is discussed, few mention it.[11] The real point is that the document provides important insight into the disinformation plans of Doty and AFOSI.

Doty's campaign against Bennewitz went beyond the creation of bogus UFO documents, however. He began to draw attention away from the actual secret installations in the Albuquerque area and planted the idea that there was an underground base near the small New Mexico town of Dulce. There was talk of human body parts stored there in vats and reports that alien abductions were associated with the collection of those parts. There was even a rumor that a murder had taken place during a UFO sighting in New Mexico.

When Major William Cunningham and Air Force Sergeant Jonathan P. Lovette were on the White Sands Missile Range searching for debris from a rocket test, they became separated by some distance. Then Cunningham heard Lovette scream. Believing that Lovette had been bitten by a snake, Cunningham rushed to find him. What he found was that some sort of long, snake-like arm or tentacle had wrapped itself around Lovette's legs and was dragging him toward a hovering UFO. Lovette was pulled inside the saucer, which then rose into the sky. Cunningham ran back to his jeep to call for help. When base security arrived, however, they found nothing. Cunningham was taken to the hospital while other teams searched for the missing Lovette, whose naked, mutilated body was found ten miles from the alleged abduction site. To add to the mystery, the autopsy report suggested that all the blood had been drained from the body.

This rather dubious report was attributed to Bill English, whose claim of military service couldn't be confirmed. The important fact here, however, is that AFOSI promoted the story and suggested that it was authentic. It is unclear if this was meant to scare away UFO researchers, or to lead them down an investigative path that would produce no evidence or results. It didn't really matter to AFOSI—or, by extension, to the Deep State—as long as UFO research was side-tracked into non-productive paths.

Meanwhile, Doty's stories of an alien presence and of alien abductions continued to expand. One of these tales claimed that a live alien had been captured and was being held in Air Force, or rather government, control. According to Whitley Strieber:

> I interviewed Mr. Doty after his retirement, although he apparently told this story while on active duty as well. In my interview, Mr. Doty repeated the same tale that he has told many times, of the capture of a live alien, who, he said, was a mechanic or engineer aboard a UFO. This being, he continued, had not been able to talk till Air Force surgeons had rebuilt his vocal chords, which was done in 1949. He stated that he had seen videotapes of the alien and is the originator of the now-famous story that aliens like strawberry ice cream.

Bennewitz's mental stability began to suffer, but Doty continued his campaign. He broke into Bennewitz's house and supplied Moore with additional, horrific information to pass along. This led to Bennewitz's mental collapse and his family had to commit him to a mental institution in August 1988. When he seem to recover after about a month, his family removed him from the facility and began an effort to shield him from information related to UFOs and alien communcations. So the plan to stop Bennewitz's UFO research was successful. Bennewitz was out of UFO research and, according to his family, a much happier man for it. Bennewitz died in 2003.

THE HOWE SAGA

Doty and AFOSI and their Deep State allies weren't through with their disinformation campaign against UFO investigators, however. Linda Moulton Howe stumbled into their clutches when Home

Box Office (HBO) executives, who were impressed by her animal mutilation documentary called *Strange Harvest*, approached her in 1983 and asked her to produce a documentary on UFOs.[12] While in New York to sign the contract, Howe had dinner with attorney Peter Gersten, who had had his hand in the MJ-12 story almost from the beginning and who later sued the government in an attempt to shake loose classified UFO-related files. The two met with Pat Huyghe, a science writer with an interest in UFOs. Huyghe and Dennis Stacy had worked together at Anomalist Books to publish materials about UFOs, strange happenings, and the paranormal.

Gersten apparently told Howe about an AFOSI agent named Richard Doty who claimed to have some very interesting inside information, and who might be willing to talk about UFO events on camera. He implied that Doty's information could establish the credibility of various UFO reports and that he even had access to a film that he could make available for the documentary. Gersten offered to set up a meeting if Howe was interested. Given what Gersten had said, she was, of course, very interested.[13] When Doty agreed to a meeting, Howe flew to Albuquerque to meet him.

According to the story, some sort of mix up at the airport kept the two from meeting as planned. Fortunately, Howe knew an officer at Kirtland and called him for help. The officer reached Doty, and the two finally got together. This whole episode sounds like a high school drama rather than a meeting scheduled between two adult professionals. But then, a great deal of this story sounds as if it was written by a Hollywood hack who didn't understand the workings of the military, the intelligence community, or the field of UFO research. Whatever really happened, a new meeting was arranged and the two agreed to get together at Kirtland.

Once at Kirtland, Doty took Howe to "his boss' office," seating her in a specific chair because "eyes can see through windows,"[14] implying that some sort of surveillance might be attempted. Howe came to believe that she was placed there so that hidden microphones could pick up her voice as they talked. Regardless of which is true, the real point here is that this meeting connects AFOSI to yet another disinformation campaign intended to divert attention from spaceship retrievals and secret government research projects. The location of the meeting and the identities of those involved also hints at a higher level of interest in this—which, of course, implies that the Deep State had a hand in the arrangements.

The meeting began with Doty telling Howe: "My superiors have asked me to show you this." He took an envelope from a drawer, opened it, and handed Howe several sheets of paper that were headed *A Briefing for the President of the United States on the Subject of Unidentified Flying Vehicles.* Since there was no date on the report and no president was named anywhere in the text, Howe had no way of knowing when or for whom the report had been prepared. But that doesn't matter here. What matters is that this was supposed to be a briefing prepared for a president. Doty then warned Howe that she could not copy the document or make notes about it. All she could do was read it. These instructions are themselves suspect and seem intended only to add more melodrama for those who don't understand how to deal with classified material.

The document Howe read mentioned the 1947 Roswell crash, as well as another that occurred near Roswell in 1949. It claimed that bodies of an alien crew, described as small, gray, and humanoid, had been recovered from both. It also suggested that an alien survived one of these crashes and was taken to a "safe house" at Los Alamos National Laboratory, north of Santa Fe, where it was befriended by an Air Force officer. The alien died on June 18, 1952—a nice detail that provides nothing in the way of verifiable evidence.

The document also mentioned other crashes—including the 1953 Kingman, Arizona incident; the 1948 Aztec, New Mexico crash; and the 1950 Del Rio, Texas event—and claimed that bodies from each of these accidents were removed and sent to various military and government facilities for study. The metallic wreckage was apparently transported to Wright-Patterson Air Force Base for in-depth analysis and attempts at reverse engineering. None of this information was new to Howe. Most of it had been circulating inside the UFO community for years and some of it had come from Bill Moore through Richard Doty, although it is unclear whether Moore told Doty about these events or whether Doty mentioned them first. Some speculate that Moore was the original source and that Doty was merely repeating what he had picked up during his conversations with Moore.

It is important to note that the other crashes mentioned in the document were all thought to be hoaxes by most in the UFO community. Only one or two witnesses came forward for each of the events and their credibility was in question. The Del Rio crash, for example, was reported by Robert Willingham, who claimed to be a retired Air Force colonel who had been a fighter pilot during part of his tour. His military records do not reflect this, however. Willingham spent thirteen months in the Army at the end of World War II and left the service as a low-ranking enlisted soldier.[15] There is no indication that he was ever a pilot in the Air Force, or even any independent corroboration that he ever served in the Air Force.

According to Howe, the document also mentioned various classified projects like Project Snowbird, Project Sigma, and Project Aquarius, as well as one called Project Garnet whose mission was to investigate alien influences on human evolution. It hinted that Nordic-looking aliens known as "Talls" or "Blonds" were engaged in a 300-year war against the "Grays," who were also mentioned in the report as being responsible for some Earth-based violence, including the cattle mutilations reported in many parts of the United States. There seemed to be no reason for mentioning these mutilations, except that Howe had been investigating similar events for a number of years.

The document further suggested that Project Blue Book was a public-relations operation intended to divert attention from real investigative projects. Doty mentioned MJ-12, but suggested that MJ stood from "Majority," claiming that it was a committee of twelve high-ranking government officials, scientists, and military officers who set the policy for covering up alien visitation and disseminating disinformation about UFOs and the government's interest in them.

There is no reason to reject Howe's version of these events. What she reported about her interactions with Doty and the trouble that ensued from them was similar to what Moore had reported about the inside workings of "real" UFO investigations. The common thread that ran between Moore's experience and Howe's was Richard Doty and what he told them about his role as an agent of AFOSI—which was supported by his office on Kirtland and the credentials he held, confirming yet another aspect of AFOSI and Deep State duplicity.

Doty had promised to provide Howe with film that would prove that alien visitation was real, claiming there were thousands of feet of film of crashed saucers, disks, bodies, and landings like the one at Holloman in 1964, which seems to indicate yet another Deep State disinformation campaign.[16] He also promised her footage of the creature that had survived one of the New Mexico crashes and its interaction with Air Force officers and various scientists. All of this was sure to prove to a disbelieving world that alien visitation was real. Then Doty went even further, saying that she might be allowed to meet with and film a third alien that was in the custody of the U. S. government, suggesting that there was something very strange about the alien.

HBO was somewhat cautious, however, and Howe was worried about possible legal fallout from these revelations, especially if Doty was exceeding his authority with his promises. To protect themselves, HBO representatives insisted on a "letter of intent" from the government with a legally binding commitment to release the promised film. Doty, when told about these requirements, said he would work on it. He suggested that it might take as long as three months for the films he had promised to be released, claiming that some sort of review process was needed, but that approval would be forthcoming. He promised to mail the letter directly to HBO when everything was arranged. Sensing some sort of trap, HBO executives said they would not release any production funds for the documentary until the highest officials in the government had backed up Doty's claims. They suggested that Howe go ahead for the time being, however, because the project was fascinating and could be one of the biggest stories of the 20th century.

Doty then told Howe that she and a small crew would be allowed to interview the retired colonel who had befriended the first alien survivor, but that she would be required to sign security oaths and undergo a background check before anything could be filmed. This all began to sound more and more like a stall to both Howe and HBO. After all, no matter how highly classified the material was, the stated purpose of the documentary was to release it to the public. So what point was there to background checks and security oaths? Delays piled up and interviews were repeatedly scheduled and then cancelled. And after several months, Doty left AFOSI, which complicated the problem, because he was the only one with whom Howe had dealt directly. In March 1984, after weeks of not hearing from anyone, Howe was contacted by a man who told her that the project would be delayed again until after the presidential election, but by then it had ceased to matter because her HBO contract had expired.

Here is the take-away from all this. Doty, an AFOSI agent, showed Howe documents that supposedly proved that alien visitation was real. He met her on Kirtland Air Force Base and promised to provide what was alleged to be highly classified information as well as thousands of feet of UFO footage that could prove the case for alien visitation beyond all doubt. But somehow, none of this ever materialized. Ultimately, Doty was transferred and Howe was left to deal with others who made similar promises but refused to reveal their identity. They strung her along until the HBO project was dead in the water and then they all disappeared—until she received one last call delaying everything until after the presidential election.

All this tells us that Doty wasn't a rogue AFOSI agent running a marginal operation. There were others involved who wrapped the whole operation in a cloak of supposed legitimacy and ultimately killed the documentary. This seems like a lot of trouble to go to to stop a single UFO documentary that would have aired only on a premium cable channel. Without the promised interviews and footage, it would have been just another UFO documentary that made some interesting claims but failed to provide convincing evidence that UFOs were really alien spacecraft flying around the Earth.

But the coordination for this operation occurred at a much higher level than Richard Doty. He had no reason to delay Howe's project. His directions had to have come from a higher echelon of government and probably originated outside the Air Force chain of command. In other words, someone in the Deep State or someone in the CIA or one of the other alphabet agencies didn't want Howe making a UFO documentary. And they did just enough to kill it without revealing their interest in it. Doty was merely a dupe charged with carrying out a campaign that he had no authority to initiate.

MJ-12

On March 1, 1989, Robert Hastings sent a thirteen-page report, along with thirty-seven pages of attachments, to many in the UFO community. Although his purpose was to show that the MJ-12 documents that had been circulating among researchers since 1984 were bogus, he also established, once again, the involvement of AFOSI in the disinformation campaign developed to divert UFO researchers onto paths that would lead nowhere. Hastings wrote:

> First, it has been established that "Falcon," one of the principle [sic] sources of the MJ-12 material, is Richard C. Doty, formerly attached to District 17 Air Force Office of Special

Investigations (AFOSI) at Kirtland Air Force Base, Albuquerque, New Mexico. Sgt. Doty retired from the U.S. Air Force on October 1, 1988.

How do I [Hastings] know that Doty is "Falcon"? During a recent telephone conversation, Linda Moulton Howe told me that when Sgt. Doty invited her to his office at Kirtland AFB in early 1983, and showed her a purportedly authentic U.S. government document on UFOs, he identified himself as code-name "Falcon" and stated that it was Bill Moore who had given him that name.

Also, in early December 1988, a ranking member of the production team responsible for the "UFO Cover-Up? – Live" television documentary confirmed that Doty is "Falcon."[17]

Of course, both Doty and Moore denied that Doty was Falcon, saying that he had been given the code name after meeting with Howe. Although this confirms that Doty and Moore had been working together at some point, it doesn't actually clarify their working relationship. In fact, Moore admitted that Howe had been the victim of a disinformation campaign hatched by Doty in cooperation with AFOSI and the Deep State.

In his 1989 speech in Las Vegas, Moore said that other people and organizations had been targeted as well—or, as he put it: "were the subject of intelligence community interest between 1980 and 1984."[18] These included Leonard H. Stringfield, Peter Gersten, Larry Fawcett, and Jim and Coral Lorenzen (of APRO). All were respected figures in the UFO community who were important to continuing UFO research. This suggests that the disinformation campaigns had been directed at these people specifically to discredit them and their research.

It is interesting that the MJ-12 documents that allege a top-secret committee created to control information about the UFO crash at Roswell may have come from Moore, but there is also good evidence that Doty may have been directly involved in this part of the plan as well. This moves MJ-12 from a hoax perpetrated by a civilian for private gain into the realm of AFOSI and, indirectly, into the realm of the Deep State.

The plan to divert UFO research into unprofitable paths was ultimately successful. Thirty or more years and thousands of dollars were wasted trying to verify the MJ-12 information. And while that was going on, research into other areas that might have proved fruitful was either reduced or ignored.

CONCLUSION

From the very beginning of the modern era of UFO sightings, the truth has been hidden by government agencies—from the super-secret Deep State to the more public AFOSI. The evidence for this has been obscured by overly zealous civilian UFO researchers who have missed the clues, and government agents whose job it was to keep everyone off balance. Anything that maintained the status quo was deemed acceptable, and anything that might expose the truth was buried as deeply as possible.

It is only recently, with the advent of FOIA and the declassification of thousands of UFO-related documents, that we have been able to learn some of the truth. The first of these truths is that AFOSI had a role in keeping eyewitnesses silent. Many of these witnesses were military personnel who experienced some sort of encounter with UFOs and whose reports came to the attention of authorities. This is what happened when people like Terry Lovelace, Jim Penniston, and John Burroughs were subjected to interrogations that would have been more appropriate for terrorists.

Penniston described chemical regressions performed by AFOSI agents and told of other civilians who used intimidation and a misapplication of military regulations to force his silence. John Burroughs, along with every other enlisted man and woman involved at Rendlesham Forest, found his life turned upside down as AFOSI worked to bury the truth about what he had seen. Personnel were transferred in the attempt to ensure their silence and to prevent them from discussing events.

We need only look back at the Roswell UFO crash to see that plan at work. After Thomas Gonzales, then an NCO at Roswell, witnessed alien bodies being transported to the base, his position at Roswell was radically altered. He was ordered off the base and transferred to another installation thousands of miles away. Why? To keep him from talking with his fellow soldiers about what he had seen. It was only decades later that Gonzales told Don Ecker and me what he had witnessed. By September 1947, nearly everyone who had been involved in any way in the retrieval operation at Roswell had been scattered to other bases around the world.

While it is true that, in 1947, there was no AFOSI, it is also true that there *was* an Army Counterintelligence Corps (CIC). We know, based on the testimony of those who were there in 1947, that soldiers were sworn to secrecy and reminded about the penalties for breaking security—fines and imprisonment for sharing what they had seen and done with those not cleared for the information. Nor were these CIC activities, and later those of AFOSI, isolated incidents, as we have seen. There were literally dozens of witnesses to the semi-legal activities that took place at Roswell. Many of them refused to talk to us even decades after the fact because of those threats. In the words of Edwin Easley: "I can't tell you that. I was sworn to secrecy."

We have also seen how AFOSI engaged in deception to suppress information. Linda Howe found herself caught up in a program designed to feed her disinformation and delay her work on an HBO documentary until her contract expired. An NCO known to be associated with AFOSI met with her at Kirtland and told her about UFO crashes and promised her film of those events, as well as testimony from those directly involved in them. In the end, neither the film nor the testimony ever materialized. Since that time, we have learned that many of the events described to Howe were hoaxes and that some of the same disinformation was fed into the UFO community to divert their limited resources into dead-end research or to discredit UFO researchers. UFO researchers have been chasing the whole MJ-12 deception for decades. Much of this disinformation can be traced back to Kirtland and to AFOSI. In fact, Bill Moore and Richard Doty produced enough disinformation to tie up resources and researchers for more than thirty years.

The evidence presented here is based on testimony and documentation that are now in the hands of UFO researchers and the public. It proves that this disinformation program was administered at the highest levels of the U. S. government and the Deep State. When researchers got too close to an important case, AFOSI intervened. The sightings by William Rhodes, Nick Mariana, and those made at Levelland, Texas all prove this assertion. And both Rhodes and Mariana were smeared by those working on the inside. But AFOSI's activities pale beside the programs designed and executed by the Deep State. These programs employed scientists and federal bureaucrats who worked at the highest levels of government to keep the secret tucked away. Both the 1953 Robertson Panel and the 1969 Condon Committee are examples of this.

The Deep State moved quickly to bury the 1952 Washington National sightings under clouds of disinformation. The press conference held by General Samford was a sham. We know this because those providing "testimony" were *not* technicians who had been in the radar rooms, or pilots who had been flying the commercial airplanes or the Air Force fighters. All those involved in the press conference had, in fact, been sitting at home at the time of the incidents. But once the temperature-inversion theory was floated, the press grabbed on to it as a way to explain the mistakes made by all those observers. This is clear confirmation of Deep State manipulation of the national media.

In fact, the *stated purpose* of the Robertson Panel was to reduce public interest in UFOs. They suggested an "education" program designed to mislead the public and convince them that UFOs were not alien spacecraft and were no more real than Santa Claus. They also suggested that teachers discourage student research into UFOs and reject projects dealing with them. Students who showed an interest in UFOs would receive poor grades and ridicule if they pursued that interest. Project Blue Book, which had tried to investigate UFOs scientifically in the early 1950s, became a propaganda tool intended to end discussion of them altogether. Cases weren't investigated, sightings were ignored, and witnesses were treated like illiterate fools. If this happens often enough, those who see something truly extraordinary won't come forward about what they've seen. Discouraging people from talking about sightings and ridiculing those who do is probably the best way to destroy any interest in UFO phenomena.

The activities of the Deep State are made clear in the creation and conduct of the Robertson Panel. The panel was packed with scientists who had no interest in reviewing UFO phenomena in a dispassionate way. Their bias can be seen in the sarcasm they directed at other researchers. Moreover, it is clear from the timing and discussions that the panel's final report was created *before* their first session was even scheduled. Given the prestige of those on the panel, the only way that could have happened is if the Deep State, working through the CIA, was running the show.

But the history of the Condon Committee is even more egregious. We have seen evidence here of the communication that occurred between members of the committee and the Air Force. Lieutenant Colonel Robert Hippler wrote to Condon giving him his marching orders: Comment positively on the Air Force investigation, deny that national security is an issue, and recommend that Project Blue Book be closed. Not long after that communication, Condon told scientists in New York that there was nothing to the UFO sightings, but that he wasn't supposed to come to that conclusion for another eighteen months. Condon clearly understood the real purpose of his investigation and that the Deep State was pulling the strings.

When Jimmy Carter campaigned for president, he made it clear that one of the first things he would do was to learn all he could about UFOs. While still president-elect, he met with CIA Director George H. W. Bush and asked him to pass along everything the CIA had on the subject. When Carter told Bush he would be bringing in his own man to head the CIA, however, Bush refused to release the information. Bush couldn't have done this without cooperation from the Deep State. His reward was apparently the vice-presidency under Reagan, and then his own term as president. And remember that Carter never revealed anything about UFOs. He pushed for information, made inquiries at the highest levels, and even consulted the Vatican. But he never revealed what he learned. The pressure brought to bear by the Deep State was clearly sufficient either to end Carter's push for information or to buy his silence. Bill Clinton, who might have pushed harder, found himself facing impeachment.

This manipulation by the Deep State—aided by the military, and especially by AFOSI—explains why, after more than seventy years of investigation, we still argue about the reality of UFOs. Evidence has been suppressed, witnesses have been intimidated or ridiculed, and scientists who know nothing about the topic have explained to us that alien visitation is a myth. We are never given a fair review of the data, but see only parts of it. We are lied to about other parts of the evidence and find some of it hidden behind a wall of secrecy, all while being told there is nothing to it. And the only reason the Deep State could have for hiding this information is that they fear they might lose their power. It is always about power.

Had the investigation of UFOs been carried out in a timely fashion and in a competent way by unbiased researchers or governmental officials, the discussion might have evolved differently. Rather than arguing about the reality of interstellar travel, we might be discussing the best way to accomplish it. Rather than planning for a mission to Mars, we might be planning a flight into deep space to another star system. But the Deep State cannot face the possibility of contact with a technologically advanced civilization, because, as we have seen, when a technologically advanced civilization contacts one that is technologically inferior, the less-advanced civilization ceases to exist. We lament its passing and acknowledge its contributions, but it is still gone, overwhelmed by technology that it couldn't understand.

And this is why—after so many years, and with so many of us no longer fearing the possibility of alien visitation—we still don't have any concrete answers. The Deep State knows that the introduction of advanced alien technology, or even the admission that this technology exists, would break the stranglehold they have on our world. So they keep the secret. And they enforce that secrecy. Why? Because they know that to do otherwise will result in the evaporation of their power.

Index of Acronyms and Agencies

AAF—Army Air Forces

AC/AS—Assistant Chiefs of Air Staff

ADC—Air Defense Command

AFOSI—Air Force Office of Special Investigations, sometimes referred to simply as OSI

AISS—Air Intelligence Service Squadron

AMC—Air Materiel Command

APRO—Aerial Phenomena Research Organization

ARTC—Air Routing and Traffic Control Center

ATC—Air Tactical Command

ATIC—Air Technical Intelligence Center

CAA—forerunner of the Federal Aviation Administration (FAA)

CIC—Counterintelligence Corps

Condon Committee—a University of Colorado UFO project funded by the United States Air Force from 1966 to 1968 under the direction of physicist Edward Condon

CSC—Center for Security Control

CUFOS—Center for UFO Studies

DATT/AIRA—Defense Attaché/Air Attaché

DCI—Director of Central Intelligence

DIA— Defense Intelligence Agency that provides military intelligence to officials in the Department of Defense and the intelligence community

EMP—Electromagnetic pulse

EOTS—Estimate of the Situation

FOIA—Freedom of Information Act

Foo Fighters—strange lights and anomalies seen by flight crews during World War II for which no explanation has ever been found

FTD—Foreign Technology Division

FUFOR—Fund for UFO Research

Ghost Rockets—strange missiles that were reported first in Finland and later in Sweden, and then across most of northern Europe for which no explanation has ever been found, although some believed them to be of Soviet origin

Hangar 18—a fictional facility that has been linked to UFO activity

JANAP—Joint Army, Navy, Air Force Publication

LCF—launch control facility

LF—launch facility

MILABS—military abductions

MJ-12—misinformation put forward by AFOSI agent Richard Doty to misdirect civilian UFO researchers

MUFON—a U. S.–based nonprofit organization composed of civilian volunteers who study reported UFO sightings; one of the oldest and largest organizations of its kind

NACA—National Advisory Committee for Aeronautics, a federal agency founded in 1915 to undertake, promote, and institutionalize aeronautical research

NCOIC—noncommissioned officer in charge

NCO—noncommissioned officer

NEPA—National Environmental Policy Act, a 1969 law that promotes the enhancement of the environment

NICAP—National Investigations Committee on Aerial Phenomena

NMC—National Maritime Command

NNSOC—Naval Network and Space Operations Command

NORAD—North American Aerospace Defense Command

NSA—National Security Agency

ONR—Office of Naval Research

OOAMA—Office, Ogden Air Material Area

Operation Blue Fly—provides logistical support for Project Moon Dust

Project Blue Book—a systematic study of UFOs carried out by the Air Force from 1952 to 1969 to determine if UFOs were a threat to national security and to evaluate UFO-related data

Project Grudge—a short-lived USAF project established to investigate UFOs; it succeeded Project Sign in February 1949 and was then followed by Project Blue Book.

UFOS AND THE DEEP STATE

Project Mogul— the classified name of the project to spy on the Soviet Union. The experiments in New Mexico run by New York University were unclassified.

Project Moon Dust—a covert project to recover returning space debris of foreign manufacture or unknown origin

Project Sign (also known as Project Saucer)—an official Air Force study of UFOs that was active for most of 1948; its name was changed to Project Grudge in 1948.

Projects Snowbird, Sigma, Aquarius, and Garnet—disinformation put forward by AFOSI agent Richard Doty to mislead Linda Howe

RAAF—Roswell Army Air Field

Robertson Panel—a panel, whose official name was the Scientific Advisory Panel on Unidentified Flying Objects, convened in 1953 to investigation and manage UFO information

SAC—Strategic Air Command

SATAF—Site Activation Task Force

SAT—Site Alert Team

SETI—Search for Extraterrestrial Intelligence

STC—Self Test Command

UAO—Unidentified Aerial Object

UAP—Unidentified Aerial Phenomenon

UCMJ—Uniform Code of Military Justice

UFO—Unidentified Flying Object

ACKNOWLEDGMENTS

This book wouldn't exist if not for the influence and assistance of many people. When I first proposed it, the idea was to focus on the classified investigations of the Air Force Office of Special Investigations (AFOSI). I had suggested, as something of an afterthought, to address some of the influence that the Deep State had on these investigations. Michael Pye pointed out that most people wouldn't know what AFOSI was, and suggested that perhaps the emphasis should be on the Deep State with AFOSI playing a lesser role. It was a good idea, and one that I embraced.

In writing this book, I was able to interview a number of people about their roles in the world of the UFO. Terry Lovelace had written a book about his experiences with AFOSI after his UFO encounter. His experience was eye-opening and important and ultimately launched the idea that culminated in this work. The same can be said for my interviews with Charles Halt, Jim Penniston, and John Burroughs, who related their experiences in the Rendlesham Forest encounter. I also had the opportunity to speak with Dewey Fournet and Al Chop about the 1952 Washington National sightings. Michael Swords's in-depth analysis of the early history of the world of UFO phenomena and his analysis of the Robertson Panel was critical in understanding this period of UFO history.

I was lucky to speak with Daniel Sheehan, who provided wonderful insight into his work inside the Carter administration, and to George Knapp, who shared his insights into the UFO crash in

Needles, California just a few years ago. I also had the privilege of interviewing Sheridan and Mary Cavitt, Irving Newton, George "Jud" Roberts, Phyllis McGuire, Walter Haut, and literally dozens of others who put the Roswell case into proper perspective.

Finally, there were many people who provided leads, information, or necessary criticism—most anonymously. Much of this can be found on my blog at *www.kevinrandle.blogspot.com.* To them, I say thanks. And to those I have overlooked, I offer my thanks and my apologies as well.

BIBLIOGRAPHY

4602nd Unit History, available through the Air Force Archives.

500th Unit History for June and July 1947, available through the Air Force Archives.

"AF Intimidates Witnesses." *The U.F.O. Investigator*, March–April 1965.

"Air Force to Explain 'Saucers.'" *Detroit Free Press*, March 25, 1966.

Akers, Doyle. "Landing Region Checked." *Santa Fe New Mexican*, April 28, 1964.

"AP Wires Burn with 'Captured Disk' Story." *The Daily Illini*, July 9, 1947.

Archer, Jules. *The Plot to Seize the White House*. New York: Skyhorse Publishing, 2007.

Arnold, Kenneth, and Ray Palmer. *The Coming of the Saucers*. Amherst, WI: Ray Palmer, 1952.

Baker, Robert M. L., Jr. "Motion Pictures of UFOs" in *UFOs—A Scientific Debate*. Edited by Carl Sagan and Thornton Page. Ithaca, NY: Amherst University Press, 1972.

———. "Observational Evidence of Anomalist Phenomena." *Journal of the Astronautical Sciences* 15 (January/February 1968).

———. *Photogrammetric Analysis of the "Montana Film" Tracking Two UFOs*. Santa Monica, CA: Douglas Aircraft Company, 1956.

Barnes, Harry G. "Washington Radar Observer Relates Watching Stunts by Flying Saucers." *New York World Telegram*, July 29, 1952.

Barron, John. *Operation Solo: The FBI's Man in the Kremlin.* Washington, DC: Regnery Publishing, Inc. 1996.

Berliner, Don. "The Ghost Rockets of Sweden." *Official UFO* 1, no. 11 (October, 1976). Privately published.

"Blinding 'Flying Saucer' 'Stops' Texas Motorcars." *Indianapolis Star,* November 4, 1957.

Bloecher, Ted. *The Report on the UFO Wave of 1947.* Washington, DC: The author, 1967.

Brown, Harold. "C. A. A. Chief Debunks 'Objects,' Radar Probably Spotted Trucks." *New York Herald Tribune,* July 30, 1952.

Burleson, Donald. "Levelland, Texas, 1957: Case Reopened." *International UFO Reporter,* (Spring 2003): pp. 3–6, 25.

———. "Looking Up." *Roswell Daily Record, Vision Magazine,* May 3, 2002.

Cannon, Martin. "The Controllers, Part I." *The MUFON UFO Journal,* No. 270 (October 1990).

———. "The Controllers, Part II." *The MUFON UFO Journal,* No. 271 (November 1990).

Carey, Thomas J., and Donald R. Schmitt. *Witness to Roswell.* Pompton Plains, NJ: New Page Books, 2009.

Carmichael, Barbara A., FOIA Manager, letter to Clifford E. Stone, May 3, 1990.

"Credulity Unlimited." *The New York Times.* November 22, 1934.

Chester, Keith. *Strange Company: Military Encounters with UFOs in WW II.* San Antonio, TX: Anomalist Books, 2007.

Clark, Jerome. *UFO Encyclopedia, 3rd Edition.* Detroit: Omnigraphics. 2018.

Darin, Paul. "The Solar Warden Covert Space Project: Fact or Science Fiction?" *Epoch Times,* February 17, 2015.

Dickinson, Terence. "The Zeta Reticuli Incident." AstroMedia Group, *Astronomy Magazine,* 1976.

"Did the Air Force Deceive the Public About the November Sightings? *NICAP UFO Investigator.* 1, no. 3 (January 1958): pp. 1, 3–4.

Dolan, Richard. *UFOs and the National Security State.* Charlottesville, VA: Hampton Roads Publishing Company, Inc., 2002.

"Evidence of UFO Landing Observed." *El Defensor-Chieftain* [Socorro, New Mexico], April 28, 1964.

Fawcett, Lawrence, and Barry Greenwood. *Clear Intent: The Government Coverup of the UFO Experience.* Englewood Cliffs, NJ: Prentice Hall, 1984.

Fenstermacher, Bruce. Testimony for the Citizen Hearing, May 2013.

"Flying Object Expert Checks Socorro Scene." *Albuquerque Tribune,* April 29, 1964.

"Flying Saucer Puts La Madera on Map." *Las Vegas Review-Journal,* January 7, 1970.

"'Flying Saucer' Reports Spread in New Mexico." *Albuquerque Journal,* April 28, 1964.

Friedman, Stan, and Don Berliner. *Crash at Corona.* New York: Paragon House, 1992.

Friedman, Stanton T. *Top Secret/MAJIC.* New York: Marlowe & Co., 1996.

Fuller, John G. *The Interrupted Journey.* New York: Dial Press, 1966.

"Gen. Butler Bares a 'Fascist Plot.'" *The New York Times,* 1, November 21, 1934.

Gillmor, Daniel S. ed. *Scientific Study of Unidentified Flying Objects.* New York: Bantam Books, 1969.

Good, Timothy. *Above Top Secret.* New York: William Morrow & Co., 1988.

———. *Alien Contact: Top Secret UFO Files Revealed.* New York: William Morrow & Co., 1993.

Greenwood, Barry. "On the Question of Tampering with the 1950 Great Falls UFO Film," *UFO Historical Revue,* September 2000.

Hall, Michael. "Was There a Second Estimate of the Situation?" *International UFO Reporter* 27, 1 (Spring 2002).

———. "Alfred Loedding: New Insights on the Man Behind Project Sign." *International UFO Reporter* 23, 4 (Winter 1999).

Hall, Michael David, and Wendy Ann Connors. *Captain Edward J. Ruppelt: The Summer of the Saucers—1952.* Albuquerque, NM: Rose Press International, 2000.

———. "Michigan Sheriffs Watch High Performance Discs." Privately published, undated.

Hall, Richard, ed. *The UFO Evidence.* Washington, DC: NICAP, 1964.

Halperin, David J. *Intimate Alien: The Hidden Story of the UFO.* Stanford, CA: Stanford University Press, 2020.

Hanks, Micah. "The Gipper's UFO." *Mysterious Universe,* January 29, 2014.

Halt, Charles I., and John Hanson. *The Halt Perspective.* Great Britain: Haunted Skies Publishing, 2016.

———. "The MJ-12 Affair: Facts, Questions, Comments." Privately published, March 1, 1989.

Hastings, Robert. *UFOs and Nukes.* Bloomington, IN: AuthorHouse, 2008.

———. "UFOs Did Shutdown Minuteman Missiles at Echo and Oscar Flight at Malmstrom AFB in March 1967." Privately published, undated.

Holden, Richard T., signed report, Project Blue Book files, Roll no. 50.

Hollings, Alex. "The UFO Question: President Reagan Was Concerned about UFOS, and He Brought It Up to Gorbarchev," *https://sofrep. com,* January 2, 2019.

Huneeus, Antonio. "The Tarija Incident: A Full Report on the 1978 UFO Crash in Bolivia." Privately published, 1993.

———. "Report on the Dexter—Hillsdale, Michigan UFO Sightings of 20–21 March 1966." Project Blue Book files, Roll no. 60.

———. "Socorro Revisited." Statement in the Project Blue Book files.

Hynek, J. Allen. *The UFO Experience: A Scientific Enquiry.* Chicago: Henry Regency Company, 1972.

"Jets Alerted for 'Saucers.'" *Washington Times-Herald,* July 28, 1952.

Keyhoe, Donald E. *Flying Saucers from Outer Space.* New York: Henry Holt and Company, 1953.

———. *Flying Saucers: Top Secret.* New York: G. P. Putnam's Sons, 1960.

Klass, Philip J. *UFO Abductions: A Dangerous Game.* Buffalo, NY: Prometheus Books, 1989.

———. *UFOs Explained.* New York: Random House, 1974.

Knapp, George. Presentation at the 6th Annual UFO Crash Conference, November 7–9, 2006.

Lammer, Helmut. *https://www.zersetzung.org,* accessed January 23, 2020.

"Local Official Questions Objectivity of Scientist.*" Hillsdale Daily News,* March 26, 1966.

Lorenzen, Coral. *Flying Saucers: The Startling Evidence of the Invasion from Outer Space.* New York: New American Library, 1966.

———. "Incident at La Madera." *The APRO Bulletin,* July 1964.

———. "The Stull Case." *The APRO Bulletin,* May 1964.

Lorenzen, Coral, and Jim Lorenzen. *Encounters with UFO Occupants.* New York: Berkley Medallion Book, 1976.

Lovelace, Terry. *Incident at Devil's Den: A True Story.* Privately published, 2018.

Maccabee, Bruce. "UFO Information from the FBI File." *UFO Investigator,* January 1978.

Madison, Lt. Col. John E. Congressional Inquiry Division, Office of Legislative Liaison, letter to U. S. Senator Jeff Bingaman, 1992.

Maney, Charles, and Richard Hall, in *The Challenge of Unidentified Flying Objects.* Privately published, 1961.

Mattingley, Jr., Colonel George M. Chief, Congressional Inquiry Division, Office of Legislative Liaison, letter to U. S. Senator Jeff Bingaman, April 14, 1993.

McDonald, James E. *UFOs—An International Scientific Problem.* Tucson, AZ: Privately published, 1968.

"The Michigan Cases." *The APRO Bulletin,* March/April 1965.

Moore, William. Presentation at the MUFON Symposium 1989. Paper was not submitted in time for publication.

Nash, William B. "An Airline Captain Speaks Out." *UFO Investigator,* October–November 1962.

Nelson, David L. "Hynek Swamps It to Study UFO's Following Report." *Daily Northwestern,* March 29, 1966.

NICAP Report. *The Ufologist,* (1958).

"Object Falls in Bolivia." *The APRO Bulletin,* May, 1978.

Olive, Dick. "Most UFOs Explainable Says Scientist." *Elmira Star-Gazette,* January 26, 1967.

Peeples, Curtis. *Watch the Skies.* New York: Berkley Books, 1994.

Penniston, Jim, and Gary Olsen. *The Rendlesham Enigma: Book 1: Time-line.* Privately published, 2019.

Pflock, Karl. *Roswell: Inconvenient Facts and the Will to Believe.* Amherst, NY: Prometheus Books, 2001.

Pope, Nick, with John Burroughs and Jim Penniston. *Encounter in Rendlesham Forest.* New York: St. Martin's Press, 2014.

Price, Carolyn W. Assistant FOIA Manager, letter to Clifford E. Stone, January 11, 1990.

Project Blue Book Administrative Files.

Project Blue Book files, Rolls no. 1, 2, 7, 8, 10–14, 40, 43, 50, 54, 73, 85, 87.

Quintanilla, Hector. *UFOs, An Air Force Dilemma.* Privately published, 1974.

"Radar and the Saucers." *The Washington Post,* July 25, 1952.

"Radar Spots Air Mystery Objects Here." *The Washington Post,* July 22, 1952, p. 1.

———. *Encounter in the Desert.* Wayne, NJ: NewPage Books, 2018.

———. *Invasion Washington.* New York: HarperTorch, 2001.

Randle, Kevin D. *Roswell in the 21st Century*. Naples, FL: Speaking Volumes, 2016.

Redfern, Nick. "The Controversy of the 'Secret Space Program.' " *Mysterious Universe*, July 1, 2019.

"Rocket Craft Encounter Revealed by World War 2 Pilot." *NICAP The U.F.O. Investigator*, August–September, 1957: 15.

Rodeghier, Mark. *UFO Reports Involving Vehicle Interference*. Chicago: Center for UFO Studies.

Rothkopf, David. "The Shallow State." *Foreign Policy*, February 22, 2017.

Ruppelt, Edward. *The Report on Unidentified Flying Objects*. New York: Ace Books, Inc., 1956.

"Saucers Swarm over Capital." *Cedar Rapids Gazette*, July 27, 1952.

Schmidt, Hans. *The United States Occupation of Haiti, 1915–1934*. New Jersey: Rutgers University Press, 1995.

"Services Try to Stop 'Disc' Talk." *Dallas Times Herald*, July 9, 1947.

Sparks, Brad. "Al Hixenbaugh Film." *http://www.nicap.org*, accessed February 15, 2020.

Steiger, Brad, ed. *Project Blue Book*. New York: Ballentine Books, 1976.

Styles, Chris. "Shag Harbor in Perspective." MUFON 1996 International UFO Symposium Proceedings, 1996.

Swords, Michael, and Robert Powell. *UFOs and Government*. San Antonio, TX: Anomalist Books, 2010.

Thomas, David E. "A Different Angle on the Socorro UFO of 1964." *Skeptical Inquirer* 25, 4 (July/August 2001).

Thomas, Dick. "'Flying Saucers' in New Mexico." *Denver Post*, May 3, 1964.

Thompson, Colonel Phillip E. USAF, letter to Robert Todd, July 1, 1987.

"The Turkish Origins of the 'Deep State.'" *jstor.org*, April 10, 2017.

Turner, Karla. *Into the Fringe: A True Story of Alien Abduction*. New York: Create Space Publishing, 2014.

Twichell, David E., *Global Implications of the UFO Reality*. Haverford, PA: Infinity Publishing Co., 2003.

"UAO Landing in New Mexico," *The APRO Bulletin*, May 1964.

"UFO Hacker Tells What He Found." *https://www.wired.com*, accessed, February 18, 2020.

"UFO Sighting Re-Enacted; No Help to Scientist." *Albuquerque Journal*, April 30, 1964.

Vallee, Jacques. *Revelations*. New York: Ballantine Books, 1992.

"Washington Blips." *Life*, August 4, 1952: pp. 39–40.

Weaver, Colonel Richard, and Captain James McAndrew. *The Roswell Report*. Government Printing Office, 1995.

WITNESS INTERVIEWS

Baca, Rick, telephone interview with Kevin Randle, March 6, 2017.

Burroughs, John, interview with Kevin Randle, December 11, 2019.

Cavitt, Mary, personal interview with Kevin Randle and Don Schmitt, January 1990 and March 1993.

Cavitt, Sheridan, personal interview with Kevin Randle and Don Schmitt, January 1990 and March 1993.

Chop, Al, telephone interview with Kevin Randle, August 20, 1995.

Exon, Arthur, telephone interview with Kevin Randle, May 19, 1990; personal interview with Don Schmitt, June 1990.

Fournet, Dewey, telephone interview with Kevin Randle, July 17, 1995.

Halt, Charles, interviews with Kevin Randle, January 11, 2017 and November 20, 2019.

Haut, Walter, telephone interview with Kevin Randle, April 1, 1989.

Knapp, George, personal interview with Kevin Randle, November 8, 2006.

Lovelace, Terry, telephone interview with Kevin Randle, April 17, 2019.

Marano, Carmon, telephone interview with Kevin Randle.

McGuire, Phyllis, personal interviews with Kevin Randle and Don Schmitt, January 1990, July 1990, and November 1990.

Meinel, Aden, email correspondence with Kevin Randle, October 2010.

Newton, Irving, telephone interviews with Kevin Randle, March 1990 and January 1991.

Penniston, Jim, telephone interview with Kevin Randle, October 23, 2019.

Roberts, George "Jud," personal interviews with Kevin Randle and Don Schmitt, January 1990, September 1990, and January 1991.

Sheehan, Daniel, telephone interviews with Kevin Randle, January 17, 2020 and February 12, 2020.

Swords, Michael, telephone interview with Kevin Randle, August 7, 1995.

Sykes, Norman, video interview with HUFON (Fred Woods), March 1997.

NOTES

INTRODUCTION

1   See, for example, *The APRO Bulletin*, July–August, 1965, p. 1.

2   Jerome Clark, *UFO Encyclopedia, 3rd Edition* (Detroit: Omnigraphics, 2018), 170.

3   Edward J. Ruppelt, *The Report on Unidentified Flying Objects* (New York: Ace Books, 1956).

4   "The Turkish Origins of the 'Deep State,'" *jstor.org*, April 10, 2017.

5   Ibid.

6   Jules Archer, *The Plot to Seize the White House*, (New York: Skyhorse Publishing, 2007).

7   Ibid.

8   Ibid.

9   Ibid.

10   Hans Schmidt, *The United States Occupation of Haiti, 1915–1934* (NJ: Rutgers University Press, 1995).

11   "Gen. Butler Bares a 'Fascist Plot,'" (*The New York Times*, November 21, 1934).

12   "Credulity Unlimited." *The New York Times*, November 22, 1934.

13   Arthur Exon, telephone interview with Kevin Randle, May 19, 1990; personal interview with Don Schmitt, June 1990.

14   Project Blue Book files, Roll no. 1, Case 46.

15 Project Blue Book files, Roll no. 50, Case 8766.

16 See chapter 11 (Alien Abductions) and chapter 12 (Rendlesham Forest).

CHAPTER 1

1 The Air Force would not be created as a separate service until the National Securities Act went into effect in September 1947.

2 Kevin D. Randle and Donald R. Schmitt. *UFO Crash at Roswell.* (New York: Avon Books, 1991); Thomas J. Carey and Donald R. Schmitt. *Witness to Roswell.* (Pompton Plains, NJ: New Page Books, 2009); Kevin D. Randle *Roswell in the 21st Century.* (Naples, FL: Speaking Volumes, 2016); 500th Unit History for June and July 1947, available through the Air Force Archives; Sheridan Cavitt, personal interviews with Kevin Randle and Don Schmitt, January 1990 and March 1993.

3 The information presented here is a consensus of data gathered by various UFO investigators. Besides those mentioned above, see also, Karl Pflock, *Roswell: Inconvenient Facts and the Will to Believe,* (Amherst, NY: Prometheus Books, 2001); Stan Friedman and Don Berliner, *Crash at Corona,* (New York: Paragon House, 1992); Charles Berlitz and William L. Moore, *The Roswell Incident,* (New York: Grosset and Dunlop, 1980). For information from a source or sources that don't agree, the specific source will be noted.

4 Phyllis McGuire, personal interviews with Kevin Randle and Don Schmitt, January 1990, July 1990, and November 1990.

5 Carey and Schmitt, 2009; Randle, 2016.

6 Cavitt confirmed to Randle and Schmitt in a personal interview that the description sounded like him, but that he hadn't been out there. But in his interview with Colonel Richard Weaver, Cavitt said that he *had* been there. See Colonel Richard Weaver and Captain James McAndrew, *The Roswell Report,* (Government Printing Office, 1995), Section 18.

7   Randle and Schmitt. 1991.

8   Irving Newton, telephone interviews with Kevin Randle, March 1990 and January 1991.

9   Marcel, in various interviews, never discussed anything other than his first trip to the debris field.

10 Friedman and Berliner, 1992.

11 Mary Cavitt, personal interviews with Kevin Randle and Don Schmitt, January 1990 and March 1993.

12 Sheridan Cavitt, personal interview with Kevin Randle and Don Schmitt, January 1990.

13 "AP Wires Burn With 'Captured Disk' Story," *The Daily Illini*, July 9, 1947, p. 5.

14 George "Jud" Roberts, personal interviews with Kevin Randle and Don Schmitt, January 1990, September 1990, and January 1991.

15 Edwin Easley, telephone interviews with Kevin Randle, October 1989, February 1990, and May 1990.

16 Sheridan Cavitt, 1990.

17 Lewis "Bill" Rickett, personal interview with Don Schmitt and Stan Friedman, January 1990.

18 This wasn't exactly the truth. Easley had mentioned the creatures once to family members, and later told me that the craft was extra-terrestrial—not in so many words, however. When I asked if we were following the right path (meaning the extraterrestrial explanation), Easley said: "Well, it's not the wrong path."

19 Pflock, 2001.

20 Sheridan Cavitt, personal interview with Kevin Randle and Don Schmitt, June 1994.

21 Weaver and McAndrew, 1995.

22 Ibid.

23 Johnny Mann, personal interview with Kevin Randle.

24 Weaver and McAndrew, 1995.

25 Charles Moore, personal interview with Kevin Randle in Socorro, NM. See also Randle, 2016.

26 Crary's field notes appear in Weaver and McAndrew, 1995.

CHAPTER 2

1 Edward Ruppelt, *The Report on Unidentified Flying Objects* (New York: Ace Books, Inc., 1956).

2 Jerome Clark, *UFO Encyclopedia, 3rd Edition.* (Detroit: Omnigraphics. 2018).

3 Ruppelt, 1956.

4 Dr. Michael Swords and Robert Powell, *UFOs and Government* (San Antonio, TX: Anomalist Books, 2012).

5 Ibid.

6 Swords and Powell, 2012. Also, Project Blue Book files, Roll no. 2, numerous cases; Ted Bloecher, *The Report on the UFO Wave of 1947* (Washington, DC: Privately published, 1967); Bruce Maccabee, "UFO Information from the FBI File," *UFO Investigator,* January 1978, *http://nicap.org.*

7 Maccabee, 1978.

8 Project Blue Book administrative files, Roll no. 86.

9 Swords and Powell, 2012.

10 Keith Chester, *Strange Company* (San Antonio: Anomalist Books, 2007).

11 Clark, 2016; Don Berliner, "The Ghost Rockets of Sweden," *Official UFO* 1, no. 11, October, 1976.

12 Michael Hall and Wendy Connors "Alfred Loedding: New Insights on the Man behind Project Sign," *International UFO Reporter* 23, 4 (Winter 1999).

13 Swords and Powell, 2012.

14 Project Blue Book administrative files, Roll no. 87.

15   Clark, 2016.

16   Ruppelt, 1956.

17   Ibid.

18   Ibid. Swords and Powell, 2012. Michael Hall, "Was There a Second Estimate of the Situation?" *International UFO Reporter* 27,1 (Spring 2002).

19   Swords and Powell, 2012.

CHAPTER 3

1   Kevin Randle, *Invasion Washington* (New York: HarperTorch, 2001); Brad Steiger, *Project Blue Book.* (New York: Ballantine Books, 1976); Jerome Clark, *UFO Encyclopedia, 3rd Edition* (Detroit: Omnigraphics, 2018); Project Blue Book files, Rolls no. 10–14.

2   Randle, 2001.

3   Project Blue Book files, Rolls no. 10–14.

4   Randle, 2001.

5   Ibid.

6   Ibid.

7   Witness statements are found in the Project Blue Book files, Rolls no. 10–14.

8   Ibid.

9   Daniel S. Gillmor, *Final Report of the Scientific Study of Unidentified Flying Objects* (New York: Bantam Books, 1969).

10   Ibid.

11   Project Blue Book files, Rolls no. 10–14.

12   Al Chop, telephone interview with Kevin Randle, August 20, 1995.

13   Edward Ruppelt, *The Report on Unidentified Flying Objects* (New York: Ace Books, Inc., 1956).

14   Chop interview, 1995.

15 Ibid.

16 Ibid.

17 Ruppelt, 1956; Randle, 2001; Project Blue Book files, Rolls no. 10–14.

18 Randle, 2001.

19 Chop interview, 1995.

20 Ruppelt, 1956.

21 Dewey Fournet, telephone interview with Kevin Randle, July 17, 1995.

22 Complete Samford Press Conference transcript of the interview
    available at *www.kevinrandle.blogspot.com*.

23 Ruppelt, 1956.

24 "Services Try to Stop 'Disc' Talk," *Dallas Times Herald*, July 9, 1947.

CHAPTER 4

1 "The Michigan Cases," *The APRO Bulletin*, March–April 1966.

2 Project Blue Book files, Roll no. 60.

3 J. Allen Hynek, "Report on the Dexter–Hillsdale, Michigan UFO
   Sightings of 20–21 March 1966." Project Blue Book files, Roll no. 60.

4 Project Blue Book files, Roll no. 60.

5 David L. Nelson, "Hynek Swamps It to Study UFOs Following
   Report," *Daily Northwestern*, March 29, 1966.

6 Project Blue Book files, Roll no. 60.

7 Gerald Ford's involvement in these events is important for another
   reason as well, one that has nothing to do with UFOs and everything
   to do with the Deep State. When Ford became president, he was ill-
   prepared to negotiate with world leaders. The FBI had been running
   an operation called Operation Solo out of its New York field office
   that was so secret that not even presidents knew about it. The intelligence acquired through this program was shared with President Ford
   to help him deal with Soviet leaders. It is not clear whether John Kennedy knew about it, but some of its intelleigence may have guided

him during the Cuba Missile Crisis. Subsequent presidents may have been briefed or they may only have learned about the operation after it was retired. Operation Solo remained secret for over thirty years. (See John Barron, *Operation Solo: The FBI's Man in the Kremlin* [Washington, DC: Regnery Publishing, Inc., 1996]).

8   Timothy Good, *Above Top Secret: The Worldwide U.F.O. Cover-Up,"* (New York: William Morrow, 1988).

9   Jerome Clark, *UFO Encyclopedia, 3rd Edition* (Detroit: Omnigraphics, 2018).

10 David E. Twichell, *Global Implications of the UFO Reality* (Haverford, PA: Infinity Publishing, 2003).

11 Daniel Sheehan, telephone interview with Kevin Randle, January 17, 2020. All quotes attributed to Sheehan are based on this interview.

12 Although not directly quoted, this information is also based on the Sheehan interview of January 17, 2020.

13 To be absolutely clear, I asked several times about these classified files and if they were part of Project Blue Book. Sheehan insisted they were, but that they had been and apparently still are classified. They are not referenced in any of the Blue Book documentation that I have seen.

14 Micah Hanks, "The Gipper's UFO," *Mysterious Universe,* January 29, 2014.

15 Alex Hollings, "The UFO Question: President Reagan Was Concerned about UFOs, and He Brought It Up to Gorbarchev," *https://sofrep.com,* January 2, 2019.

16 *https://www.azquotes.com.*

CHAPTER 5

1   Jerome Clark, *UFO Encyclopedia, 3rd Edition* (Detroit: Omnigraphics, 2018); Michael Swords and Robert Powell, *UFOs and Government*

(San Antonio, TX: Anomalist Books, 2012); Daniel S. Gillmor, *Final Report of the Scientific Study of Unidentified Flying Objects* (New York: Bantam Books, 1969); Edward Ruppelt, *The Report on Unidentified Flying Objects* (New York: Ace Books, Inc., 1956).

2 Swords and Powell, 2012; Project Blue Book Administrative files.

3 Ibid.

4 Kevin Randle, *Project Moon Dust* (New York: Avon, 1998).

5 Ruppelt, 1956. Dewey Fournet, telephone interview with Kevin Randle, July 17, 1995.

6 Michael Swords, telephone interview with Kevin Randle, August 7, 1995.

7 Ibid.

8 Ibid.

9 Ruppelt, 1956.

10 Ibid.

11 Walter Haut, telephone interview with Kevin Randle, April 1, 1989.

12 Project Blue Book files, Roll no. 8.

13 Ibid.; also Ruppelt, 1956.

14 Project Blue Book files, Roll no. 11.

15 Project Blue Book files, Roll no. 8.

16 Michael Swords, telephone interview with Kevin Randle, August 7, 1995.

17 Dewey Fournet, telephone interview with Kevin Randle, July 17, 1995.

18 Ruppelt, 1956.

19 Ibid.

20 Ibid.

21 Ibid.

22 Those who said this included Hynek, Ruppelt, and Fournet.

23 Ruppelt, 1956.

24   Michael Swords, telephone interview with Kevin Randle, August 7, 1995.

25   Ibid.

26   Dewey Fournet, telephone interview with Kevin Randle, July 17, 1995.

CHAPTER 6

1   Based on an analysis of the Project Blue Book Index, all reported UFO sightings.

2   Project Blue Book files, Roll no. 29.

3   Ibid.

4   Ibid.

5   Jerome Clark, *UFO Encyclopedia, 3rd Edition* (Detroit: Omnigraphics, 2018).

6   Project Blue Book files, Roll no. 29.

7   Donald Burleson, "Levelland, Texas, 1957: Case Reopened," *International UFO Reporter,* Spring 2003.

8   Ibid.; Project Blue Book files, Roll no. 29.

9   Ibid.; Kevin Randle, *Alien Mysteries, Conspiracies and Cover-Ups* (Detroit: Visible Ink, 2013).

10   Project Blue Book administrative files.

11   Ibid.

12   Ibid.

13   Ibid.

14   Clark, 2018; Daniel S. Gillmor *Final Report of the Scientific Study of Unidentified Flying Objects* (New York: Bantam Books, 1969).

15   Dick Olive, "Most UFOs Explainable Says Scientist," *Elmira Star-Gazette,* January 26, 1967.

16   Project Blue Book administrative files.

17 Project Blue Book administrative files. See also Clark, 2018; Michael Swords and Robert Powell, *UFOs and Government* (San Antonio, TX: Anomalist Books, 2012).

18 Swords and Powell, 2012.

19 Gillmor, 1969.

20 Ibid.

21 Chris Styles, "Shag Harbor in Perspective," *MUFON 1996 International UFO Symposium Proceedings*, 1996.

22 Ibid.

23 Ibid.

24 Ibid.

25 Michael Swords, telephone interview with Kevin Randle, August 7, 1995.

26 Ibid.

27 Gillmor, 1969.

28 Ibid.

29 Arthur Exon, telephone interview with Kevin Randle, May 19, 1991.

30 Gillmor, 1969.

31 Robert Hastings, *UFOs and Nukes* (Bloomington, IN: AuthorHouse, 2008).

32 341st Strategic Missile Wing Unit History.

33 Gillmor, 1969.

34 341st Strategic Missile Wing Unit History.

35 Hastings, 2008.

36 Gillmor, 1969.

37 Robert Kaminski, letter to UFO researcher Jim Klotz, dated February 1, 1997.

38 Robert Hastings, "UFOs Did Shutdown Minuteman Missiles at Echo and Oscar Flight at Malmstrom AFB in March 1967," Privately published, undated.

39   Gillmor, 1969.

40   Ibid.

41   Ibid.

CHAPTER 7

1   Edward Ruppelt, *The Report on Unidentified Flying Objects* (New York: Ace Books, Inc., 1956).

2   Project Blue Book administrative files.

3   Jerome Clark, *UFO Encyclopedia, 3rd Edition* (Detroit: Omnigraphics. 2018).

4   4602nd Unit History.

5   Ibid.

6   Ibid.

7   Ruppelt, 1956.

8   Project Blue Book administrative files.

9   Clark, 2018.

10   Project Blue Book files, Roll no. 73.

11   Ibid.

12   Ibid.

13   Ibid.

14   Ibid.

15   Ibid.

16   Arthur Exon, telephone interview with Kevin Randle, May 19, 1990.

17   Ibid.

18   Arthur Exon, personal interview with Don Schmitt, June 18, 1990.

19   Arthur Exon, telephone interview with Kevin Randle, May 19, 1990.

20   Ibid.

21   Ibid.

22   Arthur Exon, 1990.

23 Timothy Good, *Above Top Secret* (New York: William Morrow & Co. 1988).; Michael Swords and Robert Powell, *UFOs and Government* (San Antonio, TX: Anomalist Books, 2012).

CHAPTER 8

1 4602nd Unit History; Edward Ruppelt, *The Report on Unidentified Flying Objects* (New York: Ace Books, Inc., 1956).
2 Project Blue Book files, Roll no. 40.
3 Ibid.
4 Ibid.
5 Colonel Phillip E. Thompson, USAF, letter to Robert Todd, July 1, 1987.
6 Carolyn W. Price, Assistant FOIA Manager, letter to Clifford E. Stone, January 11, 1990.
7 Barbara A. Carmichael, FOIA Manager, letter to Clifford E. Stone, May 3, 1990.
8 Lt. Col. John E. Madison, Congressional Inquiry Division, Office of Legislative Liaison, letter to U. S. Senator Jeff Bingaman, 1992.
9 Colonel George M. Mattingley, Jr., Chief, Congressional Inquiry Division, Office of Legislative Liaison, letter to U. S. Senator Jeff Bingaman, April 14, 1993.
10 Ibid.
11 "Object Falls in Bolivia." *The APRO Bulletin*, May 1978; Antonio Huneeus, "The Tarija Incident: A Full Report on the 1978 UFO Crash in Bolivia," Privately published, 1993.
12 Ibid.
13 Ibid.
14 Ibid.
15 Leonard H. Stringfield, "The UFO Crash/Retrieval Syndrome Status Report II: New Data" (Seguin, TX: MUFON, January 1980).
16 Huneeus, 1993.

17 Ibid.

18 1127th Air Activities Group, July 1968.

19 Ibid.

20 Colonel Phillip E. Thompson, USAF, letter to Robert Todd, July 1, 1987.

CHAPTER 9

1 George Knapp, presentation at the 6th Annual UFO Crash Conference, November 7–9, 2006; George Knapp personal interview with Kevin Randle, November 8, 2006.

2 Ibid.

3 Ibid.

4 Stanton T. Friedman, *Top Secret/MAJIC* (New York: Marlowe & Co., 1996).

5 Nick Redfern, "The Controversy of the 'Secret Space Program,'" *Mysterious Universe,* July 1, 2019.

6 Ibid.

7 Ibid.

8 "UFO Hacker Tells What He Found." *https://www.wired.com,* accessed, February 18, 2020.

9 Redfern, 2019.

10 Friedman, 1996.

11 Redfern, 2019.

12 Ibid.

13 Paul Darin, "The Solar Warden Covert Space Project: Fact or Science Fiction?" *Epoch Times,* February 17, 2015.

CHAPTER 10

1 Multiple sources including United States Air Force Office of Special Investigations.

2   Project Blue Book files, Roll no. 2.

3   Ibid.

4   Ibid.

5   Ibid.

6   Aden Meinel, email correspondence with Kevin Randle, October 2010.

7   AFOSI official web site, accessed March 2, 2020.

8   Project Blue Book administrative files.

9   Jerome Clark, *UFO Encyclopedia, 3rd Edition* (Detroit: Omnigraphics, 2018).

10   Ibid.

11   Project Blue Book files, Roll no. 2. Later, Massey added: "During the Battle of the Bulge, a sergeant and myself were on guard duty and saw something that resembled this object in question. We later found that we had witnessed the launching of a German V-2 rocket. It carried a stream of fire that more or less resembled this object. This object looked like rocket propulsion rather than jet population, but the speed and size was much greater."

12   Ibid.

13   Ibid.

14   Philip J. Klass, *UFOs Explained* (New York: Random House, 1974).

15   Edward Ruppelt, *The Report on Unidentified Flying Objects* (New York: Ace Books, Inc., 1956).

16   Brad Sparks, "Al Hixenbaugh Film," *http://www.nicap.org*, accessed February 15, 2020. Project Blue Book file, newspaper clipping only, no case file.

17   Ibid.

18   Clark, 2018.

19   Ibid.

20   William B. Nash, "An Airline Captain Speaks Out," *UFO Investigator*, October–November 1962.

21   Ibid.

22   Ibid.

23   Clark, 2018; Project Blue Book files, Roll no. 11.

24   Ruppelt, 1956.

25   Daniel S. Gillmor, *Final Report of the Scientific Study of Unidentified Flying Objects* (New York: Bantam Books, 1969).

26   David Shindele, Testimony for the Citizen Hearing, May 2013. Information also presented on *A Different Perspective* radio show/podcast, February 12, 2020.

27   Ibid.

28   Ibid.

29   Ibid.

30   Ibid.

31   Bruce Fensternmacher, Testimony for the Citizen Hearing, May 2013.

32   Ibid.

CHAPTER 11

1   Helmut Lammer, *https://www.zersetzung.org*, accessed January 23, 2020.

2   Project Blue Book files, Roll no. 43.

3   John G. Fuller, *The Interrupted Journey* (New York: Dial Press, 1966).

4   Various sources used including Fuller, 1966; Jerome Clark, *UFO Encyclopedia, 3rd Edition* (Detroit: Omnigraphics, 2018); David J. Halperin, *Intimate Alien: The Hidden Story of the UFO* (Stanford, CA: Stanford University Press, 2020); Philip J. Klass, *UFO Abductions: A Dangerous Game* (Buffalo, NY: Prometheus Books, 1989); Lorenzen, 1976.

5   Fuller, 1966.

6   Terence Dickinson, "The Zeta Reticuli Incident," AstroMedia Group, *Astronomy Magazine*, 1976.

7   This section is based on Terry Lovelace, *Incident at Devil's Den: A True Story* (Privately published, 2018), and on an interview conducted on April 17, 2019 available at *https://www.speaker.com*.

8   Martin Cannon, "The Controllers, Parts I and II," *The MUFON UFO Journal.* Nos. 270 and 271 (October and November 1990).

9   Karla Turner, *Into the Fringe: A True Story of Alien Abduction* (New York: Berkley Books, 1992).

10 Lorenzen, 1976; Fuller, 1966.

11 Helmut Lammer, *https://www.zersetzung.org*, accessed January 23, 2020.

CHAPTER 12

1   John Burroughs interview with Kevin Randle, December 11, 2019.

2   Burroughs, 2019.

3   Burroughs, 2019; Jim Penniston interview with Kevin Randle, October 23, 2019; Charles Halt interview with Kevin Randle November 20, 2019.

4   Burroughs, 2019.

5   Penniston, 2019: Jim Penniston and Gary Olsen. *The Rendlesham Enigma: Book 1: Timeline* (Privately published, 2019).

6   Unless otherwise noted, this section is based on the interviews with Penniston and his book.

7   Halt, 2019; Unless otherwise noted, this section is based on interviews with Halt and his book. Charles I. Halt and John Hanson, *The Halt Perspective* (Great Britain: Haunted Skies Publishing, 2016).

8   Charles Halt, interview with Kevin Randle, January 11, 2017; Halt, 2019; Halt and Hanson, 2016.

9   Halt, 2017, Halt, 2019; Halt and Hanson, 2016.

10 Nick Pope with John Burroughs and Jim Penniston, (*Encounter in Rendlesham Forest* (New York: St. Martin's Press, 2014); Halt and Hanson, 2016.

11 Pope, 2014, as well as other sources.

12 Penniston and Olsen, 2019.

13 Ibid.

14 Ibid. Unless otherwise noted, this information came from various interviews with Penniston.

15 Penniston and Olsen, 2019.

16 Ibid 17. Halt, 2019.

17 Halt, 2019.

CHAPTER 13

1   Jerome Clark, *UFO Encyclopedia, 2nd Edition* (Detroit: Omnigraphics, 1998).

2   Ibid.

3   Ibid.

4   See also Robert Hastings, "The MJ-12 Affair: Facts, Questions, Comments" (Privately published, March 1, 1989); Timothy Good, *Alien Contact: Top Secret UFO Files Revealed* (New York: William Morrow & Co., 1993); Jacques Vallee, *Revelations* (New York: Ballantine Books, 1992).

5   William Moore, presentation at the MUFON Symposium 1989. Paper was not submitted in time for publication.

6   Ibid.

7   Ibid.

8   Hastings, 1989.

9   Moore, 1989.

10 Richard Hall in personal communication to Kevin Randle.

11 Stan Friedman, when queried about the Aquarius Telex, suggested he didn't know what that was.

12 Clark, 2018; Good, 1993; Vallee, 1992.

13 This section is based on various sources, including Clark, 2018; Richard Dolan, *UFOs and the National Security State: The Cover-Up*

Exposed (Rochester, NY: Keyhole Publishing, 2009); Good, 1993; Hastings, 1989; Vallee, 1992.

14 Ibid.

15 Information about Willingham's military record supplied by the National Archives and Records Administration (NARA) in St. Louis, which houses those records, and the Air Reserve Personnel Center in Denver, CO.

16 For more information on the Holloman AFB UFO landing, see Kevin D. Randle, *Encounter in the Desert.* (Wayne, NJ: NewPage Books, 2018).

17 Hastings, 1989.

18 Moore, 1989.

INDEX

ABOUT THE AUTHOR

Kevin D. Randle is a retired Army lieutenant colonel who served in Vietnam as a helicopter pilot and Aircraft Commander. He was commissioned into the Air Force in 1976 and served first as a Public Relations Officer and later as an Intelligence Officer. He was honorably discharged in 1984. After the attacks on 9/11, he joined the Iowa National Guard and was deployed to Iraq in 2003 as an Intelligence Officer. He retired from the National Guard in 2009. In 2013, he was awarded the Bronze Star Medal for his service in Iraq and an Air Medal for Valor for his service in Vietnam. He is a graduate of the University of Iowa and has advanced degrees from California Coast University and American Military University, including a PhD in psychology and a Master's degree in the art of military intelligence.

During his nearly fifty years of UFO research, Kevin has investigated some of the most important UFO cases, including the Roswell crash, the Levelland, Texas sightings, the Socorro landing, and some of the more interesting UFO abduction cases. He has published more than twenty-five books about UFOs, including *Encounter in the Desert* and *Crash: When UFOs Fall From the Sky*. He has been interviewed on hundreds of radio shows and appeared in dozens of documentaries as well as on many television shows, including *Good Morning America, Today,* and *Larry King Live*. He now hosts a weekly radio show called *A Different Perspective* on the X-Zone Broadcast Network. You can find his blog at *www.kevinrandle.blogspot.com*.